between shadows and noise

amber jamilla musser

sensation, situatedness, and the undisciplined

Duke University Press Durham and London 2024

Printed in the United States of America on acid-free paper ∞
Project Editor: Livia Tenzer | Designed by Aimee C. Harrison
Typeset in Garamond Premier Pro and SangBleu Kingdom
by Westchester Publishing Services

Library of Congress Cataloging-in-Publication Data
Names: Musser, Amber Jamilla, author.
Title: Between shadows and noise : sensation, situatedness, and the undisciplined / Amber Jamilla Musser.
Description: Durham : Duke University Press, 2024. | Includes bibliographical references and index.
Identifiers: LCCN 2023020971 (print)
LCCN 2023020972 (ebook)
ISBN 9781478030096 (paperback)
ISBN 9781478025832 (hardcover)
ISBN 9781478059097 (ebook)
Subjects: LCSH: Feminist theory—Political aspects. | Feminist theory. | Imperialism. | Black people—Race identity. | Queer theory. | Sensuality. | BISAC: SOCIAL SCIENCE / Black Studies (Global) | SOCIAL SCIENCE / Feminism & Feminist Theory
Classification: LCC HQ1190 .M895 2024 (print) | LCC HQ1190 (ebook) | DDC 305.4201—dc23/eng/20231011
LC record available at https://lccn.loc.gov/2023020971
LC ebook record available at https://lccn.loc.gov/2023020972

Cover art: Ming Smith, *Flamingo Fandango (West Berlin) (painted)*, 1988. Archival pigment print, 24 5/32 × 36 in. © 2023 Ming Smith / Artists Rights Society (ARS), New York.

In their own special ways,
Thomas, Carrie, and Ankur are the
architects of my luminous new life.
Thank you for the love and abundance.

Contents

Acknowledgments

JUST AS THIS BOOK SITS at the intersection of the personal and the scholarly, so too do these acknowledgments. This book was completed amid extremely difficult circumstances; yet writing provided a necessary lifeline for me. This book offered an opportunity to dwell on sensual delights and to think and feel while I rebuilt my being from the inside out. It is only because of the deep generosity of my friends, family, and community that I am here and that this book become real.

My brother, Thomas, tangibly offered me an opportunity for more life and he and his family, Ashley and Eleanor, encircle me with love. There is nothing like seeing a baby grow into a toddler to feel inspired and curious and to understand the depth of joy and inner radiance that come from living with purpose: "We did it!" My parents, John and Camille, stayed with me for many weeks—cooking, cleaning, and entertaining me. We watched the Celtics almost go all the way and wandered the summer gardens and outdoor concerts of Ditmas Park in style. Much love also to my more extended Musser and Saunders family.

Carrie Gleason makes sure that I am truly seen. Her unwavering constancy, humor, immense advocacy, and excellent organizational skills helped me find a horizon of steadiness and possibility. More than the pragmatic, I cherish her ability to insist on a future filled with an abundance of delight and love. I extend my deepest gratitude for her determination to keep me enmeshed in the beauty and realness of the world and her willingness to read and discuss draft after draft.

Ankur Ghosh has been a beacon of inspiration, comfort, and joy. He bought fake plants (real ones not allowed); he brought jelly beans and chocolate; he decorated hospital rooms; he moved me from one apartment to another; he ran copious errands and made me smile. Kadji Amin is a deeply cherished caring and kind friend. His daily care and our various adventures have been their own forms of salvation. Michael Gillespie is a delight whose care extended into daily invitations to new music. Jasbir Puar has been the best neighbor and friend the West Side can offer. Niamh Duggan and Bahia Munem have prompted many tantalizing brunch conversations. Maureen Catbagan has been a collaborator and friend extraordinaire—especially when they assured me that the no eyebrow look was hot. Stephanie Clare, Larissa Chernock, Alison Macdonald, Chitra Ramalingam, and Isaac Nakhimovsky have taught me that most acts of friendship consist of being willing to listen and to talk about things that are not necessarily what is going on and to keep sharing one's life. Avgi Saketopoulou sent me gold eye shadow and organized a private motorcycle pride parade. Many thanks also to Jordy Rosenberg, Paige McGinley, Mel Micir, Fannie Bialek, Samita Sinha, Jayna Brown, Tavia Nyong'o, Moon Charania, Beth Freeman, J. Kehalauni Kauanui, Nasser Zakariya, Eng Beng Lim, Karen Tongson, Jasmine Mahmoud, Jordan Stein, Shanté Smalls, John Andrews, Yxta Murray, Annie Howell, Jennifer Nash, Jina Kim, Britt Russert, Lyndon Gill, Kyla Wazana Tompkins, Aimee Bahng, Karma Chavez, Kiri Mah, Laurie Marhoefer, Molly Caldwell, Kandice Chuh, Jessica Rankin, Pacho Velez, Ben McKean, Alex Horowitz, Amy Carson, Arwen Griffith, Emily Bolton, Danny Fox, and Risha Lee for the ongoing kindnesses of friendship.

I do not take for granted the wealth of care that I received from NYU Langone Health. Deep thanks to the teams of nurses, nurse practitioners, doctors, physician aids, physical therapists, nutritionists, and custodians who tended to me on KP 12, KP 16, the BMT clinic, and various other outpatient units. I especially thank Dr. Hay, Dr. Saint-Fleur, Devynn Emory, Jay Swanson, Danielle, and Greg for helping me understand the strength, hope, and miracle of a bone marrow transplant. I am also extremely humbled by the generosity of those who contributed to the GoFundMe set up by Jasbir and Carrie so that I was relatively unburdened by financial anxiety. The shock of the immense kindness put forth is ongoing and I strive to live in that communal orientation to the world and keep paying it forward. I am also grateful to everyone who took the time to send me good wishes and who kept me within their hearts during all of this. And, finally, I am grateful to the loved ones of my caregivers whose labor gave them the capacity to extend care—I am especially thankful for the flexibility of Alan and Devon Cage. I recognize the multiple fortunate aspects of my circumstances.

I wrote this book between 2018 and 2023. The ideas began to germinate while I was teaching at Washington University in St. Louis. I thank my wonderful colleagues and friends there: Paige McGinley, Mel Micir, Rebecca Wanzo, Bahia Munem, Jasmine Mahmoud, Rhaisa Williams, Pannell Camp, Diane Lewis, Jean Allman, Andrea Friedman, Trevor Sangrey, Anika Walker, Cynthia Barounis, and Shefali Chandra. Much of the research for this book took place while I had the fortune of working in the American Studies department at George Washington University. Thank you for being a convivial space for conversation and thought: Nicole Ivy, Libby Anker, Gayle Wald, Melanie McAlister, Tom Guglielmo, Robert McCruer, Joe Baez, Ro Carson, and G. J. Servillano. I am especially grateful to Mona Azadi for taking on the administrative burden of dealing with my unusual reimbursements for learning alternative cosmologies. This book was completed as I began working at the CUNY Graduate Center. I extend deep thanks to Kandice Chuh and David Olan for figuring out creative ways for me to navigate the institution in illness. My students in "Black Feminisms and the Flesh" and "Black Performance, Black Visuality," were excellent interlocutors; Ben Krusling was a gem of a research assistant. I also thank the Graduate Center for supporting reproduction of artwork in this publication.

I am also grateful for other intellectual forums which benefited the book. I thank Malik Gaines and Hentyle Yapp for our brief, but productive, writing group; the Black Feminist Working Group of *Social Text*—Vanessa Agard-Jones, Aimee Meredith Cox, and Jayna Brown—for stimulating conversations; the Black Atlantic Ecologies Group at Columbia—Vanessa Agard-Jones, Marissa Solomon, Anna Arabindan-Kesson, Jayna Brown, Aimee Meredith Cox, Alyssa James, Julie Livingston, Chazelle Rhoden, and Sonya Posmentier—for multidisciplinary thought explorations. The Keywords for Gender and Sexuality Studies Feminist Collective of Aren Aizura, Aimee Bahng, Karma Chavez, Mishuana Goeman, and Kyla Wazana Tompkins and the many writers, thinkers, and activists of that volume were also instrumental to my thinking, as were my coeditors of the "Care and Its Complexities" special issue of *Signs*, Linda Blum and Martha Fineman. I am also grateful to the ASAP organization—specifically the excellent motherboard of 2021–2023—for their support and thoughtfulness. I also owe many thanks to the editors of the *Brooklyn Rail* who gave me the opportunity to refine my art writing, interview artists and thinkers, and explore in a new genre.

Thanks to Elizabeth Ault for her work on this manuscript. I have been in conversation with Elizabeth since 2016 about the possibility of this collaboration and I could not have asked for a better set of eyes to push this project where it needed to go. She found excellent reviewers, whose comments helped me refine and think and made this book what I always imagined it could be. Thanks also to Benjamin Kossak and everyone else at Duke University Press for producing this amazing, beautiful book. Special gratitude to Josh Rutner for thorough indexing (and extra eyes during proofing).

Intellectually, this book emerges from conversations I have been having about art over the past several years. I have been thinking about Samita Sinha's work in several places: in particular, a 2019 ASA panel on queer femininity with Christina Leon and Summer Kim Lee, and workshops at Danspace Project in New York. For the invitations to share my thoughts on tamarind and rest, I am grateful to audiences at the University of Chicago, including the 2022 "After Affect" conference and the history of science working group in 2021; the Future of American Studies Institute in 2021; and the Disability and Debility Working Group at the University of Pennsylvania. For my work on Jordan Peele's *Us*, I am grateful to the Gender Studies department at Queens University. I also thank the attendees of the "Sticky Films Conference" put together by the Configurations of Film research group at Goethe Universität at Frankfurt am Main for their wonderful questions and hospitality in 2023, and Michael Gillespie for the copious references to Black horror. For hearing a late version of the research on Allora & Calzadilla, I thank my fellow participants at Northwestern University's "Object Relations" conference in May 2023, who offered insights into the project as a whole. I am also grateful to share work related to broader themes of the project with the Center for Research in Feminist, Queer, and Transgender Studies at the University of Pennsylvania in 2022, ICI Berlin in 2021, Stanford University's Arts and Justice series in 2021, and Yale University's Religion and American Excess conference in 2021.

Introduction

Body Work

AGAINST THE WANING SUN, you can only see the blurred silhouettes of surrounding trees; in the foreground, a flamboyance of flamingos. They are pink elegance: long curving necks and legs ready to strut. With its saturated blacks and moody bursts of color, Ming Smith's 1988 photograph *Flamingo Fandango (West Berlin) (painted)* (plate 1) makes felt what lies between shadows and noise. The background darkness (the shadows)—enfolds multiple histories and temporalities: Cold War contours, Germany on the precipice—the Berlin Wall would fall in 1989—the eighteenth-century imperial impulse underlying all zoos, and the current moment's shifting climate, which endangers flamingos, especially in Europe.[1] Beyond grounding the image spatially and temporally, I locate these shadows in the different forms of capture lurking around the flamingos: in addition to photographic apparatus and zoological enclosure, one can sense the constructedness of leisure and the fetishization of species difference that underlie the idea of the zoo itself. These material and epistemological structures are critical elements of the viewer's perspective on these birds; they emphasize the flamingo's presence. That these differential layers of context recede into the background does not diminish the structures of meaning that they give the photograph. On the other hand, the noise of the flamingos, their flamboyance—in relation to their number, their loud chatter, their color, their being—makes felt the different ways that pink tropical birds might be excessive in the context of West Berlin. They seem out of place—with their behavior, volume, and preference for warmer climates—and this unbelonging is externally marked by their pink feathers, which Smith has rendered even pinker through paint: "I wanted to add color [the way] someone would put a ribbon on a dress or a lacy collar or a big belt—to embellish and make it more exciting."[2] In this context, the painted pink, which I consider the noise of the photograph, signals the flamingos' affective and sensual milieu not their actual coloring; the pink, the noise, gestures toward uncontained excess within the photographic image.

A less idiosyncratic description of this photograph might register it as a representation of flamingos in a zoo. From this perspective, the flamingos emerge as objects of interest to the eye as well as the mind. One might ask, for example, what this photograph might teach us *about* flamingos? If, as Kandice Chuh argues, "aboutness functions as an assessment of relevance," the question of aboutness here reminds us of how evidence offered by the visual has served as the bedrock for producing hierarchies of knowledge.[3] In other words, this reading of the photograph would position *Flamingo Fandango (West Berlin) (painted)* as a continuation of colonial and racist projects of capture and categorization; it would augur its significance to what the photograph makes visible. In this way, the objectification of flamingos is a residue of what we, following Jacques Rancière, might call the production of a "common sense" that would conjoin approaches to works of art with projects of knowledge extraction, thereby flattening a wide swath of sensory orientations, intimacies, and histories.[4]

However, even as flamingos fill the frame, the photograph is also *not* about them; the knowledge we gain is not about birds nor Berlin, but is about discipline, sense, and situatedness. *Flamingo Fandango (West Berlin)(painted)* asks us to sit with questions of perception—what are the photograph's layers and what do they tell us about the visible and invisible aspects of the world? While Smith is best known as the sole female member of the Kamoinge collective, a 1960s group of Black photographers based in New York City, and as prolific photographer of New York nightlife, the technical elements of her work are where we see her breaking open the sutures of representation in order to reveal (and revel in) a greater unruliness.[5] I began by describing how shadows and noise in Smith's photograph structure affective and sensorial aspects of our perception, but that is only part of the story. Our ability to attend to conditions of possibility and sense the cacophony of the flamingos are themselves indications of Smith's rejection of the subject-object binary that discipline expects. Instead of demarcating an object (or set of objects) to be look at, parsed, or investigated, Smith presents a blurred image whose fuzzy boundaries speak to the inseparability of flamingo from "background" and which tether the viewer affectively, historically, and geopolitically to the world of the image.[6] *Everything*, in other words, is revealed to be connected.

In an interview with Janet Hill Talbert, Smith describes her method of taking photographs as intuitive, saying, "I feel my way through things, and let the spirit guide me."[7] Later, she compares photography with dancing, saying, "You have to be in the moment, you have to be right there—it's like a form of meditation."[8] Smith's openness and commitment to a spiritual, sensual realm is evident in the moodiness of the photographs themselves—they make something present without necessarily making claims about representation. I read Smith's movement toward sense as reparative, as an intervention against the violent history of representation that has had pernicious effects for those who are not part of dominant groups. Namwali Serpell argues that Smith's aesthetics cannot be separated from the knowledge that Smith largely photographed Black people and communities. She writes, "What we might call Smith's luxuriant, deconstructive chiaroscuro also arises from her technical innovations in lighting, shutter speed, and the relative movements of camera and subject—all of which derive from immersion, an insistence on taking pictures of black people in black spaces."[9] Describing Smith's technique in conversation with Greg Tate, Arthur Jafa also focuses on her precise manipulation of shutter speed to create blur without sacrificing form: "What's unique about Ming is her ability to use this shutter thing to erase much of the distinction between the figure and the background, but at the same time, have it be very precise in its articulation of form."[10] Later, both Tate and Jafa agree that Smith's photographs enable what is depicted to escape capture, signaling what they describe as her interest in Black fugitivity:

> **Tate:** A fugitivity that's not bound up with escape but a kind of self-illumination.
>
> **Jafa:** Yeah, totally. Circular breathing.... The fugitivity of people willing to be free from being fucked with. You can't fuck with what you can't see.[11]

Just as important as the politics of emancipation are the corporeal techniques—circular breathing—summoned by Smith's swerve around representation. It is in this landscape of sensation and affect that I locate the possibilities of shadows and noise.

The term *shadow* is used to separate "light" from "dark," offering language not only for an optic phenomenon, but a system of value that would prioritize light, equating it with transparency, rationality, and "enlightenment," leaving the concept of the shadow to signify something that is either deliberately hidden from view (usually in a malevolent fashion), disavowed, or repressed; think of shadow terms, governments, processes, archives. Jill Casid argues that shadows provide a contrast to organization and discipline and offers that their devaluation is a consequence of disavowing the importance of experiential knowledge. What is described as enlightened, Casid writes, is "a way of knowing . . . that offers the dream of dispelling the shadow of vulnerability to the disorganizing somatic and affective responses that hollow out the defended fortress ego to rational, disincarnate vision and its fantasy of sovereign agency over the tremulous body and its enmeshed, interdependent precarity."[12] Against the prioritization of visibility, enclosure, and sovereignty, shadows conjure irrationality, unclarity, vulnerability, and enmeshment. Orienting perception toward shadows, then, not only makes felt foreclosed entities and relations, but allows one to grapple with underlying processes of repression, disavowal, and denial and their embeddedness in ontological and epistemological systems of valuation. Alessandra Raengo provides an example of this type of analysis when she looks to shadows to displace the overdetermined (racist) sets of referents that attach to images of Black people. Shadows, she argues, confound the way that race is perceived because they highlight the importance of context and render representation weak—moving us toward other ways of making knowledge. She writes, "As a paradigm, the shadow has the ability to bring to the fore the idea that race most prominently inhabits the *state* and not the content of the image. . . . The shadow is an indication of the body's extension into its surroundings and, therefore, calls attention to the spaces and modes of interaction between bodies."[13] In other words, shadows move us away from assertions of aboutness toward relation. Shadows allow us to ask: What are the conditions of possibility at work and how might we imagine otherwise?

While shadows offer information about hierarchies of valuation, what counts as noise is heavily contested. Many scholars in sound studies argue, for example, that the distinction between music and noise is reliant on hierarchies that depend on raced, classed, and gendered norms.[14] Beyond its circulation in the sonic, noise is conceptually related to excess, abundance, and the unruly. Notably, these are terms that correlate closely with racist attempts to demean and police the behavior (and, more often than not, mere existence) of people of color. As Jennifer Stoever argues, "the sonic color line invokes noise in direct connection to (or as a metonymic stand-in for) people of color, and particularly blackness."[15] Moreover, this conflation of being with noise highlights the particularly close tethering of processes of enfleshment with processes of disciplining and classification. In this way, understanding how and why something (or someone) has been designated as noisy gives us an affective and sensational vocabulary for grappling with how difference is (or is not) incorporated into a social body. Think, for example, of the so-called noisiest park in the world, People's Park in Chengdu, China. There, noise means loudness—sounds high in decibel that occur consistently—but noise is also an atmospheric designation linking noise with other forms of toxicity and excess associated with the megacity.[16] For sensing a different valence of noise, consider the 2012 murder of Jordan Davis, a seventeen-year-old Black teenager shot at a gas station in Jacksonville, Florida, for refusing to turn down the rap music in his car, or the group of Black women asked to leave a Napa Valley wine tasting tour for boisterous laughter, or Regina Bradley's comment: "as a black woman, the bulk of my threat is associated with my loudness."[17] This list illuminates the equation of Blackness with being out of place, such that the matter of Blackness is perceived as threatening, noisy, and dangerous.[18] In these instances, difference is met with nonrecognition, disorientation, and perhaps overwhelm. Noise, then, allows us to sense how questions of recognition, legibility, and comfort underlie reception. This version of noise is multisensory and attentive to the fabric of social relation.

Shadows and noise, then, give us two sensory modes to index the density of representation. They disrupt univocal meaning making, forcing us to navigate its edges. While these edges are often ignored, normalized, and rendered subordinate to the frame (aboutness), art critic Amanda Gluibizzi asks us to think about the specific types of affective and sensorial work that edges perform. An edge, she argues, may offer invitation, play, obstacle, utility, or signal vulnerability.[19] Here, the overarching question is *not* how to avoid the edge by shifting something out of the category of noise or shadow—there will always be noise and shadows—nor how to revalue the categories so that noise and shadow become desirable in their possibility to disrupt or subvert.[20] Instead, shadows and noise invite us into a riot of modes of being and thinking so that we might move away from asking how something might be represented "better" or more clearly and toward how we might make representation denser, overrun with contradictory information, so that signification can be multiple and promiscuous.

Beyond Representation, Toward Sense

I work with shadows and noise because they are embodied relational categories. They tell us a doubled story: what are we meant to pay attention to *and* what is devalued or deemed excessive? As Katherine McKittrick offers in *Dear Science*, "discipline is empire."[21] By this she means imperialism produces, relies on, and consists of surveillance, categorization, and hierarchization. "Science" is but one of its designated disciplines and it unfurls fractally, compounding subdivisions, methods of investigation, and categorizations. We might especially discuss the privileging of visual evidence as part of this paradigm. By asking *about* the representation of flamingos, we are asking what knowledge we might extract from these birds, what can be made transparent or useful. As I have argued, however, there is always excess—otherwise, discipline (as noun and verb) would not be necessary. As Nasser Zakariya writes, these "genres of synthesis . . . structure an approach to the production of knowledge. But they also provide a kind of grammar of ignorance, delimiting what it means not to know, shaping what progress or its lack amounts to and further indicating what might be in principle unknowable: those parts of the representation that can never be resolved or will forever be open to further resolution."[22] Shadows and noise show how the senses have been trained ("synthesized," per Zakariya's parlance) into a "common sense" while also granting insight into what has not, and perhaps cannot, be incorporated. Accessing this otherness, the undisciplined that sits alongside discipline in many of its durations, scales, and forms, including what might be described as Man, colonialism, anti-Blackness, patriarchy, homophobia, capitalism, neoliberalism, and so forth, demands methods that I describe as "body work."[23]

Fleshy methods proliferate. Kandice Chuh describes the illiberal humanisms—that which might counter the centrifugal force of common sense—as offering "a fuller, embodied accounting of reason and rationality."[24] Britt Rusert uses Deleuze's reading of empiricism, "a method that depends on sense perception, continual observations, and a mobile, searching orientation toward the world," to connect fugitive modes of science- and subject-making.[25] She writes, "Empiricism finds us always in the middle, in a line of flight or a line of escape—at the level of praxis and ongoing experiments—in the material realm of sensation and subjectivity rather than in the metaphysical plane of knowledge production."[26] As Ronak Kapadia demonstrates through his analysis of what he calls insurgent aesthetics, sensual methodologies can offer insight into covert (shadowy and noisy, perhaps?) forms of resistance and critique. He writes, "these insurgent aesthetics craft a queer calculus of US empire that makes intimate what is rendered distant, renders tactile what is made invisible, and unifies what is divided, thereby conjuring forms of embodied critique that can envision a collective world within and beyond the spaces of US empire's perverse logics of global carcerality, security, and war."[27] Here, Kapadia's use of *queer* alerts us not only to the disavowed aspects of sensual knowledge but also to the forms of attachment at work in activating sensuality as method. In a similar vein, I have previously argued that flesh summons its own ways of knowing, such that sensation acts as a critical analytic in mobilizing the world-making possibilities from the queerness of Black and Brown femininities.[28] Here, I see queerness hovering in these methods of sensory extension as well as in the communication of the particularities described.

Let us consider *[Closer Captions]* (2020; plate 2), a short film by Christine Sun Kim. Kim, who is deaf, begins by lamenting the lack of nuance in most closed captioning before offering her own captions of images that narrate a day: a bright blue sky with a few wispy clouds [the sound of sun entering the bedroom]; the reflection of the sun on water [sweetness of orange sunlight]; and, finally, a darkened hallway where we see a door slightly ajar [the sound of hurt feelings scabbing over].[29] Kim highlights how the word *music* omits many possibilities for experience while also calling attention to the wide sensual world that her descriptions hail. Kim's captions emphasize the polymorphous possibilities of representation (Chuh's illiberal humanism) while explicitly foregrounding the extensions of being (Rusert's empiricism) that undergird these landscapes of affect and sensation and, in relation to her deafness, enacting a critique of the accessibility of film and television (Kapadia's resistance). Together, these different facets of corporeality point toward how Kim's situatedness produces its own specific forms of personal representation.[30]

Simone de Beauvoir argues that the body is a situation—a set of material givens whose value shifts depending on context. While some of Beauvoir's terminology encapsulates her antipathy toward physiology—especially the impositions of menstruation, childbirth, and nursing—this framing (despite its implicit idealization of one particular mode of embodiment) highlights the ways that constraint emerges contextually. Although the social and the material are inextricable, theirs is not a deterministic relationship.[31] Writing from science studies, Donna Haraway dispenses with the universality and objectivity produced from an omniscient "God-like" view from nowhere and argues, instead, for the importance of partial perspectives that are founded on an awareness of specific privilege and oppression. Here, the body is the vantage point from which one makes sense of the world. These situated knowledges, the product of epistemological, ontological, political, and ethical positions, leads, in Haraway's words, to "a more adequate, richer, better account of a world, in order to live in it well and in critical, reflexive relation to our own as well as others' practices of domination and the unequal parts of privilege and oppression that make up all positions."[32] In Sara Ahmed's account of orientation, positionality is fused with opportunity and attachment, so "bodies take shape through tending toward objects that are reachable, that are available within the bodily horizon."[33] These forms of extension, aversion, and movement are, Ahmed argues, "how we reside in space."[34]

In addition to highlighting the imbrication of bodily knowledge with positionality and attachment, situatedness highlights the political importance of difference. Preserving this difference is how we maintain the polymorphousness within representation that emerges from these sensual methods. The importance of this difference is something we learn especially from women of color feminisms.[35] Referring to Audre Lorde and other women of color feminists, Grace Kyungwon Hong uses the term "to reference a cultural and epistemological practice that holds in suspension (without requiring resolution) contradictory, mutually exclusive, and negating impulses."[36] While Hong is particularly interested in how women of color feminists were able to preserve difference despite its disavowal within the framework of neoliberalism, I am interested in drawing continuities between women of color feminisms and the cultivation of strategies for sitting with difference as well as recognizing its infinite abundance. I see this work as complexifying our vocabularies for gender, race, and racialization, instantiating what Jasbir Puar describes as "a proliferation of race."[37]

We might also imagine this impulse alongside José Esteban Muñoz's description of the Brown commons as a "collectivity with and through the incommensurable."[38] In this way, I see sensuous methods, body work, as building the capacity for recognizing and living with difference by foregrounding ethical forms of being-with. Following Édouard Glissant, we might argue that this ethics emerges by acknowledging the primacy of opacity, the unknowability of the self and others, in relation.[39] For example, consider Pope.L's *Skin Set Drawings* (1997–present), a series of drawings with words describing people, such as "WHITE PEOPLE ARE ANGLES ON FIRE," "GREEN PEOPLE ARE HOPE WITHOUT REASON," and "ORANGE PEOPLE SUCK AND GET SOMETHING OUT OF IT" (plate 3). In describing the effect of the plethora of descriptions, Darby English argues that the drawings "imply seeing but record, or index knowing. A full picture of their representational activity accounts for its meandering epistemology and for the thrilling and textual activities it comprises—that is, the drawings know that they lack synthetic ambition, harbor no synthetic vision of a single representational strategy to contain the social whole."[40] English is especially drawn to what I would call the noisiness of Pope.L's work and the way that his project as a whole illuminates the pleasures, what he calls, "an ecstasy," of difference.[41] In the context of shadows and noise, I am also compelled by the way that each drawing emerges from a specific situatedness, which, in turn, destabilizes common sense in its emphasis on the abundance and polymorphousness of difference.

While I have offered a brief description of situatedness as an analytic rooted in amplifying the politics of difference and corporeality, it is equally important to note that I understand situatedness as operating against multiple forms of consolidation—those that would insist on flattening processes of gendering or racialization into identity categories as well as those that understand situatedness to coalesce into an individual. Working with situatedness as a rubric allows the identification of ambivalences, forces, and histories in tension with each other that need not (and perhaps cannot) resolve into one particular narrative trajectory. Instead, situatedness allows us to understand the multitudes that reside within each of us.

A Brief History of My Situations

My investment in situatedness as offering resources for theory and criticism means that I am interested in seeing how and where the personal manifests in the world around me, how this situatedness facilitates an experience of art as an invitation into other ways of being, and how this situatedness impacts my perception of what constitutes shadows and noise. One of the personally appealing aspects of Smith's *Flamingo Fandango (West Berlin) (painted)* is finding a Caribbean resonance (flamingos are the national bird of The Bahamas) in an unexpected place. The work of unpacking this perceived disjunction is part of my sensual attachment to the photograph and it informs the way that I identify the structures that comprise its shadows—constructions of leisure and colonialism are not that distant from tourism. Likewise, the noise of the pink resonates with my own experience of local Caribbean color palates. It is impossible for me to sever my investigations of Smith's photograph from my situatedness but there is knowledge in that space—knowledge about the feelings, sensations, geographies, and temporalities that comprise the densely layered now of empire as well as knowledge about the worlds that exceed it.

Here, then, are some of the complexities of my own enfleshment. I am writing this from the unceded territory of the Lenapehoking, the traditional land of the Wappinger, Canarsie, Munsee, and Lenni Lenape people of the Delaware Nation and Shinnecock Indian Nation in a time of ongoing state-sanctioned violence levied broadly at many nonwhite and gender nonconforming people with a specific murderous intensification of police violence toward Black and Indigenous people.[42] This statement is a version of one that I have encountered many times since the summer of 2020 and it offers a step toward a more collective reckoning with the foreclosures that Justin Leroy names as occurring when "slavery and settler colonialism vie for primacy as the violence most foundational to the modern social order."[43] Using the orbit of the sensual to feel for the simultaneity of these violences as well as their differences, Tiffany Lethabo King describes the unmooring she experienced as she began to come to grips with the deep entwinements of slavery and settler colonialism: "Genocide and slavery do not have an edge. While the force of their haunt has distinct feelings at the stress points and instantiations of Black fungibility and Native genocide, the violence moves as one."[44] These overlapping forms of violence are one of the durative spatio-temporalities to which I am attuned, but there are also others.

Thinking with my simultaneous past and present, I also feel the distentions of British imperialism. Here, I am speaking directly about St. Vincent and the Grenadines, the small hilly set of islands in the southern Caribbean where my mother was born. When the British attempted to impose colonial rule—setting off wars that would last throughout the eighteenth century—the islands were populated by a multiethnic coalition of so-called Caribs, maroons, and a small group of (slave holding) French settlers.[45] In this context, the use of the word *Carib* to designate an Indigenous ethnicity is fraught since the term originates not with a particular group, but in the Spanish colonists' label for the Indigenous people hostile to them, a term that, in St. Vincent, was also enlarged to account for Indigenous people who fled their settlements to avoid colonialism and ended up on these islands. The mountainous geography also played an important part in the growth of St. Vincent's African population, many of whom arrived by boat having fled sugar plantations on nearby Barbados, although there are also rumors that some Africans may have arrived before any European settlers on their own vessels from Benin.[46] This anticolonial struggle, however, is not oft-repeated, an omission that Julie Kim ascribes to the historiographic myth of Indigenous disappearance combined with British anti-Blackness that renamed the Caribs the "Black Caribs," suggesting that Africans had killed off the "original Caribs," and that they therefore had no claim to the islands or sovereignty.[47] After their defeat, the British exiled the Caribs, now known as the Garifuna, to Honduras and established widespread plantation slavery on St. Vincent. Enslavement lasted until 1838; colonialism, until 1979; and St. Vincent's status as a commonwealth nation persists.

My grandmother was from one of the Grenadines—Union Island—where they hold an annual festival for the maroons. My grandfather's mother's name was Eglantine and his father, a planter with a Scottish name, had hair that "lay down flat." As a member of the commonwealth, my mother moved to the United Kingdom at nineteen to study institutional cooking and catering at the University of Leicester. In a series of migrations that abut the Windrush generation (1948–1970) and are shaped by colonialism's condensation of respectability, economic mobility, and educational opportunity with movement to the metropole, her two older brothers (Chesley and Keith) moved to New York and a younger brother (Ronnie) went to Toronto. Her youngest brother, Adrian, however, stayed in the Caribbean, studied law at the University of the West Indies, and now lives in Trinidad where he serves as chief justice of the Caribbean Court of Justice, an intra-Caribbean court whose aim is to sever judicial ties from Britain and the Commonwealth. My mother, now living in Massachusetts, paints portraits of Joseph Chatoyer, who led the charge against the British, and, in a nod to theories that the Caribs and Taínos are actually the same people, deities such as Atabey, Supreme Goddess of fresh water and fertility, as a way to work through this legacy of colonial violence.[48] These familial negotiations with and against British imperialism testify to M. Jacqui Alexander's assessment of its temporal, affective, and regulatory legacies: "Perhaps empire never ended, psychic and material will to conquer and appropriate, twentieth century movements for decolonization notwithstanding. What we can say for sure is that empire makes all innocence impossible."[49]

These histories and relations to colonialism mediate my own more direct interactions with colonialism, which are themselves multiple. First, there are the circumstances of my being, which rely on various economic and geopolitical currents to have my parents meet in Norway and then eventually (with several peregrinations in between) move to Ecuador where I was born. While I have sketched my mother's trajectory, my father's travels have more to do with a desire to explore life and living elsewhere—a privilege attached to education, class, and whiteness. His father, a World War II veteran who was stationed in Trinidad, went to college on the GI Bill, which kept the family in the echelons of the middle class and which, in turn, provided forms of stability that enabled my father to work abroad during and after college. In this formation as a child of empire, I find resonance with Hazel Carby's *Imperial Intimacies*, which investigates the multiple entwinements of family lines through histories of colonialism and enslavement.[50] Carby, the daughter of a Welsh woman and Jamaican immigrant who grew up in Britain, is unflinching as she contextualizes racialized formations of desire, kinship, and contagion. In her narrative, racialization is a colonial texture that shapes the conditions of quotidian, not just monumental, historical life. My narrative is different from Carby's, but both involve the West Indies, the British Empire, and the United States and both also deal with the complexity of empire when one has both European and Caribbean heritage. This racialization as white, Black, in-between, or neither demands its own further contemplation, but here I will say that my own specific combination—Black mother from the colony, white father from the empire—has felt overdetermined and obvious. This is, after all, a formation that overlaps (negatively) with histories of enslavement and (positively) with aspirations toward the colorblind, post-*Loving* era of my birth.[51] The shadows of both interracial arcs haunt and inflect differently but combine to produce me as a product of these historical desires and complicities even as the specifics of my parents' narratives, relationship, and erotic autonomy exceeds this framing.

By the time I was born, my parents' accumulated wanderlust had led my father to take a job with Dole, whose founding in 1901 as the Hawaiian Pineapple Company played a large part in the colonization of Hawaii and the suppression of Indigenous sovereignty—a suturing of imperialism and corporate interest that would follow in its global expansion.[52] This job produced assignments in Guayaquil, Bogotá, Paris, Brussels, Boca Raton, and San José (Costa Rica), rendering me, for most of my youth, an "expatriate," another version of placelessness. This label, however, is also fundamentally relational—it centers a nation in a way that designates, in my case, desires for affiliation and belonging from a distance. I can best describe the shape of these feelings, directed, in this case, toward the imperial and neoliberal United States, as a form of normativity. In *Why Karen Carpenter Matters*, Karen Tongson describes moving to California from the Philippines as a girl, the fantasies of "normal" that Karen Carpenter represented, and the difference from her parents' way of living: "All I wanted, desperately, was to be 'normal'—to fit in with our new surroundings. . . . In my mind, cleanliness was the mark of prosperity. And so, like Richard and Karen, I too endeavored toward perfection, albeit perfectionism of a different kind, on behalf of my parents and the dreams I thought we shared, in the suburbs that were supposed to furnish them for us."[53] While my own specifics differ from those that Tongson offers, the imagined embrace of "the normal" can be strong for those living outside "the metropole" as well as those who have moved there in an attempt to make it their home. Even though this attachment manifests culturally, it also resonates with Ann Laura Stoler's argument that Dutch pedagogy in colonial Indonesia expanded beyond the linguistic to implicitly train for particular forms of attention, value, and behavior.[54] Some of my negotiations with respectability and authenticity, then, have do with this striving to belong to the normative, the difficulty of actually doing so, and the recognition of the complicities that produce this compulsion.

In the midst of all of this, there is also my own relationship to the Caribbean, a place I spent months at a time growing up, but where I also lived for a year as a teenager when my father took a job at WIBDECO, the Windward Island Banana Development Company, a company whose aim was to bring control of the banana business back to Caribbean countries. We lived in St. Lucia and I attended a convent school run by nuns. In lieu of the feeling of home my mother hoped for, I primarily experienced alienation. It was difficult to live with the clash between visiting and the realities of living somewhere grappling with the poverty, poor infrastructure, and reliance on tourism that marked the "aftermath" of British imperialism. In *A Small Place* Jamaica Kincaid captures these tensions well:

> What a beautiful island Antigua is—more beautiful than any of the other islands you have seen, and they were very beautiful, in their way, but they were much too green, much too lush with vegetation, which indicated to you, the tourist, that they got quite a bit of rainfall, and rain is the very thing that you, just now, do not want, for you are thinking of the hard and cold and dark and long days you spent working in North America (or, worse, Europe), earning some money so that you could stay in this place

> (Antigua) where the sun always shines and where the climate is deliciously hot and dry for the four to ten days you are going to be staying there; and since you are on your holiday, since you are a tourist, the thought of what it might be like for someone who had to live day in, day out in a place that suffers constantly from drought, and so has to watch carefully every drop of fresh water used (while at the same time surrounded by a sea and an ocean—the Caribbean Sea on the one side, the Atlantic Ocean on the other), must never cross your mind.[55]

This life between tourist and resident is born from an enormous amount of economic privilege, which, as Mimi Sheller argues, should be critiqued, since these movements impact those with less access to mobility differently: "It is *our* mobilities that cause the destruction of Caribbean environments, the exploitation of Caribbean workers, and the undermining of social welfare and human rights."[56] There are also additional frictions produced by my queerness, which as Alexander notes, disrupts the implicit heterosexuality of the state and its reliance on specific norms of respectability for Black middle-class women. Of the erotic autonomy afforded by queerness, she writes, "Erotic autonomy signals danger to the heterosexual family and to the nation. And because loyalty to the nation as citizen is perennially colonized within reproduction and heterosexuality, erotic autonomy brings with it the potential of undoing the nation entirely, a possible charge of irresponsible citizenship, or no responsibility at all."[57] Through Alexander's formulation, I can see how my queerness—especially in this particular class formation—has produced its own estrangement in claiming the Caribbean: queerness complicates the familial forms of belonging to which I have access while middle-class respectability and mobility has produced its own distancing effect from contemporary Caribbean queer communities. Placelessness and colonialism, again.

Sensual Cartographies: Or, How Not to Write an Autobiography

Between Shadows and Noise, however, is not a memoir; it is a book of theory and criticism. Even as its impulse, via the work of emplacement, is reparative and its archive is composed of art that I understand through my own attachment to the Caribbean, the book does not solely tell a story about colonialisms, the Caribbean, or me. Instead, it offers strategies for thinking and being otherwise. Each chapter is anchored by an analysis of one or two works of performance, film, or fine art. I found these artworks fascinating; they provoked in me questions about race and gender and their relationships to agency, liberation, and the transmission of knowledge. This is art that made me look and feel and look again, undoing straightforward connections between looking and thinking in their revelation of representation's density and unruliness. As works of criticism, these analyses show the interpretive possibilities offered by sensual forms of knowing, complexifying how we have thought about representation and offering an argument for critical situatedness.

Moreover, it is this very same situatedness that unfolds into the sensual cartographies of shadows and noise. While their contours are formed by the personal, shadows and noise make felt the multifaceted terrain of the uncanny, the diasporic tensions between insider and outsider knowledge, the contagion of rage, the projection of approximation, and the aesthetics of metabolism. Each of these analyses, in turn, unfurl into meditations on desire, spirituality, myth, multiplicity, and rest. Shadow and noise circulate throughout as methods of feeling and sensing into difference. It is important that this polymorphousness is routed through the personal because it enables a robust understanding of situatedness in relation to the politics of difference that animate body work. Additionally, sitting and thinking with difference *now* is imperative because it offers a bulwark against the narrowing of perspectives that underlies our global shrinkage of political and representational fields. If, as McKittrick does, we link discipline to empire, this turn toward situatedness and representational density offers methods of surviving the ongoing aftermaths of empire by feeling through what is in plain sight.

The book begins by exploring two different signs of Blackness—the figures of the Black woman and girl and Afro-diasporic syncretic religious rituals—in order to sense what escapes these overdetermined representations. The first chapter focuses on figures of Black women and girls as they circulate through *Us*, Jordan Peele's 2019 film (plates 5–7). The uncanniness that Peele invokes by mobilizing the horror of the doppelgänger enables a closer examination of Black women's fraught and multiple relations to desire, privacy, and agency. However, the fungibility and illegibility—what I am calling noise—that emanate from the Black girl in Peele's mirror offer possibilities for sensing alternate frameworks and ways of being. Here, theorizing the Black girl anchors the book in autobiographical reflexivity to make an argument for a critical deployment of the uncanny in order to sense what lies beneath representation and to highlight what attachments—personal and critical—emerge through this sensual expansiveness. The second chapter grapples with the tensions between authenticity and spectacle in *Shango* (1945), a dance choreographed for Broadway and performed in repertoire by Katherine Dunham and her dancers (plates 8–10). Dunham's ethnographically informed invocation of Vodou makes felt the tensions between exoticization and the possibility of decolonization while also preserving something of the unrepresentability—the noise—of Vodou itself. *Shango*'s movement through and distance from African diasporic spirituality complicates questions of agency, representation, and legibility. Dunham's anthropological gaze, I argue, provides a particular vantage point from which to think about the desires and tensions of diasporic belonging. In relating to Dunham's curiosity about and attachment to Vodou, I focus my analysis especially on the yanvalou, a dance of devotion that requires spinal fluidity, to ponder the appeal and enactment of liberated movement in relation to Black vernacular dance and culture. The main tension that undergirds the chapter is the friction between insider and outsider knowledge and how that friction guides interpretation. These first two chapters draw on the sense-based autobiographical to illuminate the complicated politics of recognition and legibility that surround these overdetermined signifiers in order to draw attention to how these figurations of Vodou and the Black girl and woman have circulated and to sense other ways of being and knowing that reside within these representational categories.

The third chapter delves into the work of attunement as critical corporeal method. The chapter analyzes *This ember state* (2018; plate 11), a performance by sound artist Samita Sinha that reworks the myth of Sati, the self-immolating Hindu goddess, to highlight rage and its entanglements with combustion in relation to colonialism, racism, and heteropatriarchy. Employing an aesthetics of deconstruction, Sinha uses breath and sound to attune (and to invite audience members to attune) to inner and outer landscapes of infinity. Attunement, here, is not just an analytic suggestion but a practice of giving attention to how and where sensations, feelings, and sounds aggregate internally. Working with and through Sinha's methods of body work, in turn, fuels attention to the sensational realm of critical reflexivity stimulated by the performance. Here, it is the sensual, felt details that matter.

The next set of chapters mark another shift in the book, one that moves away from the embodied negotiations that racialized people undertake, in which shadows and noise function as a preservative of multidimensionality, toward sensing the workings of racialization when people are not the focal point. In these chapters, I critique the disciplining actions of multiculturalism, diversity, and colorblindness and I use attunement to attend to what is felt and what can be mobilized when race is not personified. The apocalyptic is the theme that holds together the fourth chapter: beginning with an analysis of Teresita Fernández's *Puerto Rico (Burned) 6* (2018; plate 12), which offers burnt paper as a representation of palm fronds, the chapter probes the conditions that enable approximation, from the use of "like" to the invocation of surrealism and Aimé Césaire in Allora & Calzadilla's gallery installation *Cadastre* (2019; plates 13–14). Approximation, I argue, mobilizes sense memory to suture different things together while also preserving the noise of this difference and the political possibilities posed by frictional engagement. The fifth and final chapter examines representations of different regimes of racialized labor through an analytic of metabolism. Using Titus Kaphar's *A Pillow for Fragile Fictions* (2016; plates 15–16), a sculpture that deconstructs the myth of George Washington by positioning his bust on its side and filling it with rum, tamarind, molasses, and lime, I argue that the presence of Tom, an enslaved man whom Washington exchanged for the aforementioned West Indian products, can be found in the condensation on the glass—a visibilization of his labor. Looking to tamarind, however, a tree crop unaffiliated with sugar's economy of extraction, enables us to sense a shadow economy of rest, a balm, I argue for neoliberalism's own efforts to invisibilize racialized labor with deadly consequences. These last chapters move us toward political orientations that become available when one engages critically through attunement and its sensualities.

Originally, I wanted to conclude with a meditation on the beach—to mark a Caribbean arrival, if you will. From the veranda on my grandparents' house in Cane Garden, we could look south at the horizon and see a series of small islands—Young Island, Fort Duvernette, and Bequia, followed imperceptibly by rest of the Grenadines—including Union Island. We could also look up and see the vast sky, but my mind's eye remains trained on the sea. I remember spending hours looking at the outlines of mountains that arose from stretches of vast blue. Our house in St. Lucia also provided a vista of another island—Martinique this time. It was a more distant view, but from our perch on a mountain we could see unmistakable specks of silvery gray even if we could never not see the surrounding parched earth. Neither of those houses was technically far from the water's edge, but it still took us at least a half hour to get to a beach. As a result, it became a (maybe) weekly trip to play in the sand, take walks, swim, visit with friends or family. We were never there for more than an hour or two. We weren't people who brought food (other than soft drinks) with us; the beach was a break. Now, my closest beach (Riis) is best for swimming during July and August and most of what happens there is lounging and eating—because it is a whole day effort to get there and the water is too cold for me to swim for long. These beach days are their own scenes—I go to marvel at fantastic swimwear (or the lack thereof), listen to other people's music, and graze on varieties of food and drink brought by me, others, or bought on site. I appreciate the spontaneity, fun, and extended chill of those outings.

Each of these moments, however, offers insight into different valences of queer sociality. Convening at Riis is in some ways more overtly queer, as that part of the beach brings together people of multiple orientations and genders to form an informal community already attached to the sign of queerness. My childhood beach days, meanwhile, offer queerness as a rejection of mandates for productivity and orient us toward the abundant possibilities of beach activities. Neither the beach nor time there is scarce; instead, the beach functions as a resource for renewal. There are many ways, however, that my association of the beach and queerness is fraught, haunted by overdetermination. As Lyndon Gill notes, the beach and its abundant vegetation functions as a way to understand how the Caribbean has been produced as a "postlapsarian sexual paradise . . . one of the primary global locations for both heterosexual and homosexual sex tourism" with the lush landscape serving "metonymically for the wild, abundant, and available sexuality of Caribbean 'natives,'" which governments play up in order to boost tourism.[58] However, in *Erotic Islands*, the beach still functions as a pulsing heart for Gill's exploration of eros as "the confidence that political, social, and cultural exclusions can (and must) be confronted through community building, through touch, and through faith."[59] Much happens against the backdrop of the beach—"We are preparing for today's barbecue on the beach . . . a benefit and a fashion show"—as the gay and lesbian artists and activists he follows create their own cultural institutions and fellowship while also negotiating various forms of violence.[60] Likewise, Vanessa Agard-Jones describes a response by an interlocutor named Karine to her query about a night at Anse Moustique, an isolated beach that serves as one of Martinique's cruising spots: "'*Seigneur* (God), I woke up this afternoon with sand in my ass and all I could think about was that hot little *chabine* that I had on the beach.' Powerfully mediated through her experience of sand lodged in an uncomfortable place, Karine's corporeal association of the beach with her lovemaking made me wonder anew what the sand might offer us as a repository for queer memory."[61] Sand, Agard-Jones argues, offers a way to grapple with the complex and overlapping temporalities, emplacements, and presences of queerness at work in the Caribbean: "Ever in motion, yet connected to particular places, sand both holds geological memories in its elemental structure and calls forth referential memories through its color, feel between the fingers, and quality of grain. Today's sands are yesterday's mountains, coral reefs, and outcroppings of stone."[62]

In both Gill's and Agard-Jones's descriptions we see the beach as queer in ways that resonate with my own beach descriptions—through sex, community, leisure—but also as relations with place that rebuff a fixed idea of queerness and of Blackness. I see this as part of the work of complexification that results in *a proliferation of races*, though also more Black queerness and more queerness too. Gill himself writes, "If it is that blackness and queerness are articulated differently depending on the meaning systems within which they appear, then might it not follow that each contributes its internal dynamism to the conjunction of black queerness?"[63] In this conceptual expansion of Blackness, queerness, and their overlaps, both Gill and Agard-Jones build on the provocations of Omise'eke Natasha Tinsley's "Black Atlantic, Queer Atlantic," which asks "What would it mean for both queer and African diaspora studies to take seriously the possibility that, as forcefully as the Atlantic and the Caribbean flow together, so too do the turbulent fluidities of blackness and queerness?"[64] Tinsley uses the oceanic to develop a version of queerness as Black resistance to their fungibility: "They are one way that fluid black bodies refused to accept that the liquidation of their social selves—the colonization of oceanic and body waters—meant the liquidation of their sentient selves."[65] *Queer*, in Tinsley's parlance, "mark[s] disruption to the violence of normative order and powerfully so: connecting in ways that commodified flesh was never supposed to, loving your own kind when your kind was supposed to cease to exist, forging interpersonal connections that counteract imperial desires for Africans' living deaths."[66] It is important, I think, that Tinsley insists on the difficulty of deciphering these formations given that they are themselves resistances to various violent colonial and racist mandates for transparency. In the essay, she writes that "The subaltern *can* speak in submarine space, but it is hard to hear her or his underwater voice, whispering . . . a thousand secrets that at once wash closer and remain opaque, resisting closure."[67] As you might guess, I see this task of interpretation as that of attuning to shadows and noise.

But the beach really shows up for Tinsley in *Ezili's Mirrors*, which was written after "Black Atlantic, Queer Atlantic." The book includes Madame

Laveau's infamous beach party, but the beach takes a more central place in the book as backdrop for the facility (Crossroads Centre in St. John's Antigua) that Whitney Houston chooses for rehabilitation.[68] Tinsley takes pains to narrate Houston's relationship to this place: "When Whitney told Oprah that she once contemplated 'going to an island and having a fruit stand . . . me and my daughter, living on a little beach on a little island,' was Antigua the island she imagined?"[69] Tinsley also connects the beach to her description of Houston as an iteration of Lasiren, the Ezili deity often described as a mermaid: "Was this where she fantasized she and daughter Bobbi Kristina—herself an avid swimmer—could live the peaceful life of mermaids? *My fantasy, I'm your baby tonight.*"[70] Neither time at the beach nor being a good swimmer could save Houston, but through the lens of Lasiren, we see the beach as orientation. In this particular case, it offers Tinsley a way to describe narratives of addiction and fantasy, formations of attachment, pleasure, and want.

In these multiple beach scenes what jumps out at me is the plethora of verbs—swimming, having sex, gathering, eating, drinking, walking—that the beach enables, each of these verbs, in turn, producing different formations of selfhood—plural, communal, familial, and so forth. That the beach solicits verbs offers its own insight into Hortense Spillers's famous description of Black women as the "beached whale of the sexual universe, unvoiced, unseen, not doing, awaiting their *verb*" (emphasis mine).[71] What Spillers means, of course, is that the beached whale is outside of its natural habitat—it cannot breathe on land. We might even think with Alexis Gumbs's invocation of the endangered North Atlantic right whale who is wounded and killed by commercial fishing vessels. Thinking with Spillers, Gumbs's statement, "Maybe you know something about what it means to bear the constant wounding of a system that says it's about something else entirely," offers an affective connection to the vast repertoire of violences that Black women must bear.[72] But, given Black attentiveness to the politics of refusal and imagination, the beach might offer something else. Specifically, I see this beach, this beaching, as offering a way to think into the densities of representation, which I see as profoundly connected to the reorientations made possible when thinking with shadows and noise. Then I received a diagnosis of acute myeloid leukemia (AML), and I could not travel, could barely imagine the beach, and so turned my thinking on shadows and noise toward cancer in order to attend again, but differently, to the importance of one's situation—especially as a theorist without the triangulation of art object (plate 4).

I
Us, the Uncanny, and the Threat of Black Femininity

ENTICED BY THE PROMISE OF a new Jordan Peele film starring Lupita Nyong'o, I made my way to the theater for an early evening screening. Unlike *Get Out*, whose plot twists provided some of the film's shock, the trailers for *Us* foreground the film's conceit: a family comes home from a day at the beach to find murderous doubles outside their home. While the film complicates this reveal, the sense of dread that it activates—I still screamed—comes not from suspense but from the uncanny. Even before the doppelgängers are introduced, the sense that something is amiss percolates through the film—especially upon repeat viewing. Nyong'o's character, Adelaide, snaps off beat; wide-eyed and nervous, she surveys her surroundings; a high angle shot of the family at the beach emphasizes their elongated shadows; teenage twins speak in tandem; the clock reads 11:11. The coincidences add up and the anxiety that Adelaide registers transmits from actor to audience, even though we all know what's coming. Underlying the unease, anxiety, and dread is the creeping sense that what we thought we knew cannot be trusted. In this case, the uncanny highlights the threat that Black women and girls present; people might not be who you think and much lurks beneath the surface. By focusing on Black women and girls' complex relationship to desire, possession, and the domestic, *Us* reveals the ways that fungibility's uncanniness produces uncertainty—not only in the realm of representation, but in formations of the bounded individual.

When we meet the doppelgängers, Red, Abraham, Umbrae, and Pluto, they are shrouded in shadow. This is the first time that this anxious feeling is personified in the present. Jason spots the group first and offers a warning: "There's a family in our driveway." The family inside, Adelaide, Gabe, Zora, and Jason, become nervous; paterfamilias, Gabe, ventures outside to offer the group what turns out to be an ineffective threat: "Now, I thought I already done told you all to get off my property." What follows are sequences of captivity, chase, and death in which each of the central actors—Lupita Nyong'o, Winston Duke, Shahadi Wright Joseph, and Evan Alex—runs away from another (terrifying) version of themselves. The film eventually explains these doubles—two bodies sharing (and connected by) a soul—but it may be easier to understand them in the language that Red uses when she confronts Adelaide and her family: "Once upon a time, there was a girl. The girl had a shadow and they were connected . . . tethered." In this life in and of shadows, food is raw and toys are sharp. While Adelaide (above ground) falls in love and has two beloved children, Red is forcibly joined with Abraham in a union that produces two monstrous children and includes a self-performed Caesarean. Red's narration lays bare the specific horrors that attend life without bodily autonomy; the story resonates with plantation slavery's severing of kinship through forced reproduction and rape. In other words, Red, Abraham, Umbrae, and Pluto appear to index the return of a repressed past, activating a notion of the uncanny that Sigmund Freud describes as "nothing new or foreign, but something familiar and old—established in the mind that has been estranged only by the process of repression. . . . Something which ought to have been kept concealed but which has nevertheless come to light."[1] Here, the casting of Nyong'o, who won an Oscar for her role as Patsey in Steve McQueen's *Twelve Years a Slave,* offers its own anchor into this interpretation (see plate 5).

This historical echo is especially evident in the primary lack that Red, the only double with a specific complaint, vocalizes, which is that things happen to her *without* her choosing them; she does not consent. This inability, explained by the tether in the film, registers as racially significant, such that Red's dilemma resonates with a historical understanding of the constrained agency of Black women and girls. Take, for example, Harriet Jacobs's *Incidents in the Life of a Slave Girl*, the 1861 autobiography that describes Jacobs's attempts to navigate the sexually predative man who enslaved her, his vindictive wife, and a white neighbor with whom she engages in a sexual relationship in a narrative of confinement and escape. In *Scenes of Subjection*, Saidiya Hartman uses Jacobs's chosen (and controversial) seduction of her neighbor to argue that conditions of enslavement freight both desire and consent in ways that illustrate the need for an alternate understanding of what constitutes agency. As Hartman argues, "The nexus of desire, consent, and coercion that situates the discussions of the slave girl's sexuality perhaps entails a consideration . . . that attends to the agency of the dominated in terms other than those we have previously considered, for if not a conspiracy of power, seduction in this instance enables opportunities for disruption and offers a glimpse of possibility in the context of peril."[2] What Hartman points toward is a reading of actions and wants that may be constrained, but that are still thoughtful—something that Hartman describes as "deliberate calculation" that "reckons with the possibilities for agency that exist under conditions of duress, coercion, dispossession, manipulation, and constraint."[3] And *deliberate* is, indeed, the best word that describes Red's behavior in *Us*. As the narrative unfolds, it becomes clear that she is the mastermind behind the uprising, coordinating the matching jumpsuits, single leather gloves, and strategy for untethering. Her movements are precise and calculated and her plan—a very literal cutting of the cord—makes evident the lengths to which the desire for bodily autonomy persists even in conditions of deep deprivation. This iteration of the uncanny in *Us* is an overt commentary on the ways that history overburdens possibility, allowing us to consider the ways that the film's "two bodies tethered by a soul" illuminates the racialized shadow structures that underlie agency, desire, and liberal subjectivity.

For these reasons, Emily Owens draws a line of continuity between the impossibility of consent under conditions of enslavement and the difficulty Black women find when seeking justice in cases of sexual violence, arguing that this negation of sexual agency continues to mark the experience of Black women: "The history of consent['s] ability to protect only *certain* women is directly tied to whose consent historically mattered, whose consent was imagined as legible—who could be considered a victim of gender-based violence. And that history certainly informs which women consent will (or won't) protect in the present."[4] Owens further suggests that Black women will never really be able to consent given the ways that this history of sexual exploitation shapes the legibility of Black women's communication, not only to any immediate parties but also other external assessors (jurors, for example). The problem of consent, then, reveals the way that desire is inextricably linked to recognition, to the legibility of one's person. In *Sensational Flesh*, I argue that the cleavage between desire and recognition that surrounds Black women is fundamental to the question of who is allowed to be imagined as a sovereign subject and, therefore, whose desire is permissible.[5]

These tensions over desire and recognition are also specifically embodied in the film's climactic showdown between Red and Adelaide. The scene is set to a version of Luniz's "I Got 5 on It" that is pared down to strings and horns; in the soundtrack's liner notes, Shana Redmond describes the song as "a microcosm for how we survive our racial present—it's a deconstruction of what we know in order that it might be anarranged for new purposes."[6] The scene begins when Red backs quickly out of the classroom where she has lectured Adelaide on her (their) origin story. Adelaide follows with big, wild motions. Red moves evenly, conserving energy as she sidesteps Adelaide's frantic lunging. In naming the inspirations behind Red's movements, the film's choreographer, Madeline Holland, describes looking for embodiments that register as not quite human. In an interview with *Vanity Fair*, she notes, "There's no bounce in her step at all. . . . She can balance a book on her head. The way that she turns is usually the way that would not be intuitive, or isn't necessarily efficient. She'll turn three-quarters of the way around instead of one-quarter around. . . . We were looking at cockroaches and [creatures] that would be skittering."[7]

Spliced between this scene of cat and mouse is a flashback to Red and Adelaide's teenage ballet—the moment that Red identifies as "the miracle . . . when I saw God and he showed me our path." In the flashback, the roles are reversed, however; the teenage Adelaide (portrayed by dancer Ashley McKoy) is poised and controlled as she moves across the stage in a performance of *The Nutcracker*. Underground, teenage Red (also McKoy) moves as if she were a puppet. She is pulled through the corridor; she crashes into walls; she dances upside down on her hands; and, finally, she falls. Holland explains that they wanted the teenage Red to move "as if there was a magnet on the feet of the ballet dancer up above, shifting and tossing and throwing the dancer below."[8] The sequence is spliced together so that it feels like watching a duet across time (youth and adult) and space (above and below). One of the film's producers, Ian Cooper, notes that McKoy's dance fuses together elements from what is taken to be the ballet's climax—the "Dance of the Sugar Plum Fairy" with her partner, the Cavalier.[9] Combining their solos highlights bodily control and precision while also alternating between expansion and contraction, producing an embodied tension that fills the scene. Indeed, Cooper notes that this fusion gives the dance "this precariousness—as if you should have a partner but you don't."[10]

In the sequences featuring the adults, the duet is not implied but happens in real time. Red moves while Adelaide reacts; their gazes lock as they circle each other in the tunnels. But what starts as a tight lockstep devolves. Peele continually pulls the cameras back so that we witness the tussling in silhouette. This happens in the flashback, too. After following Adelaide's movements from the rear of the stage, the camera begins to only register her shadow in the stage lights. The teenage dancing Red, however, takes up more of the screen as she begins to dance with less distortion such that the movements above and below come closer to synchronizing. This is the miracle of self-determination to which Red alludes when she says that she saw God and found her faith—a statement that gives us insight into Red's understanding of her relationship to agency. In the adult timeline, Red also seems to have the upper hand—wounding Adelaide and luring her into the darkened bunkroom. She raises her arms to deliver the fatal blow when Adelaide turns suddenly and stabs her in the stomach (see plate 6).

While the other doubles pursue more direct forms of disposing of their aboveground counterparts, Red's elaborate game of chase not only defers the possibility of her freedom in favor of explanation, but also, we could argue, shows the limits of deliberate calculation. Red's several long monologues seem to suggest that her untethering might have a psychological, not just physical, component. The forms of action available to Red, it seems, can only do so much. Moreover, the prism of faith and arrested development—note Red whistling "The Itsy Bitsy Spider" before she is strangled and her fixation on scissors as opposed to more obvious objects of murder—ask viewers to consider the paucity of resources that she has at her disposal. I see Red's extended expositions (first in the house and then in the subterranean tunnels) as emphasizing her need for Adelaide to acknowledge her as a subject, a process akin to the relation between desire and recognition that G. W. F Hegel postulated with the Master-Slave dialectic (hence the un-utility of the scissors). This is to say that Adelaide's refusal to recognize Red's boundedness as a subject—encapsulated by Red's voiced outrage that Adelaide could not imagine that they both could live above ground and share resources instead of having one of them consigned to shadow living—is the underside to Red's complaint about being unable to act. In other words, desire is intrinsic to the maintenance of the bounded body, which Red wants and which Adelaide is working to defend. Red's frustration, then, reveals the ways that desire signals subjectivity's reliance on both the fiction of agency *and* the idea that one is separate from (and can act upon) the world.

Notably, there is a fierceness to Adelaide's attempts to claim desire—both as a means of individuation and as a drive toward normalization. Even before the elaborate chase sequences, Adelaide clings to property—self, family, and house—such that we can register the anxiety she voices to Gabe early in the film about a "black cloud hanging over me" as her fear that the girl in the mirror is after her possessions as much as her life ("My whole life . . . she's still coming for me"). By the end of the film, we understand that the retribution Adelaide fears has to do with the fact that she exchanged places with girl Adelaide, confining her to a subterranean life—effectively, at least through the lens of property, "stealing" what had been hers. This is to say that *Us* also understands desire and possession to be inextricably linked—something we can also feel when we read the film through the horror subgenre of "home invasion" narratives, a trope triggered by Gabe's injunction to "get off my property." Since this genre activates the fear of a border being breached alongside a submerged acknowledgment that securitization is a futile endeavor, the terror of unboundedness hovers alongside the uncanny, providing an alternate valence to Freud's description of the uncanny as *unheimlich* (unhomely). This version of the sensed uncanny produces something more akin to vertigo, the dizzying sensation of being unmoored, mobilized here by the impossibility of home.[11] We can even put this unhomeliness into a broader racial socioeconomic perspective. The Wilsons—Adelaide, Gabe, Zora, and Jason—are, as Sheri-Marie Harrison reminds us, "the black petit bourgeoisie, who have job security and vacations but are still less well off than their white counterparts."[12] Harrison locates this racialized class stratification in the differential effects of the United States' falling GDP between 1984 and 1990, a time period to which the film makes several references.[13] This precarity underlies the Wilsons' relationship to home and property, showing how property is an important aspect of liberalism's "ascendency to whiteness" even as the shadow of black dispossession overwhelms.[14] This precarious relationship is also evident in the bankrupting of cities in the United States and, as Tiffany Lethabo King argues, "ongoing struggles against gentrification and [displacement caused by] disasters like Hurricane Katrina, which . . . continue to reveal the tenuous relationship that Blacks have to land tenure."[15] These literal forms of being unhomed suggest, as Harrison argues, that Red and her family be understood through the lens of Frantz Fanon's lumpenproletariat: "the landless peasants" who "circle tirelessly around the different towns, hoping that one day or another they will be allowed inside" and around the promise of mass uprisings by an underclass.[16] Through this lens, the exploitation of an underclass and the concept of property are the shadow sides of what it is to be an "American," as Red names herself and her family.[17] These relations of race and property also allow us to register the ways that having Black protagonists upends the home invasion genre itself—by focusing on what happens when *home* itself is unstable, such that the parameters of invasion are endlessly mutable—and thus illuminate the ways that *Us* functions as Peele's own particular deconstruction of that genre from the inside out.[18]

Domesticity, Privacy, and Passing Strange

Thinking further with Peele's disruption of genre, *Us* also makes palpable the uncanniness that undergirds Black women's relationships to the domestic. It is not just the shadow of dispossession that renders the home unstable, but also Black women's fraught relationship to the domestic that operates as a threat from inside. While the horror genre makes abundant use of the precarity of the domestic precisely because the home often acts as a metonym for safety and belonging, *Us* brings our attention toward the threat that Black women present when they are, in fact, ensconced in domestic, family life.[19] Interestingly, *Us* does not use these complex relationships to critique domesticity; instead the film provides a meditation on the multiple forms of anxiety that Black women can incite. In this production of Black women as threat, I align *Us* with other recent films including *Ma* (2019; dir. Tate Taylor), starring Octavia Spencer, in which Black women's maternal affects terrorize others. However, despite Adelaide and Red's status as mothers, the aura of threat in *Us* comes from how Black women use the privacy afforded by domesticity.[20]

In Adelaide and Red's cultivation of family and resistance, we find an echo with Angela Davis's 1971 essay "Reflections on the Black Women's Role in a Community of Slaves," where she argues for the importance of living quarters as offering respite from work and surveillance: "We can assume that in a very real material sense, it was only in domestic life—away from the eyes and whip of the overseer—that the slaves could attempt to assert the modicum of freedom they still retained."[21] While Davis is forthright about the labor of this extra burden for Black women, she is quick to assert its centrality to practices of resistance, sociality, and survivance. She writes, "Even as she was suffering under her unique oppression as female, she was thrust by the force of circumstances into the center of the slave community. She was, therefore, essential to the survival of the community. Not all people have survived enslavement; hence her survival-oriented activities were themselves a form of resistance."[22] In the film's foregrounding of Adelaide and Red's different creative practices of survival, we can read the two women as occupying two sides of the same coin (Janus heads). But in this portrait of inversion (we might consider Red to be Adelaide's negative, thereby providing some rationale for her name), they both remain sutured to the sense of Black women as threat.[23]

Initially, the film focuses on the danger posed by Red and her murderous underground army. The viewer, infected by Adelaide's anxiety, spends much of the film worrying about Red's plans for uprising, strategies that we might read (in a continuation of other resonances) as proxies for the unanticipated (by slavers) resistance produced by the enslaved. Notably, however, Davis's "Reflections" emphasizes the ways that rape and sexual coercion were employed against enslaved Black women. These violences against body and spirit serve as disincentive (or punishment) for resistance while simultaneously activating cleavages in the fabric of Black belonging—motivating distrust from Black men as to Black women's perceived relationship to power. Indeed, Red's narrative of forced coupledom with Abraham, although at the behest of tether rather than slaver, produces a glimpse at the aftermath of such disciplining. That Red does not survive, then, might be Peele's commentary on these tactics and the perceived severity of the threat Black women incite. Of course, by the time Red is killed, we understand that Adelaide is the more dangerous figure and her menace more covert; Adelaide is passing. In this way, *Us* invites us to consider the moment the *heimlich* becomes the *unheimlich*, a transition that underscores the representational instability of the uncanny and what it says about the ontological nature of the threat posed by Black women.

Peele signals the movement between the *heimlich* and *unheimlich* by lingering a bit too long on girl Adelaide's smiles in the flashbacks, giving them time to curdle, this extra beat acting as a visual and affective sign of difference. Tellingly, at the end of the film, Adelaide smiles in the same way at Jason. He then pulls down his wolf mask and the whole family drives off in an ambulance. The audience is left to assume that he will keep his mother's secret—his mask signaling his performative return to "normal," yet another sign of the uncanniness that hovers. The film teases the porosity of the border between Adelaide and Red several times, but it is only in these last few minutes when we see the flashback of girl Adelaide being dragged through the tunnels and chained to the bed that it all falls into place. Suddenly, we are given a way to re-read Adelaide and Red's practices of survival and resistance—both are honed by childhoods underground, which are, notably, marked by the quality of overdetermination. In addition to upending what viewers may have thought they understood, this nested series of smiles, their own masks, invites us to think about the link between privacy, passing, and the imposter.

As a trope in cinema and elsewhere, the imposter's facility with belonging incites paranoia; danger or difference are not only unrecognized, but they lurk within interior (private) contours. Of course, Adelaide is not the only impostor in *Us*; one of the reveals that complicates reading the film through the lens of the return of a racialized repressed is the presence of other doubles. Before this point, viewers might be able to imagine that Red, Abraham, Umbrae, and Pluto are alone—although the non-arrival of the emergency services signals broad disturbance—but eventually we meet the Tyler family's doppelgängers, who murder the family just before Adelaide, Gabe, Zora, and Jason arrive at their home. That this family, unlike the Wilsons, is taken totally unaware offers insight into Adelaide's difference, as does the contrast between Red, Dahlia, and Tex. Although we spend more time with Dahlia (Kitty's doppelgänger) than with Tex (Josh's), viewers are invited to read Tex's last-second retrieval of his outstretched hand to slick back his hair as an exaggeration of Josh's immature jocularity. Likewise, Dahlia's grazing of her face with scissors can be read as a more extreme version of Kitty's plastic surgery endeavors. It is this preening, however, that offers the clearest insight into Adelaide (and Red's) difference. Dahlia's self-absorption trumps all. While Adelaide works to save her family and Red seeks emancipation with a side of retribution, Dahlia smiles and playacts with the mirror. In lieu of freedom or survival, her goal, it seems, is to be an admired object. We can, and I think we should, read this solipsism through the lens of a white feminism which pivots around individual rights and privilege instead of a broader dismantlement of pernicious systems.[24]

Dahlia's mirror scene also offers several ways to understand how racialization itself activates schisms between public and private selves. In Jacques Lacan's description of the mirror stage, the reflection in the mirror (*objet petit a*) offers the subject an opportunity to imagine a coherent bounded self.[25] Dahlia's self-surgery and makeup application in the mirror could, then, be read as a way of integrating Peggy and Dahlia into one coherent individual. Fanon, however, points out the ways that the racialized subject must also contend with external forms of objectification through the projections of others—incorporating "the look," as it were, into the idea of self.[26] For Fanon's racialized (and colonized) subject, this means a constant negotiation between these multiple versions of self. In the context of *Us*, this split between the racialized public and private versions of self help us consider the differences between Red and Adelaide. If Red surfaces the overdetermined imago of a dispossessed, nonagential Black woman, Adelaide appears as a rare figure in popular culture, a "normal" (and, not incidentally, vacationing) member of the Black bourgeoisie—loving, playful wife to Gabe and protective, nurturing mother to Zora and Jason.[27] Conjoining these images through the tether reveals their mutual imbrication, their friction, and just how much both projections are undergirded by how much we do not know about these women; everything is hidden beneath their visage. This is "privacy" in its uncanny mode—produced as ominous because of racialization. Thus, the film's real reveal is that the distance between these positions is not very far at all.

From the perspective of those who are attempting to "defend" access to privilege, passing narratives are often framed as morality tales—written as warning to those who might pass—in an attempt to endow categories with an ontological certainty that their performativity undercuts.[28] Especially since, as Gayle Wald argues, it is this performativity that allows race to be deployed in the service of social mobility, "we need to acknowledge that identities, though not etched in permanence or transcendence, nevertheless have multiple and competing histories, and that they likewise can be deployed to serve a variety of interests."[29] Given this performativity, there are also ways to read passing narratives as critiques of the social.[30] This perspective presumes the performativity of identity and uses it to illustrate the hypocrisy of differential value based on perception. Reading passing narratives as a form of social critique became especially pronounced after the 1950s when, as Wald argues, questions of racial integration and belonging occupied a more central locus in the public sphere. She argues that these stories "[mediate] collective fantasies and hopes regarding the inclusion of African Americans within national narratives of democratic community, meritocratic reward, and economic opportunity."[31]

Whether circulating as morality tale or critique, however, the aura of the uncanny suffuses these narratives, underscoring the threat posed by the passer—either as alien or critic. The alien attempts to contain its unfamiliarity, fearing exposure, while the critic wishes to expose the ruse underlying the familiarity of the system. In this regard, the uncanny feeling that Adelaide activates as a passing figure registers multiply. There are several moments—

her propensity toward excessive use of force, her grunting, and her loss of language—where she moves from the familiar to the unfamiliar. Likewise, in the vein of social critique, her ability to infiltrate the upwardly mobile Black middle class invites anxiety about the artifice of its borders and its value more generally. Here, Mikal Gaines's argument about how race and class function in horror films resonates: "Buppie horror stages contests in which the promise of projecting oneself through time runs headlong into the realities of an anti-Black world where ontological security for Black folks has been undermined or outrightly obliterated."[32] Moreover, reading Adelaide as a passing figure invites a comparison to Douglas Street, the protagonist of *Chameleon Street* (1989; dir. Wendell B. Harris Jr.), who impersonates a surgeon, Yale graduate student, journalist, and politician as a form of racial transgression attached to class mobility rather than skin tone. In Michael Gillespie's reading of the film, Street's successful impersonations, "affectively attuned to place, race, and being," illuminate not only Street's brilliance—a threatening mimicry on its own—but that Street's continuous and overt mimicry "fumes with disdain for whiteness and antiblack standards of normativity."[33] "The menace of the film," Gillespie argues, is that "Street's performativity disputes compulsory measures of class, privilege or power, and access to knowledge."[34] Notably, these frictions between interior and exterior duplicate Frantz Fanon's (and W. E. B. DuBois's) theorizations of the schisms inherent in occupying a minoritarian subjectivity—marking ways that the affective terrain of passing is already part of a racialized landscape and that the threatening aspect of its uncanniness is felt most acutely by those with more proximity to power and therefore more to lose.

However, *Us* stops short of critique. Adelaide is never punished for her transgression; nor does she divest from the systems in which she is embedded. Unlike Red, who is fighting to liberate those below ground, Adelaide prefers escaping the United States in favor of Mexico rather than revolution. Adelaide's full integration—including her suggestion to settle in another country—suggests a further uncanny aspect of the Black domestic, one with echoes of what Joy James defines as the captive maternal and what Erica Edwards describes as "imperial grammars of Blackness." For James, the captive maternal are those who are "most vulnerable to violence, war, poverty, police, and captivity," and whose "very existence enables the possessive empire that claims and dispossesses them."[35] James, however, is less invested in victimization and more interested in the harnessing of "their productivity and consumption" for projects of "governance, prisons, police, and the military."[36] What is useful about James's captive maternal is the way it uncovers the co-optation of the possibilities of the domestic that Davis outlines. Edwards's "imperial grammars of Blackness" also captures this uncanny twist on the Black domestic but embeds it within a specific post–World War II framework.[37] The historical arc that Edwards traces shows how "through the verbal and visual language of Black achievement, Black suffering, and Black resistance . . . the United States has justified invasion, occupation, perpetual detainment, and other military-carceral modalities of counter-terrorism."[38] Like James, then, Edwards is interested in the co-optation of the labor of the dispossessed; her focus, however, is on the specific horizons of possibility mobilized by the idea of Black inclusion especially when used to mark others as unassimilable subjects or targets of war. In this complex imperial project, Black women, especially, signify multiply—as radical threats or model patriots.[39] In the mode of patriot, Edwards provides a close reading of Condoleezza Rice, who served as George W. Bush's secretary of state (2005–2009), emphasizing the attention paid to her interior life (symbolized by piano playing) as emblematic of what Edwards terms "*Black imperial agency*—a term I am using to refer to the inner life of Black service on behalf of empire-building in the era of the high war on terror."[40] Edwards argues that these forms of creativity and interiority have been harnessed into performances of "preparedness," which are required in the face of amorphous threat, and that these performances index ways that Black female proximity to power has been entangled in imperial projects. She writes, "Black women's *empowerment* has been framed as neatly compatible with US public policy aimed at dismantling the aims of the civil rights movement, the military-industrial complex and its structuring fictions of safety, bourgeois notions of Black women's roles in reproducing viable Black families, and the development of a US visual culture in which Blackness could be simultaneously valued as an aesthetic object and disarticulated from both US citizenship and radical challenges to the violence that secures it."[41] Edwards's vast framework of complicity and ambivalence is important to casting a critical eye toward the relationship between the fostering of Black domesticity and its redeployment in the service of imperialism.

Both Edwards and James, then, give us another way to read Adelaide's assimilation. That which marks her as a member of the petite bourgeoisie—vacation home, boat, intact family—signify incorporation (however messy) into the social body of the United States via consumption.[42] That which has been rendered unassimilable (Red and her collectivist impulses) has been expelled.[43] The labor of the Black domestic has been co-opted and rendered uncanny—terrorizing the marginalized rather than acting in solidarity. Drawing on Edwards further, we might ask what it means that Peele unleashes this narrative now. There is no catharsis—we cannot read Adelaide as triumphant racial icon—which is the point, but it may also explain the confused box office response to the film. In contrast to the triumphant legibility of *Get Out*, Peele has produced a narrative that illuminates ambivalence and Black complicity with empire (complete with Mexican expansion) and he has couched it within a narrative of Black achievement and inclusion—the characters' race is not discussed or remarkable within the film.[44] This is, perhaps, an uncanny moment of coincidence with contemporary racial and class politics in the United States.

Us: Black Girls and the Politics of (Mis)Recognition

In *Us*, the uncanny surfaces the overlapping and contradictory shadow discourses that surround Black women—the tethering to histories of enslavement and the accusation of being a domestic threat—but the film also leaves us with their fundamental illegibility as subject positions. For me, this inscrutability coalesces into the figure of the Black girl, whose presence operates as a noisy excess to the film. Throughout the film, her appearances convolute linear temporality, anchoring the present narrative into a past moment, only to render both more opaque. The film begins with the reflection of young Adelaide (Addy), played by Madison Curry, in a flickering television before moving to the Santa Cruz boardwalk. There, we see her wander away from her family into "Vision Quest," an attraction containing a hall of mirrors, where Addy encounters her not-quite reflection. The first time we are presented with this moment, the camera shoots from behind to show two pairs of shoulders and pigtails before cutting to Addy's wide-eyed reaction. The second time, the adult Adelaide recounts the event to her husband, Gabe, and we see that instead of a reflection, Addy and the other girl turn to face each other. The third time is a brief flash to Addy's face when the adult Adelaide enters the hall of mirrors (now named Merlin's Woods). The fourth time we see them look at each other face to face—we are privy to the girl in the mirror's perspective, allowing us to see the fear in Addy's eyes as she registers that the girl in the mirror is not her reflection. And, finally, when we return to the event in the aftermath of Adelaide and Red's showdown, we observe the encounter from a neutral perspective in its entirety: the girl from the mirror subdues

Addy, drags her underground, and then chains her to a bed. Within these repetitions with difference there is much to consider. Narratively, these scenes inform the feelings experienced by characters in the present giving insight into Adelaide's anxiety, Red's desire for revenge, and Adelaide's subterfuge by offering a prelude to the actions we are following. In addition to bolstering this scene's narrative and affective significance, the effect of returning to this moment, to this girl, reveals something about the uncanniness, what I am describing as the noisy excess, of the Black girl. Each time we return to Addy, she grows less and less familiar to us, in ways that activate a riot of significations, movements, and attachments to the Black girl (see plate 7).

While Black boys receive much concerned attention—especially vis-à-vis aggressive policing, excessive surveillance, and premature death, Black girls do not, remaining, as Aimee Meredith Cox argues, "illegible."[45] Some of this illegibility has to do with the more general estrangement that Blackness produces from conventional categories of childhood. In the context of enslavement—perhaps exemplified in Jacobs's *Incidents in the Life of the Slave Girl*—sexual violence, labor, and, one could argue, shrewd interpersonal negotiation, contrast with the imaginary of girlhood as a time of innocence and play. However, this merger between the categories of youth and adulthood persists. For example, in her analysis of nineteenth century literary figurations of Black girls, Nazera Wright argues that they were seen as allegorical figures for Black struggles for progress and liberation.[46] In this framing, it is their status as "'not-yet' subjects"—one suspended on a threshold before citizenship and before womanhood—that undergirds this representational possibility. Contemporary discourses on Black girls also reference this theoretical space betwixt and between, positioning Black girls between "can-do" and "at-risk," or as Cox argues, defining them "primarily by their status as both female and adults in the making."[47] We can even see the ways that this malleability underlies the trajectories that Edwards outlines in her discussion of the imperial grammars of Blackness—the Black girl will either persist in her disruption of the system or be disciplined into it.[48] It is this amorphous quality, its own version of fungibility, that makes the Black girl so compelling in *Us*. Each time we return to the mirror, we change orientation—a movement into different imaginaries and futurities that Peele's deliberate shifts in perspective literalizes.

In addition to indexing the fungibility underlying how the Black girl signifies, however, these moments at the mirror remind viewers of the connections between the girl in the mirror, Addy, and Adelaide and Red, suturing the

Black girl with the Black woman, allowing us to consider temporality through the dimension of age, which is its own distinct embodiment of polytemporality. While it differs from Uri McMillan's attention to the co-presence of histories of enslavement for Black female performers, what he calls "mammy memory," and Daphne Brooks's emphasis on the importance of creative archiving for female performers, age offers its own analytic richness.[49] In her description of Black age, Habiba Ibrahim argues that "a fluid relation to the past, present, and future constitutes the womanist subject. She is at once the female child who can only be 'like a woman' and the female adult for whom the mimetic relation to womanhood persists."[50] The "untimeliness of black age," Ibrahim argues, "is the evidence of things not seen," offering critical insight into vectors of oppression and possibility for Black feminisms.[51] Ibrahim argues that the 1970s offered radical Black feminists a profound understanding of the ways that gendered adulthood "would not get them free" (perhaps in ways that we can again relate to Edwards), positioning "Black women's developmental lives [as] never completely individuated nor synced to the timeline of civic and national belonging."[52] These are the polytemporalities of enslavement to which McMillan refers and the ambivalent relationship to the United States that Edwards periodizes.

These different versions of the Black girl—amplified when we consider the ways that one of the film's pleasures is knowing that the actors are embodying doubles and that these characters may be in dialogue with what we may know about their other roles and their own lives—allow us to revisit the Lacanian mirror stage, to dwell not only on the difference between interior and exterior that Fanon identifies but on the lamella, the fleshy container, which Michelle Stephens describes as "fl[ying] off the body rather than assimilating into word or image."[53] The lamella enables these performances of Black femininity, but it is also where we find that which does not conform. In other words, the repeated mirror scenes make apparent the ways that Black women and girls are bound by the projections foisted upon Black femininity, as well as the ways that their being cannot be captured by them. As Stephens writes, the lamella "is, therefore, everything about the living being of the subject that cannot be captured by word or image and symbolized as difference."[54] This excess, which is noisy in its illegibility and uncanny in its disruption of an imagined ontological stability, is where we locate both the threat of Black women and the radical potential of Black girls. One both is and is not what one seems, which is one of the persistent threads of this chapter.

Age, then, is part of the noisiness of the Black girl. As Ibrahim argues, "Black age does not always presume that there is a knowable, retrievable subject—such as the Black girl—that can be recovered through empirical methods."[55] This is to say that the Black girl is not quite separable from the Black woman and not quite separable from the external projections foisted upon her. Further, if we cannot quite know the Black girl within the developmental narrative of aging, without it, things become even more challenging. Here, I briefly mention Zora, the other Black girl in the film, whose presence thwarts straightforward analysis. Her primary defining characteristic is her athletic ability; most of the film sees her (or her double) running or immersing herself in her phone, itself a portal into an offscreen world.[56] Either because the character is shallowly written or because her character's connection with Red or Adelaide is underdeveloped, she deflects my own attempts at further scrutiny. In other words, she is noisy.

By invoking the specter of the Black girl within figurations of Black women and Black feminisms, Ibrahim's prism of age allows us to consider the dynamics activated in encounters with the Black girl and to see different types of attachments and frictions. In *Us,* tying an analysis of the uncanny to that of age allows us to sense the ways that the Black girl functions as a sort of cinematic screen or mirror, generating temporally complex forms of (mis?)recognition. Beyond the world of the film, the presence of Black girls, as Ibrahim argues, punctures the work of theorizing by activating polytemporality in complex ways—thus broadening the "me" or "us" found in these Black girl mirrors. While the bulk of my analysis of *Us* unpacks the stakes of the uncanny as an affective, sensorial, and aesthetic schema that reveals layers to thinking about how Black women and girls circulate both within the film and more broadly, here, my move toward critical reflexivity, promised by the book's introduction, sutures that analysis to the personal, magnifying the sense of the uncanny as a mode of critical embodiment that informs the process of theorizing itself.

Throughout *In the Wake,* Christina Sharpe returns repeatedly to a photograph of a Haitian girl with the word *Ship* written in tape on her forehead; Sharpe is compelled by her face and the historical echoes that she produces—the uncanny, again.[57] The first resonance Sharpe identifies is with Louis Agassiz's (in)famous daguerreotypes of the enslaved women Delia and Drana. After first pondering the meaning of the *Ship* label, Sharpe finds herself returning to the girl's eyes because they draw her into the question of her interiority and her specificity:

What is the look in her eyes? What do I do with it?

> When I stumbled upon *that* image of *this* girl child with the word *Ship* taped to her forehead, it was the look in her eyes that first stopped me, and then, with its coming into focus, that word *Ship* threatened to obliterate every and anything else I could see. . . . Her eyes look back at me, like Delia's eyes, like Drana's. I marked her youth, the scar on the bridge of her nose that seems to continue through one eyebrow, her eyes and eyelashes, the uncovered wounds, a bit of paper, and a leaf. In this photographic arrangement I see her and I feel with and for her as she is disarranged by this process. I see this intrusion into her life and world at the very moment it is, perhaps not for the first time, falling apart. In her I recognize myself, by which I mean, I recognize the common conditions of Black being in the wake.[58]

In Sharpe's recognition of the girl in the image through the condition of "being in the wake," which is to say, in the temporal always of the injury of enslavement, we see how the transit of age (between adult and girl), historical moment (1850, 2010), and place (South Carolina, Haiti) are mapped onto the figure of the Black girl. This quality is what creates continuity between the disparate aftermaths of enslavement, disenfranchisement, dispossession, objectification, and sexualization. Later, when Sharpe returns to the girl, she puts her into conversation with yet other Black girls: "And so this Girl from the archives of disaster in the first month of the second decade of the twenty-first century is evocative of another two girls on board that slave ship *Recovery*. . . . And they are evocative of other contemporary girls, as they, too, are mis/seen and all too often un/accounted for."[59] The girls Sharpe references aboard *Recovery* are those that Saidiya Hartman documents in "Venus in Two Acts," an essay that outlines the historical impossibility of knowing the specifics of these girls because of their unremarkable status as commodities: "One cannot ask, 'Who is Venus?' because it would be impossible to answer such a question. There are hundreds of thousands of other girls who share her circumstances and these circumstances have generated few stories."[60] Hartman also, however, cautions against fixating on the violences, which have tended to give the Black girl her shape but which overwhelm her actuality.[61] For Hartman, this results in a turn toward critical fabulation, a speculative method that we see enacted in *Wayward Lives*, which features unnamed Black girls at the start of the twentieth century as the central protagonists: "Each new deprivation raises doubts about when freedom is going to come; if the question pounding inside her head—Can I live?—is one to which she could ever give a certain answer, or only repeat in anticipation of something better than this, bear the pain of it and the hope of it, the beauty and the promise."[62]

Ibrahim positions Hartman's resurrection of these two girls as its own form of immortalization, arguing that "Hartman's 'two girls' themselves have an archival function: neither one of them 'vanish[ed] into the heap of obscure lives scattered along the ocean's floor'; both are 'immortalized,' . . . both continue to 'live' as evidence of a story that cannot be told."[63] This quality of immortality hovers around the images of Delia and Drana as well, allowing them to become legible as evidence of violence. These complex projections are vibrant, pointing toward the forms of thought that are enabled by these forms of attachment and identification. And, of course, as both Sharpe and Hartman note, there is always the something else that evades not only capture by violence but capture even by care.

Although Sharpe and Hartman transform these practices of looking at and looking for these Black girls into a type of mirror gaze, the fact that *Us* is a film—a moving picture—activates different coordinates vis-à-vis the Black girl and her noise: the kinetic.[64] In *Us*, I see these kinetic strategies of bodily movement and extension in the film's deployment of whistling, which figures prominently in the film. When young Addy enters the hall of mirrors, she is visibly unnerved and begins to whistle "The Itsy Bitsy Spider." When she rounds the corner, she hears distorted whistling returned to her, which sets the stage for the encounter between the girls. Later, just before Red enters the home, we hear her whistling "The Itsy Bitsy Spider" again, and finally, Red whistles the tune just before she is strangled by Adelaide. The whistling acts as a mark of identification (and time travel), connecting girl Addy to adult Red; it offers a sonic clue for audiences even before the final scene's confirmation of this twist.

While voice offers more emotional nuance, it is also a more vulnerable instrument because the larynx requires using many interconnected muscles to operate. As we can hear in Red's strangled voice, which Nyong'o modeled on the speech patterns of people with spasmodic dysfonia, a condition in which the muscles that control the larynx are rendered dysfunctional either because of trauma or lack of use, much can impede vocalization.[65] Whistling, on the other hand, is the sound made when breath is exhaled through puckered lips. The tongue helps guide the air to produce different pitches, enabling a tune. Since it is not reliant on the maintenance of muscle tone, whistling more faithfully reproduces pitch than voice.[66] Whistling offers the ability to produce messages that accurately span distance, acting as a specific type of expansion of self, in which its fidelity to pitch heightens the intensity of connections. In this way we can register young Addy's whistling for comfort as a way to link herself to the space of emotional security (another imaginary landscape). On the other hand, the same whistled song brings Adelaide back to her girlhood (and her insecurity) even as it brings dying comfort (or a final stab at Adelaide) to Red. What we see is that the Black girl has reconfigured the landscape sonically so that it has contours that only she will understand. In whistling, then, I find an echo of Katherine McKittrick's argument about the illegibility of Black female geographies: "The dispossessed black female body is often equated with the ungeographic, and black women's spatial knowledges are rendered either inadequate or impossible."[67]

Perhaps because I am the same age as Jordan Peele, the sight of young Addy in 1986 speaks to me in particular ways. Her hair ties and pigtails feel familiar and the *Thriller* T-shirt that her father wins at the boardwalk reminds me of watching the video for the first time with my uncle, brother, and cousins in the (less scary) bright afternoon. I remember and don't quite remember the 1980s, which means that Addy provides insight into some of the specifics of a girlhood that still resides in me, somewhere. Perhaps I recognize her shock that the world is different than she expected? Still, she haunts in the ways that Ibrahim, Sharpe, and Hartman describe. Further, in this externalization of the Black girl, who attaches to me, but is also not me—she is uncanny—I sense some of her resistance to transparency. I have access to memories, but not my own thinking, my own unruliness. Because of this uncanniness, it is easier to graft this noise onto others.

"Tra la la la la . . . something about a sugar plum."[68] My mother's soft Caribbean lilt comes through the telephone. I have asked her if she knows the song "Brown Girl in the Ring" and she responds by singing. When it was her turn in the middle of the circle, she said she would shake her hips; "wind up she waist," she says and we giggle. When I think of a Black girl, it is my mother whose image pops into my head. I think of this skinny child with knobby knees, mischievous eyes, a grin that is slightly too wide for her face, with hair neatly plaited with ribbons. In the photographs I have seen, I always recognize her immediately. She is the one who always looks slightly off camera as if she had better things to be doing. This girl is anchored deeply within my tenderness. I feel protective over her though I already know who she has become, but it is those parts of her that I can't access—the uncanny—which interest me the most. How are we different? What is she looking at?

Which fruit did she just eat? Her thoughts and visions are infinitely more mysterious than those of my own girlhood, which I maybe half remember but which arrive already attached to emotions and circumstances with which I am familiar. This space of difference (even and especially) in familiarity is the other side of (mis)recognizing the Black girl.

This is to return to Sharpe's question ("*What is the look in her eyes?*") without seeking the recognizable. It is also to remember that this unruliness means that something actual, interior, is always missed. To find this, Sharpe performs her own strategy of alternative sight: annotation; "I saw that leaf in her hair, and with it I performed by own annotation that might open this image out into a life, however precarious, that was always there. *That leaf is stuck in her still neat braids*. And I think: *Somebody braided her hair before that earthquake hit.*"[69] As figuration, the Black girl exists in this space between representation and misrecognition. Locating her, as Tammy Owens and LaKisha Simmons have argued, requires creative reading practices. While Owens looks toward the gaps in popular culture to find evidence of girls in what is left unsaid but presumed, Simmons delves into "rich black counterpublics" to see how Black girls were representing themselves to understand more about the actual textures of their lives, despite the paucity of information.[70]

My mother is the girl I recognize and also do not. Some of this oscillation has to do with diaspora and the tension between the desire for belonging and the differences produced by time and geography (among other things). In teasing out the vicissitudes of diaspora, Nadia Ellis emphasizes this quality of difference, naming it the spacetime of elsewhere: "In my account black diaspora is characterized by a distinctive desire to belong 'elsewhere' which desire produces. A productive tension between attachment and a drive toward intense and idiosyncratic individuation."[71] My mother was a girl in St. Vincent, a place I only know as a visitor, and so while I can register some embodied similarities between me and my mother, it is this sense of belonging to this place that I can't fully understand. It is also much easier for me to flatten out these contours into a simplistic form of attachment than to grapple with her migration and the aftermath of histories lived here and there, diaspora producing its own version of the uncanny (*unheimlich*). I concluded *Sensual Excess* with the question "Is the mother a place?" in order to situate orientations toward indivisibility, care, and femininity within a non-Oedipal psychoanalytic framework. By foregrounding my relationship to the Caribbean as both real and imagined place, I am showing my own specific negotiations with the maternal as place—both as ground for my investigations and as site of expansion beyond discipline (including Oedipality). This sensed Caribbean might not tell us much about the actualities of Caribbean life, but it gives an example of how places and temporalities live in people.

So, in this girl, I am looking for belonging, but when I look in her eyes I see things that I cannot place—uncanniness, again. A disconnect compounded when she tells me stories about finding and tampering with Jack Spaniard wasp nests on lazy afternoons. "But why? Did you get stung?" "Oh, yes, maybe I wanted attention," she shrugs over the phone. She will laugh and say that she used to get stung so much and it was painful and that they would often go for her face. Once, she was stung so extensively and the swelling so bad that her mother was forced to cancel a family outing because she couldn't see. I did some research on these wasps and saw that they build paper nests near water, but in the shade, and I knew immediately which gutters they would be near—some on roofs and some to help the rainwater ease its way down the hillsides—places where I hid from cousins during games. And so, it is in this act of remaking sight and place with wasps—an act that is on its surface indecipherable to me—that I find the possibilities and noise in the uncanniness of the Black girl.

2

Inside Out

Shango and Spectacles of the Spirit

THE FIRST TIME I SAW the forty-second clip of Tommy Gomez slithering across the stage, I was enthralled. The silent excerpt from Katherine Dunham's *Shango* begins with Gomez crouching and moving his entire body to the rhythm of the nearby drums—up and down he undulates before the movement becomes horizontal. Gomez's feet propel his body forward but his spine continues to roll, each vertebra articulated in turn. The scene then abruptly cuts to members of Dunham's company—all clad in white—hoisting Gomez atop a large drum in the air and, led by Dunham, dancing exuberantly in formation around him.[1] Gomez makes his motions look effortless, but achieving this kind of spinal movement is difficult. It requires a spinal anatomy in which the spinous process, the part of vertebrae that sticks out through the back, is not too long or too thick so that it can withstand the compression caused by this motion. The movement also requires one to have enough cushioning in the discs between the vertebrae, so that bones are not rubbing up against each other. But the spine is not the only thing; executing this movement requires a coordinated effort between muscles—the abdominal muscles pull the pelvis forward and under, allowing shoulders (and cervical spine) to follow. Gomez then uses the momentum of untucking the pelvis to propel his body forward and begin the movement anew. This is a feat of anatomy, body intelligence, and muscle control (see plates 8–10).

Although I was watching the clip to gain insight into Dunham's translation of Afro-syncretic ritual, my admiration for Gomez's physical feat produced its own set of attachments, since such spinal fluidity feels, to me, like freedom.[2] This is because the S-curve of my spine—scoliosis—has left me with a knot on the right thoracic side. It isn't necessarily noticeable to others, although I think it is partially responsible for hiking up my right shoulder a bit higher than my left. In lieu of a visual presence, however, the knot is an experience. It thickly connects neck to shoulder to pelvis so that they move and feel together. The knot gets tighter when I am guarding against danger, against exhaustion, against any number of aggressions that I sense require hardness. It offers an emotional shield of sorts. In these moments, the knot also hurts. This is not a pulsing pain, but a dull throbbing—exacerbated when I try to move beyond it or stretch by leaning forward. I always thought it was an unremarkable part of my landscape until it started to disappear. The loosening started during a massage. The person was actually working on my left hip and digging deep into the immobile tissue of the IT band. That area was numb, but I felt a release in my chest—the front part of the knot had unraveled. It turned out that the knot had encircled my heart. What I felt in this slackening was not only mobility, but waves of feeling that had been crystallized, caught, and transformed into density. More specifically, in this letting go, I felt a combination of grief and shame for my specific embeddedness within multiple frameworks of colonialism. As the fascia softened, the shame was accompanied by anger at having felt shame and anger at the hierarchization, objectification, and violence that have enabled colonialisms' formations.

That I felt Gomez's movements in my core speaks not only to my body's specific structure; it illuminates something about how *Shango*'s evocation of a Caribbean context aligned with my own enmeshed diasporic longing and anticolonial feelings. Yet, *Shango* is spectacle, originally part of a Broadway show, and as such traffics in entertainment rather than the conveyance of factual information about the Caribbean or Afro-diasporic syncretic religions. This tension between representation and lived experience, both my own and Dunham's, animates my reading of *Shango* as a noisy representation. The dance number acts as a site for many different forms of projection, including those which might experience alignments as partial, diffuse, or fictional. These gaps between experience and representation offer room for individual investments in addition to, perhaps, cover for spiritual dimensions of the dance, which might be felt by those who *know*. In other words, *Shango* thrives on the tension between insider and outsider knowledge, which enables noise to obfuscate any transparency of message while allowing shadow attachments to proliferate.

Dunham, Afro-syncretic Spirituality, and Black Diaspora

Shango refers simultaneously to the Yoruba deity of thunder, the Trinidadian religion that blends Yoruba and Catholic traditions, and the name given to a ritual of possession. The dance number, meant to flesh out the Trinidadian setting of *Carib Song*, a musical choreographed by Dunham, includes her—she played the lead—but she is not the dance's focal point.[3] Instead, the narrative tension occurs between the High Priest, played by La Rosa Estrada, and, as Gomez is referred to in the program, the boy. The villagers gather, the priest begins the ritual, the boy sacrifices a chicken, and the drumming becomes more intense. The villagers begin to convulse and chant in rhythm with the drums. Then the boy falls to the ground, flicks his tongue, and begins to undulate, indicating that he has been possessed by Damballa—the snake deity. The boy stands at an altar where he is worshipped by the villagers while the priest controls his movements with incantations. Eventually he faints and is carried into the jungle, there is more dancing, and then he returns, hoisted atop the *mama* drum while the rest of the villagers, led by Dunham, dance in celebration alongside him.[4]

Although *Carib Song*'s brief Broadway run in 1945 coincided with the US military presence in Trinidad (1940–47), it does not invoke this time of cross-cultural intimacy and exchange, dwelling instead on an isolated rural Black village seemingly untouched by the contemporary.[5] With a book and lyrics by William Archibald, the play tells the story of a woman who cheats on her husband, a farmer, with a fisherman, whose wife turns the rest of the community against her. Subjected to scorn and gossip, the woman is ultimately murdered by her husband. Joanna Dee Das argues that the play aims to "demonstrate that black life had serious, dramatic, and tragic dimensions unrelated to racism."[6] Refracted through the imperial context, however, we can also see how the play's punishment of Black female sexuality might serve as a proxy for anxiety about local women's involvement with US military men.[7] And, although Archibald left Trinidad for New York in 1937, we can register the nostalgic presentation of the Trinidadian village as emblematic of a rising nationalism that would prioritize the Afro-diasporic as offering an alternative to colonial or corporate incursion. These tensions, which vibrate through *Shango*, emerge especially in Archibald's "Note on the West Indies" in the program for *Carib Song*, in which he offers brief contextualization for the staged ritual: "The lives of West Indian natives often find expression in dances that, while being uninhibited have certain ritual foundations.... At the Shango... the people often go into a trance."[8] Devoid of the sensationalism that generally characterized engagements with syncretic religion in that era, the presence of the note within the playbill accentuates the degree to which Archibald and Dunham view the performance as having a pedagogical function—offering Broadway's predominately white audiences a more accurate portrayal of Afro-diasporic life absent lurid imaginings. Both the traditional white clothing (for Damballa) and the drumming signal an apparent fidelity to Shango rituals, even as the stylized jungle background and spectacle of possession muddy the authenticity invited by knowledge of Dunham's anthropological research in the Caribbean and permit an aura of exoticism.

Born in Chicago and raised in Joliet, Illinois, but best known for her promotion of Afro-diasporic dance, Dunham conducted fieldwork on ritual dances in Jamaica, Martinique, Trinidad, and Haiti in 1935.[9] She arrived in Haiti just after the occupation ended and was in Trinidad a few years before the US military presence began.[10] Although her research agenda counters an imaginary of "primitive" Blackness and is more overtly aligned with the political and pedagogical approaches of other anti-racist anthropologists at the time, it is not separable from US imperial currents. As Das argues, for Dunham, the Caribbean, and Haiti in particular, represented the possibility of locating Black cultural practices that were unmarked (or less marked) by colonialism—noting, in particular, Dunham's enthusiasm that "'the dances of peasant Haiti today might well be those of slave Haiti in the seventeenth century' because they had 'fortunately resisted the strong impact of European culture.'"[11] This was especially the case in the early twentieth century as disenchantment with racism and capitalism grew alongside a nascent pan-Africanism. In this moment, the Haitian Revolution and Afro-diasporic religions—Vodou, especially—acquired a particular sheen for Black people in the United States who looked toward its historical example for models of Black empowerment.[12] In that framework, Vodou became an integral part of a genealogy of Blackness that began before the transatlantic slave trade and spoke to practices of survival and resistance.

In *Dances of Haiti* (1947), Dunham outlines the findings of her early ethnographic work, drawing a distinction between sacred (religious rituals included) and secular (for pleasure or seasonal rites—like Mardi Gras) dances, which often look similar, but serve different social and personal functions. Dances of possession are especially unique within this pantheon because they "indicate the presence of the *loa* in the individual."[13] But, in contrast to the cultural imaginary of uncontrolled volatile movements, these dances proceed under the attentive and orderly guidance of the High Priest and the *mama* drummer who "regulates the tone and pace of the dance, who decides when it is appropriate to introduce the breaks or feints which so often induce possession, and who, by fixing his attention upon and directing his drumming toward a particular individual, invokes the *mystere* to enter that individual."[14] While the specifics of each possession vary, "both dance and behavior are according to formula, so much so that an outsider, after frequenting the dances, can determine almost as readily as an official which loa has entered."[15] This balance between the specific and the general is pervasive in Dunham's ethnographic account. One might recognize a movement, for example, but rhythm and song are critical to being able to discern which *loa* (more typically known as *lwa* today) is being honored: "In general, each family of the *mysteres* has its own special drum rhythm; each *mystere* has one or more songs sung to this family rhythm. Each rhythm has also a characteristic dance it accompanies."[16] The resulting knowledge, Dunham argues, is specific to each community and its set of interpersonal and historic intimacies.

This tension between insider and outsider destabilizes our understanding of Dunham's own accounting for her knowledge. While she declares uncertainty, she still positions herself within a framework of belonging, not only through her interpretive abilities, but also because of her status as Vodou initiate. The first of her three baptisms into Vodou took place in 1936 when she underwent her lavé-tête. Though she later ascended to other ranks—including *mambo-asegue* (the highest rank)—it is this first initiation that she recounts in *Islands Possessed*, a hybrid memoir-ethnography published in 1969. Throughout the book she details the multiday ceremonies while interspersing them with memories of what happened to objects, people, and situations in later years. The result is a meandering narrative whose culmination—the dance of "possession"—is described over the course of twenty pages. After setting the scene, the narrative begins: "Our feet on the hard-packed, hot earth, we were ready to venerate our loa in dance, nervous at the anticipation of a 'possession' but confident that we would not be mistreated or embarrassed because of our new, hard-won status."[17] Then, it sputters; Dunham becomes hungry, uncomfortable, tired, sweaty, seemingly untouched by the ecstasies, "even the grace from which the others benefitted."[18] Finally, she is overcome, though not necessarily possessed:

> The joy of dancing overwhelmed me and I found myself sometimes in front of Doc, at other times in front of Téoline or La Place or Georgina in the ruptured movements of the feints, then gasping, stumbling, teetering on the verge of rhythm- and fasting-induced hypnosis, returning to the sheer joy of motion in concert, of harmony with self and others and the houngor and Damballa and with all friends and enemies past, present, and future, with the wonders of the Haitian countryside and with whatever god whose name we were venerating, because by then a number had been honored and I had lost track.[19]

Dunham's narrative produces a density of description, but it seems to draw circles around many aspects of the experience. Dunham's ethnographic writings on possession are likewise elliptical regarding the experience of the participant, emphasizing the degree to which an "I" would be evacuated: "The person possessed has no recollection of his conduct or motor expression while under possession. . . . The nearest approach to analyzing the function of the *loa* dances from the participant's point of view would be that they acknowledge unity with the *mystere* to such an extent that the body of the possessed becomes a temporary abode of the god."[20] In this context, "I had lost track" might actually include the possibility of possession, but we as readers can never actually know, because of both the impetus to preserve insider knowledge and the undoing of the "I" induced by possession itself. Sarah Jane Cervenak's analysis of wandering is especially apt for assessing the effect of this textual and representational meandering because it sutures physical and mental roaming to practices of Black freedom.[21] Cervenak is particularly interested in the way that we might gauge these acts of waywardness as affronts to various forms of control and discipline. In the context of this chapter, I read Dunham's circumnavigatory prose as telling us something about Vodou's resistance to representation.

Additionally, Dunham's complicated experience of possession is tinged with a bit of disappointment because possession, as Marina Magloire argues, "in Dunham's youthful conception of the practice, is the ultimate marker of belonging. Her possession by Danbala [Damballa] would proclaim—to both her observers and herself—the authenticity of her belief in Vodou."[22]

Magloire emphasizes Dunham's own oscillation between an exoticized understanding of Vodou as it had been represented in the United States and her experience as an initiate. Dunham had expected possession to feel a particular way—to announce a total lack of control—which she did not quite experience. However, Magloire, citing Karen McCarthy Brown's concept of "possession-performance," hints at different modalities of possession (some involving theatricalized ritual) and suggests that Dunham—in the fevered dancing that she does recount—may have experienced more than she initially understood.[23] Further, Magloire understands Dunham's idealization of one version of possession as related to her desire for diasporic belonging. Possession, Magloire writes, "would make her into the believer rather than the scientist in this formulation and put to rest all those unsettling fears about whether she really 'belongs.'"[24]

These complex currents become evident in her reflections on the initiation ceremony, in which Dunham draws parallels to several different understandings of the sacred to articulate her feelings: "I felt weightless like Nietzsche's dancer, but unlike that dancer, weighted, transparent but solid, belonging to myself but a part of everyone else. This must have been the 'ecstatic union of one mind' of Indian philosophy, but with the fixed solidarity to the earth that all African dancing returns to, whether in assault upon the forces of nature or submission to gods."[25] Invoking the Dionysian elements of Nietzsche's philosophy and understandings of the oneness of the universe brought forth in multiple strains of South Asian philosophic traditions, Dunham fuses spirit and ecstasy with an idea of corporeal groundedness that she affixes to African dancing traditions.[26] By describing the feeling of being at a ritual through this mélange of traditions, Dunham is gesturing toward a philosophical undercurrent to the dances (although not providing the specific content), thereby positioning Vodou in conversation with disparate traditions rather than exceptionalizing and exoticizing it.[27] There are, however, ways that Dunham's ascription of groundedness to African dance traditions abuts a mind-body separation that would designate Blackness as the space of an unthinking corporeal, the very threat announced by the fervent US discourse on possession.[28]

While *Shango* may be based on Dunham's research and personal experiences, it (like her prose) is not a transparent representation of a possession ritual. *Shango*, in fact, is a deliberate amalgamation of different island cultures and religious traditions—Halifu Osumare identifies components of rituals from Haiti, Cuba, and Trinidad—as well as movements from multiple modern dance lineages, with Alison Kraut noting that "Dunham, who was trained in both ballet and modern dance, integrated, and at times even foregrounded, Eurocentric dance forms in her choreography. The result, exemplified in dances like her 1938 L'Ag'Ya, was a fusion of diasporic folk idioms and ballet technique that also invoked both Afrocentricity and hybridization."[29] While this mélange resulted in criticisms that the work lacks authenticity, we can also see how these representational choices are not only reflective of Dunham's creativity, but that they work to protect the integrity of Afro-syncretic rituals even as they mobilize a complex and problematic field of attachments.[30] As Das notes, "Dunham told a radio interviewer that she 'hesitate[d] to do the strictly authentic in ritual" in *Shango* because she felt "a little superstitious.'"[31] Tellingly, Dunham herself does not dwell on questions of accuracy, moving instead to the emotions conveyed by the narrative of the ritual. On the occasion of the company's 1948 performances in Mexico City, Dunham spoke on emotion in a conversation reported by Peter Waddington: "Presentations of this kind, she said, not only help to explain the African people to us but they help us to establish a bond of sympathy because the fears, aspirations, loves, and reverences of the Africans are also common to us."[32] In addition to pedagogy, Dunham imagines that *Shango* can provide a necessary emotional connection to African people (and implicitly, the broader Black diaspora). In parsing the complexities of Dunham's work, VèVè Clark argues that her work is "at once a celebration of Caribbean memory and history preserved in dance form and a reminder of cultural artifacts one should not forget."[33] Weary of critics who take Dunham to task for a perceived gap between authenticity and representation, Clark argues that "Criticism of this kind is irrelevant, because it fails to understand that Caribbean dance has been stylized and transformed throughout its history. More important, stylization has been a tradition in American modern dance since its inception."[34] To counter reductive assessments of Dunham's work which hinge on the question of accuracy, Clark invites critics to think about specific race, gender, and class components of the audience, individual variations between performers inhabiting the same role, and techniques for conveying mood and movement.[35] What Clark draws our attention to is the tension between Dunham's invocation of the reality of diaspora and the affective and technical workings of the aesthetic, which solicits connection to the dances on multiple levels, thereby mobilizing diverse politics and affinities. Eschewing the ethnographic frame, Susan Manning argues, for example, that "For those who were looking, Dunham's dances made legible the performance of diaspora and of black sexual dissidence during the war years."[36] Das concurs, underscoring the radical politics of Dunham's choreography, extending

Dunham's anticolonial stance to include an embrace of female sexuality, vernacular dance, and Afro-diasporic syncretic religions. In Das's reading, Dunham "did not accord with black respectability politics of the mid-twentieth century," thereby "broadening the field of representation for people of African descent, particularly women, [making] Dunham's choreography . . . its own form of social protest."[37]

However, there are ways in which Dunham's emphasis on the timelessness of the Afro-diasporic dislocates these practices and people from their current contexts—contexts in which these rituals might themselves serve as critiques of or resistance to imperialism—therefore facilitating a flattening of the Caribbean into an exotic, erotic, and primitive spectacle to be consumed by a global audience.[38] For example, writing about Dunham's influence on Kazuo Ohno, the Japanese midcentury butoh dancer, Michio Arimitsu argues that Ohno's use of chickens and some movements were based on having seen the company perform—either live or on television—in 1957. Dunham's performances captivated audiences, with critics emphasizing the eroticism of Blackness. One critic describes Dunham as showing "robust, sensual, energetic, and thrilling dance with its ingenious use of the distinct movements of the shoulder and the hip, which are peculiar to the Negro dance."[39] *Shango*, in particular, is singled out for its invocation of sensuality and primitive Blackness: "'With a huge jungle tree constituting the background,' the article continued, 'the most primitive, ritualistic, and incredibly dynamic dance unfolded mystically to the rhythm of the drums and to the shouts of the dancers.'"[40] In large part these critics are responding to the atmosphere of eroticism summoned by the dances and the idea of Blackness and the Caribbean, especially Haiti and Vodou, as it circulates in Japan. We should also note that this eroticization extends to readings of Gomez, whose Black masculinity signifies differently through the filter of the Caribbean. In his examination of midcentury calypso performances, Shane Vogel argues that perceptions of Caribbean Blackness produced expectations of different racialized performances of gender and sexuality. Even as most of the performers (like Gomez) were US-born Black performers "imitating Afro-Caribbean sounds and gestures," the fantasy of the Caribbean still carried weight and enabled forms of agency for Black performers and expanded formations of Black diaspora: "In embracing and acknowledging the inauthentic, such performances modified inauthenticity itself and allowed for the possibility of an authenticity through inauthenticity. Disclosed in and as performance, this authenticity momentarily shimmers through the vulgar time and idle chatter for mass media and the anxiety of US racial antagonisms."[41]

Notably, some, such as dance critic Tobi Tobias, were left uncomfortable—not because of the aforementioned arguments about inaccuracy or qualms about respectability, but because they perceived Dunham to be commodifying spirituality and the Caribbean. Responding to Alvin Ailey's restaging of *Shango* in 1988, she writes: "The production is an uneasy combination of anthropological investigation and commercialized exoticism. Strictly observed on their native turf, such rites are meant to be secret, for participating initiates only, here they are being offered as spectacle, and the thrill we experience is indeed a theatrical, not a spiritual one."[42] And, although he does not specify his rationale, dancer Vanoye Aikens, who was the leader of the *Shango* dancers in *Carib Song*, eventually refused to perform in *Shango* when it became part of Dunham's revues: "And after a while I just refused to perform in *Shango*. I just wouldn't."[43] His silence speaks volumes about the piece's contradictions and complexities.

"Ah Wan Soca"

When I first saw the clip of Gomez, I had yet to learn about Dunham's complicated relationships to Vodou, but what caught my attention was the familiarity of movement and the feelings of release I associated with it. More specifically, Gomez's undulating spine returned me to the sensuousness of playing carnival as a child. Most of my carnival memories are of watching people dance through the streets of Kingstown from the second-floor window of my grandparents' shop. My cousins and I would drink soft drinks—red Ju-C preferably—and play—only somewhat paying attention to the gathering. I was intrigued by the costumes and delighted when one summer my mother signed us—the cousins—up for a band. My brother and cousins wore black flared trousers and shirts that tied at the waist while I wore a neon yellow ruffled skirt and top—accessorized by a silver sequined band. We were not expected to dance in the street, but to dance with the other young members of the band on stage during Junior Carnival.[44] Faced with a crowd, in a crowd, I froze—the danced expression of joy feeling outside my reach, perhaps foreign to someone like me who came to visit, but for whom understanding always lay a bit outside (an anthropological feeling perhaps also experienced by Dunham). Such are the tangles of belonging and isolation that are part of diasporic identity.

Some of my feelings of recognition are not incidental. St. Vincent's carnival was first tied to the liturgical calendar; the celebrations were timed to begin the Tuesday before Ash Wednesday in anticipation of Lent's abstentions. Carnival dance is dancing in order to let loose. As Dunham observed of her experience participating in Mardi Gras in Haiti in 1936, "All of the things that you have ever been curious about + suppressed, dreamed of but not thought of—wished without being conscious of wishing. These you do know and find that your neighbor too has been wanting to do them."[45] The size and length of the festivities grew, especially with the addition of calypso and steel pan, so carnival was moved to the summer to avoid clashing with other islands' carnivals and to more easily accommodate the ten days of sprawling events including various music and costume competitions as well as J'Ouvert and Mardi Gras.[46] Remembering Dunham's observation that many dances are performed in both sacred and secular contexts and across different islands, Gomez's movements might be inserted into a pantheon of Black movement vernacular, which is its own diasporic formation.

In a review essay on "Negro Dance," Dunham herself is explicit about the multiple places—rituals, carnivals, and dance halls—where one might encounter these fluid forms of spinal articulation:

> In the more formalized of secular dances, in the dance halls at carnival time, the young people of Haiti perform what they refer to as *do-ba* dances, whose characteristic feature is a wavelike motion of the spine performed in a squatting position, back forward, body bent double. The *do-ba* begins in an erect position, but gradually, by a simultaneous forward movement of shoulders and back, is lowered until the dancer is in an almost squatting position. Anyone who has seen the dance to Damballa, snake-god of the Rada-Dahomey cult, will certainly recognize the secular do-ba as a derivative of the ritual in imitation of the undulations of the snake-god.[47]

This is to say that the dances I observed probably did look a lot like the dances performed by Dunham's company and the dances of Vodou ritual. For me, Gomez's movements also activate specific feelings of embodied knowing. This is not just about visual recognition; when I close my eyes, stop thinking, and let myself be transported, my spine can flow, producing my own version of these movements. I understand this motion and this form of consciousness as coming from the body's connective tissue—the fascia. *Fascia* is the term used to describe ligaments and tendons, but it is also the three-dimensional webbing that covers everything inside the entire body. Described by physiologists as a "fluid crystal," fascia consists of collagen, elastin, and ground substance, a viscous liquid that changes consistency depending on where it is in the body and its surrounding conditions.[48] Fascia "support[s] individual cells, tissues, and other organs," because "it is woven together to create the movable frame which supports our posture and from which everything else is suspended," making it integral to movement.[49] It remembers how to hold the body so that one can move without thinking: fascia is why one can stand up in the morning without having to remember exactly what goes where and which muscles should be activated. As such, it is an important part of body intelligence or what we might call a sensory engram: "Engrams are built up largely from the life experiences of every individual, and are in many ways unique to that individual . . . they are a means of arranging into meaningful sequences the firings of these primitive reflexes units; they are an *organizing factor* that cannot be materially pinpointed."[50] Importantly, this ability to render movements effortless can produce static patterns and repetition that are not necessarily efficient. Further, in order to allow ease of motion, the connective tissue must be able to glide over itself—something that becomes difficult if there is trauma, if the body is unused to mobility or if there is stress. In these situations, the hyaluronic acid which aids in movement becomes tightly coiled—producing knots in the fascia and restricting movement. Relaxation, here, means the ability to move without restriction. It is important to note that there are "archetypal engrams" that exceed one's known experience: "Possession of our thoughts and actions by an archetype may be thought of as the sudden appearance of a 'spontaneous engram' of a full-blown and highly complex nature. It is almost as though the *experience of another* has entered our neural precincts, dramatically changing the hue of our perceptions and our reactions, often pushing us into feats of strength, or agility, or sensitivity that are quite alien to us in our normal state."[51] Here, we encounter another form of possession. This one I link to ancestors because I think this movement is already in my fascia—it can bypass colonial, racist, patriarchal, homophobic constriction to produce fluidity, its own version of freedom.

This place between memory and embodiment is also the location of the gesture—movement traces that convey constellations of selfhoods and orientations toward the world that belong to historical and imagined encounters. José Esteban Muñoz describes gestures as "atomized and particular movements [that] tell tales of historical becoming. Gestures transmit ephemeral knowledge of lost queer histories and possibilities within a phobic majoritarian public culture."[52] While gesture offers a way to access an archive, especially in Juana María Rodríguez's reading of Muñoz, he is especially invested in the way that gestures permit survival—hints of critique and liberation.[53]

Describing Kevin Aviance's voguing, Muñoz writes, "I am proposing that we might see something other than a celebration in these moves—the strong trace of black and queer racialized survival, the way in which children need to imagine being Other in the face of conspiring cultural logics of white supremacy and heteronormativity."[54] The gesture, for Muñoz, is multifaceted—communal but not quite divorced from the realm of spectatorship. In parsing this further, Ramón H. Rivera-Servera argues that "Muñoz pursues 'the pathos that underlies some of these gestures,' Aviance's in particular, despite their seemingly libidinous celebratory nature. It is gesture as resource, as a mode of performance that both plays the surface of the fabulous and reaches the depths of the marginal, material, and affective alike, what Muñoz positions as the potential political promise of this queer way of moving."[55] It is the uncertainty of gesture that enables its political potency. As Rivera-Servera further notes, "In this theorization of the utopianism of gesture, Muñoz invests in its incompleteness as a politics . . . dwell[ing] in its supplementary cultural capacity, as offering a performance that may not necessarily cohere into the grids of intelligibility."[56] This pathos is what I am describing as the noise elicited by these spinal undulations, which attach to Black vernacular dance as well as the sacred. These movements are emblematic of the slippery significations of movement that enable Black diasporic survivance through the mobilization of multiple onto-epistemologies, only some of which we may think we know. As much as I want to feel the freedom of a supple spine, which I understand as an embodied diasporic connection as much as a personal movement, there is also part of me that understands that my emphasis on freedom misses the point. Not just because, as Elizabeth Anker argues—citing evidence that British philosopher of democracy John Locke ran plantations in Barbados—freedom always implies an undercurrent of violence, but because, in this case, it operates in relation to a particular formation of self in which belonging and freedom are things to be attained.[57] Here, it is important to remember that the noise of *Shango* also engages with other understandings of the self and freedom.

Yanvalou, Supplication, and the Movements of Vodou

Gomez's spinal movements, yonvalou or yanvalou (or, more technically, yonvalou-do-bas, to describe "the low bending of the back"), are meant to look like an awakening snake, testament to the presence of Damballa, the lwa responsible for creation.[58] Yvonne Daniel explains that in Haiti, snakes became associated with "ongoing and profound life" because they are found both low to the ground (a place of nourishment) and near to the sky (nearer to notions of infinity) and because they eat eggs, which also symbolize life.[59] The yanvalou, Daniel argues, physically invokes these elements of fertility and infinity.[60] Notably, Damballa is the lwa to whom Dunham is pledged—even as Dunham could "never overcome a fastidiousness since childhood when near serpents."[61] Nevertheless, Damballa accepts Dunham as bride with the understanding that she will serve him whenever and wherever he desires; as Dunham writes, "she must remember that Damballa stood for no nonsense and expected to be rewarded for his gifts and to be offered at regular intervals the food and drinks of his taste no matter where in the world she might be."[62]

Indeed, Dunham's acts of service are frequent narrative interruptions in *Islands Possessed* where they exist on a continuum with personal possession—when a lwa controls one's body—giving readers a sense of the range of practices and attitudes meant to signify deference and devotion toward the lwa. Elaborating on what it means for a lwa to "mount the horse"—the local framing used in lieu of "possession"—Alessandra Benedicty-Kokken argues that "In a sense, the body, that is the *kò kadav*, like the morpheme or the phoneme, is nothing more than a signifier waiting to receive its meaning from a relational experience that depends on location.... The body in Haitian Vodou is a domicile in continual displacement whose denizens are also continually displaced to make way for the spirits."[63] While Benedicty-Kokken is largely invested in theorizing possession as a mode of processing the individual and collective trauma of dispossession, her description of a cosmology that pivots around corporeal porosity emphasizes the communal orientation of this devotion. In this vein, Roberto Strongman argues that "Afro-Diasporic religions operate under a transcorporeal conceptualization of the self that is radically different from the Western philosophical tradition. Unlike the unitary soul of Descartes, the immaterial aspect of the Afro-Diasporic self is multiple, external and removable."[64] It is important, for example, that any purported moments of union benefit the community who has gathered—the ecstasy is not contained within any individual but shared. As Daniel writes, "I knew that the dance ritual's ultimate purpose was to bring transformation of the believing community, such that particular spirits would appear in the bodies of ritual believers."[65] And, as Daniel points out, music and dance are key elements of this ecstasy: "The fastening of the human world to a spiritual world, and thereby the bonding of differing spheres of existence, occurs *through or as a result of* dance performance *and/or* music practices."[66] Moreover, these elements of connection persist even in contemporary contexts evacuated of explicit Vodou context, which Dasha Chapman explores in her ethnography of a contemporary Haitian dance class, where she argues that the "legacies of racial formation and historical imagining materialize through the bodily labor of dancing" to produce "collective bodily practice as a form of diasporic re-membering."[67]

Yanvalou physicalizes these relational dynamics through movement and rhythm. In describing the technical effort involved in the dance, Daniel writes that "dancers allow the entire body to simultaneously relax and work: the dance movement follows the normal inhalation and exhalation of breathing, but expands the breath movement throughout the entire body toward a series of undulations on a vertical axis."[68] In drawing energy from the earth and routing it through the body, yanvalou feels both grounded and liberating. Movement originates from the pelvis; the knees are bent and arms are moved in whichever way feels most comfortable. While the feet may move, the legs and pelvis provide stability, which allows the upper body to feel light and loose. This steadiness permits the undulations to continue unabated. The lack of tension in the trunk lets the spine move as it wants and the breath to move freely throughout. The dance is designed to allow people to follow the polyphonic rhythms and move for extended periods of time. In this way one submits to the rhythm and the bodily whims that it summons. Daniel describes the dance as a set of "'choreographed improvisations' because they utilize movement sequences, much of which are improvised artistic materials, but in a conscious organization."[69] In yanvalou, the specific rhythms are important; they are meant to evoke a form of spiritual connection. Jerry Giles writes,

> The drummers depict our world by playing one constant beat, which is then followed by the shattering called kase. It is at the point of kase by the mother drum player that contact is made between our world and that of the spiritual realm. In Dahomean tradition, the guardian of that contact is Legba because it is he who was chosen by God to be the patron spirit of communication and of music. In Vodou services, the talented manman drum player mimics the role of Legba by providing the kase that permits contact with the spiritual world. After this contact, the music is played in such a manner so as to show resolution of tension.[70]

Eventually one is given over to the beats and the spiritual energy that they contain, producing a dance that enacts a porosity to collectivity and spirits.

Daniel writes, "the [yanvalou] movement in repetition went beyond mere inhalation and exhalation to communicate the sense of reaching out and giving in, or yearning and accepting."[71]

Echoing Daniel, Dunham, in *Islands Possessed*, describes the yanvalou as "a prayer in the deepest sense" and invokes her earlier description of the dance in notes for her thesis as "a psycho-narcotic and catharsis of the nervous system" that leaves the dancer "in a state of complete submission and receptivity."[72] The movement, she writes, is fluid, "issuing from the base of the spinal column, mounting the spinal column to the base of the skull, at the same time penetrating and involving the solar plexus, the plexus sacré, the pelvic girdle, and when this circuit is finished, mounting to the chest and head."[73] Dunham's mention of the solar plexus is not incidental. While Das argues that Dunham's interest in this nerve center has to do with her understanding of its proximity to the uterus (and therefore creation), in Dunham's description of it as "the first great active centre of human consciousness," we also hear her knowledge of the chakra system and South Asian cosmology.[74] Indeed, in the Western chakra system, *solar plexus* is one of the terms given to the energy center that comprises the third chakra, *Manipura*, which governs individuality—ego, personality, and personal choice.[75] The first three chakras establish the foundation for being—they are related to feelings of stability, creativity, and self-esteem—while the higher chakras are related more explicitly to spiritual forms of connection. That Dunham connects the consolidations of ego and its related mechanisms of digestion and metabolism to the yanvalou rather than the third eye chakra is intriguing. In some ways it underscores the deep connections between dance as an extension of Afro-diasporic spirituality while also calling attention to the importance of fleshiness (mounting the horse, as it were) for serving a lwa.

Thinking about yanvalou in terms of devotion allows us to see the movements not as mere muscular contraction but as a window into the energetic dynamics of being. Rachel Wyman, a dancer and student of Haitian cosmologies, argues that the dance moves energy throughout the body, bringing awareness to one's internal state. She writes: "Yanvalou's continuous undulation shifts one's state of concentration inward, to the center. And indeed, as my teacher explained it, everything about Yanvalou is circular. Its path of energy moves up from the floor through the bottom of the mover's feet, courses through the legs, pelvis, spine, neck, and out of the top of the head, returning to the earth to be pulled back up again through the feet."[76] For Wyman, it is this movement of energy that connects the dancer to the world happening inside themselves. Reflecting on her experience with the dance, she writes, "Yanvalou opened me up to the possibility of embodying fluidity and strength, flowing within containment, and feeling at times boundless and removed from time yet deeply within the here-and-now of my own body. I have come to experience my body concretely in all its pain and pleasure, while also sensing that much of what or why or who I am remains unknown to me."[77] Importantly, however, the yanvalou also connects dancers to something greater. In the case of ritual, it enables a sociality that signals a particular way of being in the world. Wyman writes: "One is free to be deep inside oneself and also with others—it is not a performance but the creation of solace within group action. . . . It is not a loud, flashy change but a quiet, internal shift. It looks like [one] has realized a new way of being in the world—more vitally alive, more attuned, and more connected to [one's] full, feeling bodily self and its relation to others."[78] While Wyman is describing a secular experience of yanvalou, several, including Daniel, would argue that the secular-sacred distinction is facile—lending some weight to criticisms of *Shango* as spiritually exploitative.[79] Elaborating on the impossibility of this spiritual-secular division, Celia Bambara writes that "Accepting the spiritual presence in choreographies is a political act that suggests different views of diaspora as ancestral linkages and excavates complicated histories of travel and presence of alternate spaces."[80] For example, Bambara describes her own sensitivity to the spirituality in performances of the yanvalou as a form of "spiritual pulling," which "occurs when one is not possessed but feels the spirits 'pulling' on the head, emotions, and body."[81] Bambara's description of spiritual pulling, in turn, casts a shadow on Dunham's representation of the yanvalou—the dance meant for Damballa, whose movements she incorporates into *Shango*. Namely, Bambara invites us to reflect on what Dunham is *not* quite saying—what is being occluded in her dance and her description, but which may be felt in multiple different ways by different viewers.

3

Noise and the Body-Place

This ember state and the Critical Encounter

WHEN HORTENSE SPILLERS DESCRIBES the violence of the transatlantic slave trade, she borrows from Freud the term *oceanic* to indicate "an analogy for undifferentiated identity: removed from the indigenous land and culture, not-yet 'American' either, these captive persons, without names that their captors would recognize, were in movement across the Atlantic, but they were also *nowhere* at all."[1] Under these conditions, we might reflect further on the suturing of placelessness and fungibility that Frantz Fanon describes in *Black Skin, White Masks*.[2] In the book's famous scene of interpellation, a boy points to the narrator and says, "Look a Negro!" In reaction, the narrator offers fragmentation: "I burst apart"; "the corporeal schema crumbled"; "my body was given back to me sprawled out, distorted, recolored, clad in mourning in that white winter day."[3] What Fanon has described is the narrator's encounter with Blackness.[4] Lurking alongside this terror, Darieck Scott argues, is a displaced body. Fanon describes, Scott writes, "a body which is no longer altogether a body or rather which is doubly a body since it is beside itself with terror."[5] For Scott, this doubling does away with the fiction of individuality, or what he describes as "the 'I' narratives of an intact ego," and results in muscular tension, which we can position alongside terror as a sensation related to fungibility, as a way to index the difficulty of inhabiting psychic multiplicities.[6] Reading with Scott, Stephanie D. Clare further emphasizes the spatial dimensions of this tension, writing that "Fanon posits the existence of a distributed form of vitality that exists between the lived body and the more-than-human earthly spaces on which life depends. This distributed vitality explains why, when human beings face dispossession (which Fanon explicitly links to hunger), they come to experience a lack of mobility, a form of death-in-life, in a word: muscular tension."[7] Through Clare, we see the extended network—from colonialism's metropole to relations with the earth (Clare speaks of gardening as a decolonial practice)—of Fanon's estrangement from spatiality. Taken together, we see the embodiment of nonindividuation is inextricable from multiple forms of dispossession.

Moreover, working through Fanon's spatial estrangement allows us to sense the ways that modernity itself produces a broader cleavage between "Man" and place. While Sylvia Wynter dwells most extensively on the production of different genres of the human, embedded in her argument is also a severing of people from place, which results in a discourse of the environmental as background rather than understanding the depth of connection between living and nonliving entities and processes held in proximity.[8] This, too, is one of the violences that M. Jacqui Alexander invokes in relation to "archaeologies of dominance."[9]

As a mode of repair that favors the possibilities of multiplicity and expansion over individuation, I arrive at the body-place, which, I argue, allows us to feel for fuller modes of enfleshment, moving beyond subject-object divisions and the spatial, spiritual, and temporal cleavages that produce "Man." These dispersals of being occur at multiple scales—"above" and "below" the individual—while acknowledging the impossibility of separating "my" movements from those of my extended kin and spiritual network, each relation producing conditions of possibility, forms of knowledge, as well as constraints and challenges.[10]

Because body-places call attention to the practices and politics of reincorporation based on enfleshment as being in and of the world, they are in conversation with Mishuana Goeman's theorization of (re)mapping, which she defines as "the labor Native authors and the communities they write within and about undertake, in the simultaneously metaphoric and material capacities of map making, to generate new possibilities. The framing of 're' with parentheses connotes the fact that in (re)mapping, Native women employ traditional and new tribal stories as a means of continuation."[11] Goeman emphasizes both the violent disciplining (of gender, intimacies, and spatiality) that accompanies what she terms (following Mary Louise Pratt) "European planetary consciousness" and the wide array of practices that "mediate and refute colonial organizing of land, bodies, and social and political landscapes."[12] In Goeman's textual analyses, (re)mapping emerges as a diverse set of negotiations between violence, reclamation, and subversion. The importance of "(re)" is that it allows Goeman to contextualize these practices within particular tribal traditions and specific histories of violence. (Re)mapping is not a utopian wish for "before," but a set of engagements that draws on practices and knowledges that have been foreclosed in order to exist in the imperfect "now." In this way, (re)mapping is not curative—these are divisions and histories that cannot be undone—but about invigorating paths and thinking otherwise in their midst.

Like Goeman's (re)mapping, some iterations of body-places may resolve into a strategic narrativization of selfhood and relation; others, however, veer toward the disintegrative, voiding possibilities of coherence and moving around ideas of self. These political and ontological ambivalences are why shadows, noise, and their amorphous qualities are such important aesthetic and sensational categories; they enable personal practices of enfleshed spatial and temporal organization—of sensing structures of power, disavowal, and belonging as well as highlighting what is kept illegible. In what follows, I elaborate on the critical and enfleshed potential of the body-place through an analysis of *This ember state*, a work by sound artist Samita Sinha.

Combustion, Abundance, and the Power of Myth

The audience files into the small gallery at the Asia Society. Benches line three of its walls; the fourth, which breaks for the entryway, is filled with a large drawing made from charcoal. Spectators wearing scarves and shawls provided by the museum sit on benches and cushions on the floor. The small white room is spare and cold. In one corner there is a large pile of charcoal. Once everyone is seated, Samita Sinha enters the space from the adjoining gallery. She wears a gray oversized sweater, calf-length black skirt, a necklace that falls to mid-chest, and thick socks. Her long black hair is pulled back into a low ponytail. She sits cross-legged facing the coal and begins to sing. At first the notes sound like phonemes, distinctive parts of words, that might be recognizable to some, even if not me specifically. As she sings these syllables, Sinha makes eye contact with members of the audience. There is a slight smile on her lips in these moments of connection while her hands move through a series of mudras.

Gradually the syllables begin to lose their edges and the sound gets louder and more guttural. At this point, Sinha has moved to the pile of charcoal. Before she sits, she raises her skirt to reveal an unclothed lower body.[13] She keeps singing as she writhes exposed on the charcoal, the sounds increase in volume and depth. With her bent legs opening and closing, her arms draped over the pile of coals, her head tilted back, and her eyes often closed, Sinha appears to be disintegrating. The tension in the room is high and then it stops. There is silence. Sinha makes eye contact with the audience then she stands and moves toward the exit. She opens the door and moves toward a sound box under one of the benches. She sings a few syllables and allows these to reverberate in the space for a while with distorted echoes coming from the machine (see plate 11).

Sinha describes *This ember state* as "a radical deconstruction of Indian classical music to investigate psyches of sexuality and gender [that] uses as a point of departure the myth of Sati—the Hindu goddess who self-immolates in sacrifice—and the idea of dark matter."[14] The specific musical form that Sinha begins with is the raga, an improvisational genre of singing known for its ability to elicit specific emotions from the listener.[15] In *This ember state*, one hears repetitions of tonal blends rather than phrases, which become shorthand for emotional arcs, although the sounds fall into a distinct sonic and emotional pattern. There are the introductory melodic tones, the wilder, deeper, more intense sounds, silence, and then the mechanical playback. The wilder sounds that I describe as guttural align with Sinha's writhing on the charcoal and deliberate revelation of nude lower body. As she sounds, the whole of her body thrashes. Then, there are only echoes of what came before.

Sati, the goddess of marital felicity, is potent. Myth holds that she was upset with her father for insulting her husband and threw herself upon the sacrificial fire in a fit of rage, so that she could be reborn to a more deserving father. Shiva, distraught at his wife's death, carries her corpse with him until it is broken into pieces, leaving sacred areas throughout the landscape.[16] In an interview with *Sound American*, Sinha offers her own narration of the myth of Sati emphasizing the contradictions of femininity that she embodies:

> Sati sacrifices herself by burning herself from the inside with the heat, or concentration, of her mind, and then she becomes the universe, reality

> itself. There's this loaded image of Shiva (her lover) holding her calcified body and dancing his dance of fury and grief. To stop him from, through this dance, throwing the universe out of balance, the gods cut up Sati's body, which falls to the ground in pieces. The last thing to land is her ashen vulva, on a site that is now a holy place. It's an intense and foundational image. So the myth becomes both a focus and a portal. It resonates with real life questions of agency and spirituality and sexuality, the shape of missiles, the question of what power is.[17]

In these phrases, we see that Sinha's attention is less on the mechanics of Sati's sacrifice in relation to the men around her and more on what the myth can tell us about power, energy, and gendered dynamics. Sinha is especially interested in Sati's transformation into abundance, a shift that Sinha describes narratively as "and then she becomes the universe, reality itself." When taken in tandem with explorations of agency, spirituality, and sexuality, the myth of Sati becomes a way to uncover possibility within constraint.[18] Despite being tethered to her husband and father, Sati innovates a path toward transformation and abundance. This is evident in the exchange that Sinha singles out between Sati and her father:

> "where shall I find you again" the helpless father asks
> Before becoming sacrifice itself
> Sati answers
> "everywhere, in every time, in every place, in every being.
> there is no thing in the world where I shall not be."
> and by her own heat burns into a column of ash.[19]

These amalgamations of deconstruction and creation vis-à-vis combustion are also manifest in the sounds that Sinha makes. Broadly, one could describe them as noise because they are not decipherable, but they are felt. Sinha specifies that these sounds are emotional distillations, they are intensity without language that illuminate her movement into multiplicity. While she begins the performance as a legible singularity, these moments in the middle dissolve sonic and physical unity to leave the audience with electronic residue—its own form of ash perhaps?

Myths are about survival and world-making; their potency lies in endowing narrative with possibility. In her analysis of the work of myth in psychoanalysis, Shoshana Felman argues, "Myth is something we cannot be sure we are seeing clearly, but we work with it because it works. Myth is thus a mediation between action and cognition, between theory and practice, a narrative negotiation of difference and self-difference in the very practice of a discourse that purports to be cognitive and theoretical."[20] For Felman, myth is important because it is not attempting to make particular truth claims but is, instead, working to offer an alternate form of explanatory framework, one that functions as explanation precisely because of its relation to the unknown. Myth, therefore, emerges from that space of interiority that has not been (and perhaps cannot be) mapped. In other words, myth is noisy. In this regard, Nasser Zakariya reminds us that myth speaks to unruly ways of being in and understanding the world: "Myths shoulder histories, persons, and practices foreign to even the most expansive formulation of the task of science."[21] By this, I mean that questions of true or false or progress or not are not at issue. In this way, myth is akin to Tavia Nyong'o's formulation of afro-fabulation in that it upends universalisms and logics that have purported to be neutral: "The proposition here, against all liberal universalisms and scientific positivities, is to insist that we do not yet know what a human outside of an anti-black world could be, do, or look like. The critical poetics of afro-fabulation are a means of dwelling *in* the shock of that reality without ever becoming fully *of* it."[22]

Sinha also explicitly connects her interest in Sati to negotiating diasporic connection. And, although Gayatri Gopinath does not describe myth, its functions and possibilities align with her argument that queer diasporas suggest "alternative understandings of time, space, and relationality that are obscured within dominant history."[23] Part of Sinha's narrative of diaspora, in fact, enfolds the mythical within the matrilineal as a source of artistic inspiration. She says, in an interview with *Sound American*, "Perhaps the greatest artistic influence in my early life were the intense women around me—mother, sister, grandmothers, goddesses we understood vaguely whose rites we experienced viscerally on childhood trips to India. It's an amazing and difficult female energy: conflicted, contradictory, full of raw power that can go in any direction."[24]

This explicit gendering of myth finds kinship with Clarissa Pinkola Estés's use of Jungian techniques to describe "*la Voz mitologica*, . . . the mythical voice who knows the past and our ancient history and keeps it recorded for us in stories."[25] *Women Who Run With the Wolves*, however, dwells largely on rereading the stories that have cast women as villains in order to see the myths' shadow side. Estés's argument is that what has been disavowed must be acknowledged and accepted in order to heal. She describes this shadow knowledge as originating from "los ovarios" (the ovaries) and discovering "a knowing from deep within the body, deep within the mind, deep within the soul."[26] Of specific import are the understanding of cycles of life, death, and rebirth and the multiple ways of knowing this "wild, innate and instinctual Self," bringing together story, movement, and sound: "She comes to us through sound as well; through music which vibrates the sternum, excites the heart; it comes through the drum, the whistle, the call, and the cry."[27] Using the figure of the wise old woman, Estés summarizes the healing work of mythology:

> The old woman sings over the bones, and as she sings, the bones flesh out. We too "become" as we pour soul over the bones we have found. As we pour our yearning and our heartbreak over the bones of what we used to be when we were young of what we used to know in centuries past, and over the quickening we sense in the future, we stand on all fours, four-square. As we pour soul, we are revivified. We are no longer a thin solution, a dissolving frail thing. No, we are in the "becoming" stage of transformation.[28]

Estés's attention to revaluing difficulty and cycles of destruction resonates with Sinha's investment in the ways that Sati's rage becomes a creative force of transformation, and Estés's argument that myth heals through sonic enfleshment gives us further insight into some of the work that Sinha's performance is doing.

Although it is an exploration of Sati, *This ember state* also allows us to examine some of the affective geographies of racialization. In an interview with *Sound American*, Sinha describes the "psychological residue from religion, colonialism, multiple patriarchies, [and] assimilation" she encountered growing up as the child of Bengali immigrants in a predominately white and Catholic area of Long Island, thereby allowing us to situate some of the rage of *This ember state* in relation to diaspora.[29] Sinha's mention of assimilation brings us, in turn, toward racial melancholy and the narratives of unbelonging that it invokes. Anne Anlin Cheng uses the term to tease out the complex psychoanalytic dimensions of racialization produced by having to assimilate to a white culture. This work to belong induces melancholy at the unattainability of whiteness for Black and Brown subjects while the simultaneous necessary repression of racial otherness (to sustain white dominance) manifests as melancholy as well.[30] The combination of these formations of unbelonging and racial melancholia undergird Sinha's comment that "sometimes letting in so much life becomes too much—I guess those are the breaking points when energy cannot be contained."[31] In her use of the phrase "too much," I register *This ember state* in relation to her own emotions at these forms of othering. While Cheng is invested in melancholy, there is a connection between these tensions and the emotions occasioned by powerlessness. Further, the tensions that Sinha describes—"religion, colonialism, multiple patriarchies, assimilation"—are not only about the challenges of racialization, but also those of second-generation immigrants who must navigate social belonging with parents who grew up with different relations to colonialism, religion, and gender dynamics. This is a form of belonging betwixt and between that involves trying to grapple with familial histories while also attempting to assert one's place in a predominately white, patriarchal present.

These negotiations over locatedness are also amplified by the idea that there is a persistent charge of foreignness that hovers around Brown women. Karen Shimikawa, for example, discusses Asian Americans as perpetually external to American-ness through the suturing of nation, race, ethnicity, and bodily identity.[32] Sinha's soundings call attention not only to the persistent foreignness of her Brown Asian body and the impossibility of assimilation, but also to what possibilities lie in between, a space that Shimikawa describes as "a movement between visibility and invisibility, foreignness and domestication/assimilation."[33] This space, notably, is not one seeking inclusion; instead, it asks us to think with noise—both Sinha's and our own—and to make something from the gift of illegibility. Noise, here, is an investigation into attuning to various body-places.

What we see and hear in *This ember state* is what happens when one accesses the abundance of a body-place. In the pause that Sinha inserts between "the universe" and "reality itself" we can clearly see the importance of noise's function as world-making. What is important is not that this reality is decipherable, but that it is a universe. To get here, however, we must take a step back to examine Sinha's technique for discerning and amplifying the universe within.

While Sinha's formal training in classical Indian music gives us some framing for her soundings, her more recent work with Baul devotional singers offers another way to think about her processes of sonic deconstruction. The Bauls are generally nomadic singers, who have traditionally held a type of outsider status within Bengal to the degree that Kristin Manring argues that people "may even describe themselves as a Baul to signal noncomformity to social expectations."[34] Traditionally the Bauls renounce conventional forms of status such as property and marriage yet earn money by singing for middle class elites. In this framework, we can register the Bauls as presenting a rejoinder to norms of respectability fostered both by colonialism and patriarchy.[35] Using a one stringed instrument (an *ektârâ*) for tuning, the Bauls practice a particularly embodied form of singing, using each part of their bodies—hair, throats, ankles, guts—to practice devotion. Devotion, in this context, being not only a reverence for the abundance of the universe, but an active engagement with abandoning the "I" in favor of this infinity. Explaining Baul philosophy, Rabindrath Tagore described the Bauls in the 1930s as "similar to the Buddhists in their belief in a fulfillment which is reached by love's emancipating us from the dominance of self."[36]

Sinha's turn toward physical expressivity is also drawn from her own investigations into various somatic techniques, some of which have been adapted from her training with French American choreographer Daria Faïn, who focuses more on Qi Gong and yoga. Sinha's system overlays tenets of Chinese Traditional Medicine and its understanding of energetic meridians along which *Qi* (life force) flows with the chakra energetic system. Though they produce different somatic mappings, both describe a direct connection between energy flowing within to the energy that constructs and flows through the universe.

In the chakra system, *Sushumna Nadi* is the energetic channel that links to universal energy. *Sushumna Nadi* runs along the spine and is concentrated in seven (or twelve, depending on the particular system) chakras or energy centers that lie along the torso. Each chakra, in turn, is related to a different scalar and emotional orientation toward the universe and is associated with a specific color, sound, area of the body, and smell. The root chakra (*muladhara*) represents the energy of being grounded in a particular space in the universe; the sacral chakra (*svadhishthana*) mediates our ability to connect to new experiences and people; the solar plexus chakra (*manipura*) modulates issues of confidence and feeling in control of one's life; the heart chakra (*anahata*) relates to love; the throat chakra (*vishuddha*) enables communication; the third eye chakra (*ajna*) facilitates perspective; and the crown chakra (*sahasrara*) governs spirituality. The energy of a chakra might become inhibited or excessive, stopping the flow of energy (*prana* or breath) through the channels and manifesting behaviorally. Resolving imbalance is a matter of confronting emotional patterns in addition to activating a chakra's specific energetics for better overall alignment.[37]

In Chinese Traditional Medicine, each person is born with a specific amount of *Jing* (Essence) and a particular elemental (fire, wood, metal, water, and earth) combination. Staying healthy means maintaining that particular balance so that blood (nutrients) and *Qi* (life force) can flow through each of the meridians without impingement. There are twelve meridians—Lung, Large Intestine, Stomach, Spleen, Heart, Small Intestine, Bladder, Kidney, Pericardium, Gall Bladder, Liver, and *San Jiao*, or Triple Burner—each of which is designated as yin or yang and each of which also correlates with a particular emotion.[38] Physical or emotional imbalances are designated as illnesses and might be caused by multiple external and internal factors such as too much dampness in the atmosphere, the consumption of excessively spicy food, worry, or grief. Each of these types of input will affect the balance of the body's *Qi*, causing stagnation (excess) or deficiency.[39]

Neither the chakra system nor Chinese Traditional Medicine establishes a normative baseline for health or being; instead, they focus on attaining individual modalities of balance. Bodily tendencies or temperaments cannot be shifted, merely managed according to situation. To take this as the site of the performing body means thinking about what balance can be; it also means confronting multiple layers of imbalance, which may constantly be unfolding. These are practices that explicitly foreground the ever-changing landscape of the body.

Sinha's warm-up starts with rolling the ankles, the wrists, the neck. There are vocalizations that accompany specific movements and palpitations of internal organs. Some motions are for the heart or lungs, others for the jaw. The warm-up's purpose is to warm up not only muscles, but to unblock any stuck energy and emotions. In the combination of sounding and movement, Chinese Traditional Medicine and the chakra system come together. When energy is not moving, it may manifest as tension in a particular part of the body, which may itself be a corporeal memory of physical or emotional trauma. When encountering these blockages, there may be bloating, muscle soreness, or repeated negative thoughts. When breath and *Qi* flow, these pains and emotional patterns can dissipate. The warm-up, then, reorients bodily awareness toward the energetic and emotional. It uses breathing as a mechanism to unlearn habits and to enable an openness to other forms of expressivity. This training is a form of unlearning in that it attempts to help find instinctual, rather than intellectualized, emotions and expressions. This process also, however, can be imagined through the prism of healing in that it can reveal internal places of hurt and rage while also unblocking alternate strategies. We might say, then, that this energetic and breathy introspection uncovers unknowns within the self and underscores the universe that lies within.

In *This ember state*, these processes of unblocking find an outlet in the fusion of sound, emotion, and movement. The performance speaks especially

PLATE 1. Ming Smith, *Flamingo Fandango (West Berlin) (painted)*, 1988. Archival pigment print: paper, 24 5/32 × 36 in. Nicola Vassell Gallery, New York.

PLATE 2. Screenshot from *[Closer Captions]* (2020). Christine Sun Kim, director.

ORANGE
PEOPLE
SUCK AND GET
SOMETHING
OUT OF IT

PLATE 3. Pope.L, *Orange People Suck and Get Something Out of It*, 2010. Marker on paper, 11 ⅜ × 9 in. Mitchell-Innes & Nash, New York.

PLATE 4. Author reflected in Ming Smith's *Flamingo Fandango (West Berlin) (painted)* (plate 1 above) at Nicola Vassell Gallery, New York, May 22, 2021. Photograph by Michael B. Gillespie.

PLATE 5. Abraham, Umbrae, Pluto, and Red in the living room.
Screenshot from *Us* (2019). Jordan Peele, director.

PLATE 6. The climactic fight between Adelaide and Red. Screenshot from *Us* (2019). Jordan Peele, director.

PLATE 7. Young Addy and the mirror. Screenshot from *Us* (2019). Jordan Peele, director.

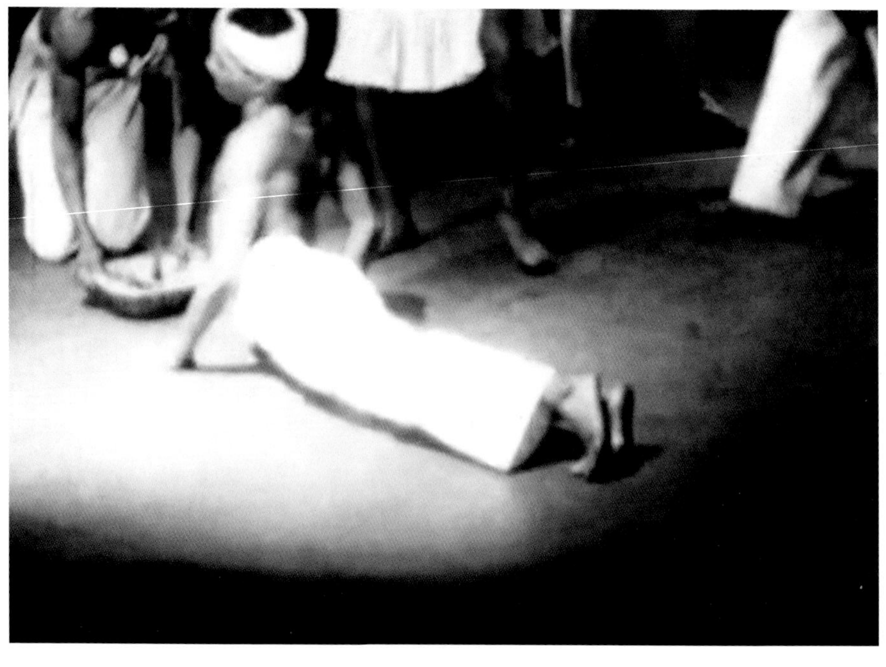

PLATES 8–10. Tommy Gomez in *Shango*; Katherine Dunham, choreographer. Screenshots from Ann Barzel's film of a 1947 performance at the Studebaker Theater, Chicago. Library of Congress, Washington, DC.

PLATES 8–10. (continued)

PLATES 8–10. (continued)

PLATE 11. Samita Sinha, *This ember state*, 2018. Performance for the Asia Society, New York, with Cenk Ergün and Dean Moss. Photograph by Dean Moss.

PLATE 12. Teresita Fernández, *Puerto Rico (Burned) 6*, 2018. Burned and cut paper, 22 ½ × 30 ¼ × 1 ½ in. Lehmann Maupin, New York.

PLATE 13. Allora & Calzadilla, *Cadastre* (exhibition), 2019. Installation view, Gladstone Gallery, New York.

PLATE 14. Allora & Calzadilla, *Graft*, 2019. Recycled polyvinyl chloride and paint forming 17,500 *Tabebuia chrysantha* flowers: largest flower, 3 × 3 × 3 in. Installation view, Gladstone Gallery, New York.

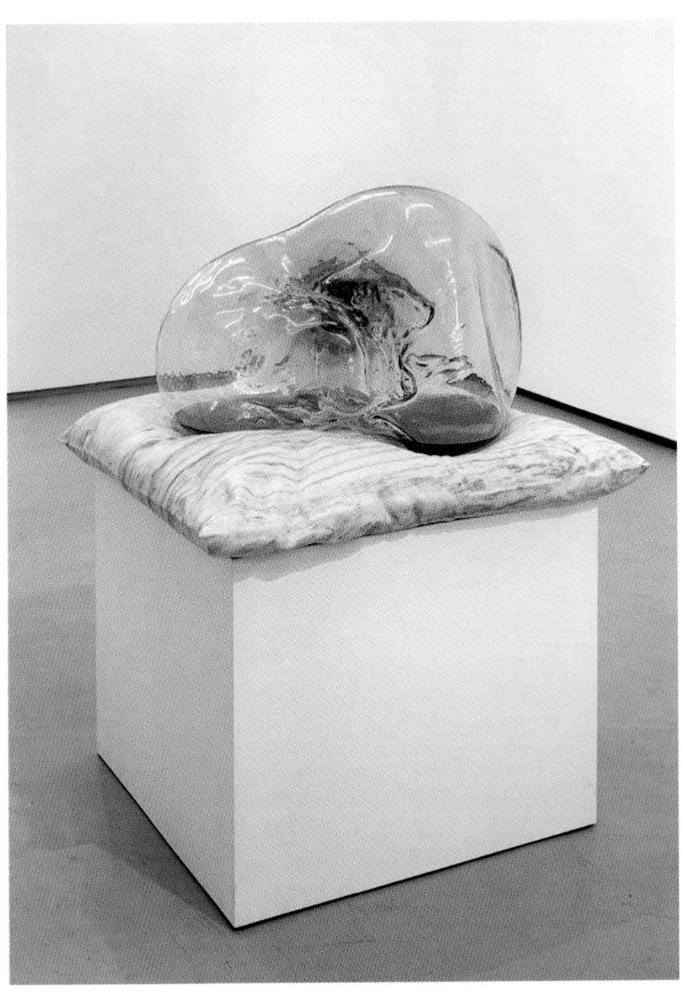

PLATE 15. Titus Kaphar, *A Pillow for Fragile Fictions*, 2016. Blown glass with rum, tamarind, lime, and molasses on marble base: glass, 19 ½ × 28 × 19 in.; base, 6 × 37 × 37 ¾ in. Kaphar Studio, New Haven.

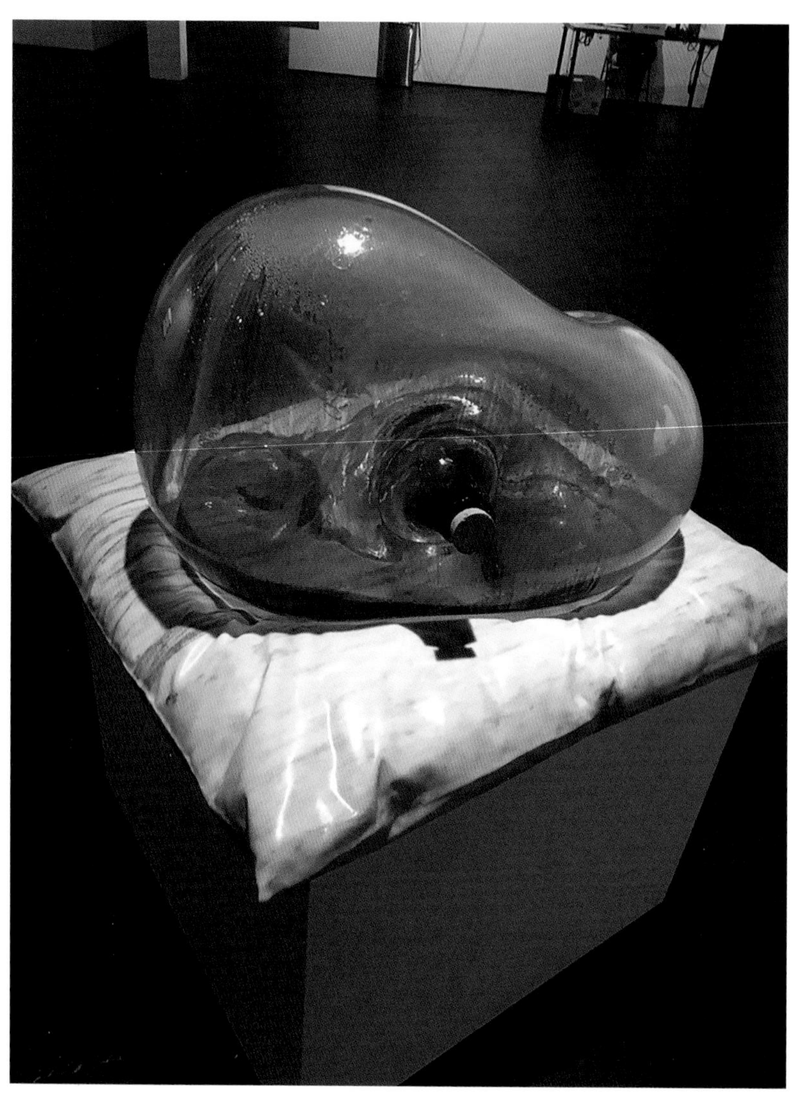

PLATE 16. Titus Kaphar, *A Pillow for Fragile Fictions* (2016), at The Kitchen, New York, 2018. Photograph by the author.

to the dense intelligence and untranslatability of the various geographies of the flesh. I like to think of the inextricability of interior and exterior through Gilles Deleuze's description of the fold. He writes:

> If the world is infinitely cavernous, if worlds exist in the tiniest of bodies, it is because everywhere there can be found "a spirit in matter," which attests not only to the infinite division of parts but also to progressivity in the gain and loss of movement all the while conservation of force is realized. The matter-fold is a matter-time; its characteristics resemble the continuous discharge of an "infinity of wind-muskets."[40]

This work of moving through the noise of one's internal planes is orienting in that it is knowledge producing and capacious because it illuminates just how much is yet to be known. The noise—of joy, rage, grief, and more—that emerges in Sinha's postures and vocalizations differs for each performance because the soundings are informed by the specific emotional and physical space that Sinha inhabits at that moment. There is an outline of deconstruction, but in keeping with the improvisational space of raga, there is no firm map toward any particular place. Frequently, Sinha's eyes are closed in order to better attune to her needs as they exist in that moment. The choreography as such is what comes from movements and positions that energies require in order to be properly accessed. What we hear in *This ember state*, then, is a complex layering of interiority and exteriority. It is the reveal of multitudes within the self *and* their inaccessibility to others. As a form of external projection, specifically a performance, I also see a relation between these explorations and Baul devotional practice. These are expressions of the abundance of the universe and the displacement of the "I." This dislocation speaking, again, toward a different way of thinking with the power of rebirth within the myth of Sati. Moreover, in summoning this abundance spatially, these processes also illuminate how the body-place might enable repair of the ruptures of belonging—by understanding the concept not through the distentions of nation-state but by reinvigorating inseparability from the universe.

Attuning to Rage

I saw *This ember state* three times over the course of roughly a year (2017–2018). Each iteration has substantial differences. The first, in August 2017, was a workshop conducted at the Asia Society. The second, the version I have described most extensively, was during its two-week run at the Asia Society in April 2018; this version was a formal collaboration between Sinha, Dean Moss, and Cenk Ergün. Moss codirected the performance and some of its visual styling while Ergün was responsible for the live composition of electronic music. The third iteration, in September 2018, was as part of a showcase organized by the journal *Women and Performance* at the Performance Workshop in Williamsburg, Brooklyn. When I saw *This ember state* for the first time, I was unsure of what to expect because I was not familiar with Sinha's performances. In this first iteration, Moss was physically present. He began the performance under a fur blanket, gradually uncovering himself and silently beginning to draw in charcoal while Sinha pondered the audience after her sounding and thrashing. I was surprised by the calm, the rage, and the moment of nudity. The last time I saw the show, Sinha performed without an elaborate set or Moss or Ergün's accompaniment. Instead, she handed out blindfolds to the audience, instructing them to put them on at the start of the performance. As such, she entered unseen, sat on the floor and sang into a microphone. Absent visual cues—like the nudity and charcoal—the narrative of Sati emerged in a different form. Whereas previously Sinha's eye contact invited the audience to connect with her and the grammar of the piece before it is broken apart, its absence made me feel as though I was listening in on a private moment. The blindfold acted as a shield against the incursion of prying eyes and stands in strong contrast to Sinha's previous nudity.

There are likely other subtler differences between the performances, but I have only been able to take stock of the whole rather than individual parts. This is due to the particularities of my memory and because the nature of an improvisational performance is to create a whole affect that shifts according to numerous types of intangibles—the composition of the audience, the performer's own physical and emotional state, and the set, among other elements. What is impressive about *This ember state* is how much coherence remains despite the obvious changes in staging. Though these alternate versions emphasize disparate aspects of the performance's complexity, the core, which is a sonic story that moves from singularity to abundance, remains untouched. To hear this narrative, especially in the absence of the visual, is to feel it.

Here, we might wish to think with Gayatri Chakravorty Spivak's suggestion in "Can the Subaltern Speak?" to move beyond recognition as a framework. If the female subaltern does not have access to a nuanced subject position because she is the site of projection and contestation, Spivak reminds us to look for the silences and gaps where we might find otherness. What

Spivak suggests as a solution to this lacuna of agency and subjectivity is a move away from language toward a practice of attunement—a being with—that she describes as "learning to speak to (rather than listen to or speak for) the historically muted subject of the subaltern."[41] By instructing us to speak to this subject, who has been rendered mute by various forms of overdetermination, Spivak is telling us to become comfortable with noise and to find ways of sitting ethically with this indecipherability. In her essay, Spivak turns toward Derrida and his methods of deconstruction, specifically catachresis because it offers a way to see the illegibility, the noise, at the heart of representation. This is to say that contradiction inheres in the concept. It is this appropriation of noise that offers possibilities for a conversation, to use Spivak's idea of "speaking to." Spivak writes that Derrida, in this way, is politically useful because he not only calls attention to the impossibility of representation, but also "he calls for a rewriting of the utopian structural impulse as 'rendering delirious that interior voice that is the voice of the other in us.'"[42]

There are ways that attunement and listening converge. I see both as practices that utilize multiple forms of sensory input that require extension. For example, Jean-Luc Nancy describes listening as "enter[ing] that spatiality by which, at the same time, [the I] is penetrated, for it opens up in me as well as around me, and from me as well as toward me. . . . To be listening is to be *at the same time* outside and inside, to be open *from* without and *from* within, hence from one to the other and from one in the other."[43] Here, Nancy describes listening as a coproduction of self and other. Listening in this mode emerges from vulnerability and curiosity; Nicole Furlonge describes listening as "an artistic, civic, and interpretive practice that emerges from a place of wonder, curiosity and *not knowing*."[44] But in this yoking of listening to discernment, listening has multiple sides. The listening ear learns through what Jennifer Lynn Stoever names "surveillance, discipline, and interpretation, [such that] certain associations between race and sound come to seem normal, natural, and 'right.'"[45] And industries have been able to manufacture their ideal listener, a process that Roshanak Kheshti describes through the elevation of the white female listener as "the topos of the American world music industry," writing that "her aurality motivates the industry at the level of hardware, sound, and affect design."[46] As Robin James notes, the sonic episteme is not neutral.[47]

However, attunement is about cultivating the awareness of multiplicity rather than discernment. I think of attunement in relation to the hunger that I describe in Lyle Ashton Harris's photographic self-portrait *Billie #21* (2002).

There, hunger is born out of the plural selfhood that Harris's citation of Billie Holiday produces. In *Sensual Excess*, I wrote that this hunger "reveals a sensuality or mode of being and relating that prioritizes openness, vulnerability, and a willingness to ingest without necessarily choosing what one is taking in. This is not the desire born of subjectivity (in which subject wishes to possess object), but an embodied hunger that takes joy and pain in this gesture of radical openness toward otherness."[48] Attunement, I argue, allows us to move toward this radical openness. I see attunement as a process of learning, opening up, and sitting with difficulty. More specifically, attunement amplifies one's capacity to sit with what is not necessarily understood but is known through feeling, building certainty in and of enfleshment. The goal of attunement more generally is not mastery, but continually finding that which one does not know as well as those places of resistance, where we might locate difficulty or negativity. Attunement can uncover previously learned patterns, narratives, and habits with curiosity—so that one can work toward letting go or simply sitting with these densities of shadows and noise.

This awareness of multiple (and perhaps incoherent) ways that the body absorbs information is, I think, an important way of attuning to noise. Noise demands that we pay attention to affect and sensation as we trace the contours of emotion. This is not something one can think one's way through. This attention to somatic reactivity is especially important when we are talking about the energetic body. Its language is not necessarily on the register of the visible or verbal. The sounds that Sinha makes may hit the ears, but they do not stay there; their meaning hits one's entire physicality. To witness the deconstruction of self is to also be willing to break oneself open to absorb this energy and see how it rearranges one's own body-place.

Some of this ethical engagement happens through the detail, especially as theorized by Alexandra Vazquez, who writes that details are "events that instantly reveal and honor what can't be said—as well as agents that also withhold what can."[49] In describing the methodology that she terms "listening in detail," Vazquez argues that the technique moves beyond "the service of instant allegory, to signify sweeping historical truths, or as a point of departure for more legible discourses about race and nation."[50] Though sound emerges from and can be understood in relation to the specific contexts of race and nation, listening in detail calls into question an overreliance on context and instead urges us to really theorize with the epistemologies brought forth by listening, which means paying "attention to this past, present, and unheard future."[51] This is to say that the methodology focuses on the sonic elements that stay with *the listener* and open fields of meaning. This version of listening, I think, says a great deal about what it feels like to attune to a performance. Things are transmitted in a way that makes it difficult to pinpoint what exactly is going on, what is being transmitted. This is where description becomes an asset—it allows one to think less of capture and more of networks of emotions and sensations that are ever perceiving disparate relations.

For me, an example of what it is to attune to a live performance can be found in Joshua Chambers-Letson's reflections in *After the Party*. For example, he enfolds a taxi ride, the weather, and the placement of benches into his description of Eiko Otake's performance at Philadelphia's 30th Street Station. Addressing his companion for the outing, Karen Shimikawa, he writes,

> You and I are in a cab riding through afternoon traffic in downtown Philadelphia. There's a light drizzle outside; everything is gray. I press my forehead into the glass to watch the buildings through the window as we talk. . . . I admit to you that in spite of the fact that I profess to be a professor of performance studies, I don't always sit all the way through durational performances. . . . I tell you about the only other time I've seen Eiko dance . . . Looking through the holes into the interior space, you see Eiko & Komo lying together and dancing naked in the center of a nest, a pile or crater of grass, feathers, and earth. There was a passage into the interior, where you could rest on a bench and watch them dance at a glacial pace to the soundtrack of dripping water and the noises made by the people in the museum. . . . Time is out of joint. Arriving a few minutes late, we missed her entrance.[52]

I dwell on Chambers-Letson's description to show the different entanglements—indeed, this is from a chapter titled "Eiko's Entanglements"—that circulate when we talk about listening in this way. In detailing their surroundings, his past encounters with Eiko, and his thoughts in anticipation of the performance, we are given access to how his body is meeting Eiko. These occur in lieu of much description of the performance itself, which, as he notes, is difficult to represent because of its slowness "as a practice that evades capture, while inhabiting, moving through, across, and exceeding incommensurable temporal, spatial, and bodily coordinates."[53] In this version of attunement, we get a sense of the breadth of attention and the importance of attending to all of these nuances as things that inform the performance.[54] Chambers-Letson is bringing his body to the encounter and making that explicit, which, in turn, invites us to dwell in what is felt in the ways that the detail reveals unexpected connections and feelings while still preserving the noise of the performance.

Returning to *This ember state*, April 21 was a cold, clear spring day. A detail—earlier in the week, on a flight from St. Louis to San Francisco, I read Junot Díaz's essay "The Silence: The Legacy of Childhood Trauma," where he describes being raped as a boy and the aftermath of that trauma: a swirling of anxiety, depression, rage, and difficulty being accountable for his own actions.[55] In Díaz's self-framing as passive, I recognized my own strategy for grappling with the repercussions of unwanted sexual encounters in adolescence. His analysis cut deep, revealing assumptions I had made about myself and unmooring my sense of internal cohesion. As a result, when I sat on the floor of the Asia Society, I was freezing and discombobulated and had to arrange myself into a seated position that I could withstand for a length of time. My back and hip flexors screamed. For this performance I was all body and Sinha's interpretation of Sati resonated.

More specifically, I felt her performance in my psoas—the muscle that connects leg and spine, attaching at the lumbar spine, winding through the abdominal core, and attaching again at the top of the femur. The psoas is a very emotional muscle—its contractions are often cued by the fear and anxiety of "fight or flight." If one is in a prolonged state of anxiety or fear, the muscle is very hard to release, resulting in an ache in the hips and a feeling of being "ungrounded"—resulting in timidity or anger. Because it winds through the abdomen, the psoas is in proximity to the gut—the so-called second brain because it has its own nervous system. The gut, associated with viscera, instinct, a language that is the body's own, has its own social world. It acts as a mediator between inside and outside—bringing in food to transform it into energy and expelling that which no longer serves. It is functional and yet also very reactive; it constricts in moments of anxiety and relaxes in moments of joy. It is also an area of great bodily vulnerability since it is not protected by a shield of bones—hence its great responsiveness. To attune with the gut is to sit with the space of somatic reactivity, it is to cede the brain's control over thought to this other organ. The psoas also travels close to the kidneys linking it to the Kidney meridian, which brings *Qi* from the rest of the body to be infused with spirit. This meridian finds its most externally accessible points on the inner legs and it governs fear. Too much results in rigidity, phobia, and a withholding of spirit while too little results in an attachment to dangerous thrills.

Remember my tight and aching hips and back? Those sensations of constriction were my psoas speaking to and through me. I was attuning to Sinha with my own recognition of the emotions that Díaz described and that I was realizing I felt. Most specifically, however, this ache was bringing me toward rage, an emotion whose province is often described as a combination of impotence and injustice. While some feminists, including Audre Lorde, Brittney Cooper, and Soraya Chemaly, have reclaimed rage and anger, arguing that its potency can (and does) ignite social justice campaigns, the charge of being angry has long been used to discipline and vilify women.[56] This tension is evident in Cooper's statement that "rage and respectability can't exist in the same space."[57] Anger unexpressed, however, produces its own distortions. Some argue, for example, that when turned inward, anger manifests as a type of masochism, depression, or grief—emotions that find kinship in their prioritization of powerlessness and passivity.[58] Indeed, there are some who argue that sadness is the manifestation of rage turned inward because its cause has not been sufficiently acknowledged.[59]

We can think, for example, about the ways that assimilation and racial melancholy might also provide cover for anger and rage. In bringing together individual psychic and somatic negotiations with the broader frames of geography and history, we can consider the scalar implications of the body-place and the reparative work that it performs conceptually. Sinha's feelings of unbelonging and the repair that abundance affords finds resonance with my own way of making sense of the rage I encountered in attuning to her performance. I was not specifically angry with any individuals—there is an unfortunate prevalence to unwanted sexual encounters—but I was filled with rage about the structures of racism and colonial violence that enabled others to consider me not only available, but receptive. I felt this violence when being exoticized—hailed as a "muñeca caribeña" (Caribbean doll)—and also when approached under the guise of ethnic solidarity. It is impossible to separate my upbringing as a Black circumcolonial subject and second- (or first-)generation immigrant from scenes of assault because the specific ways that a Black girl in those spaces is approached and given value has everything to do with where she is sensed to belong—in these cases, somewhere between an elsewhere and a nowhere of consequence. Tiffany Lethabo King, notably, offers the framework of colonial racism in her interpretation of Díaz: "One way to frame Díaz's trauma, as well as his alleged sexual predation and how it shows up in his work, ethically is to think about it structurally and as a legacy of conquest."[60] I say this not to assert priority over one type of trauma over another, but to show that they might be layered. When I encountered *This ember state*, then, I recognized placelessness. I felt creativity, pleasure, and sadness, in and through Sinha's unfolding, a layer of noise resonant with my own emergent landscape of rage.

4 On the Brink

Approximation, Difference, and Ongoing Storms

WHEN YOU HAVE BEEN THROUGH a hurricane or tropical storm, the feeling stays in your body. When I was fourteen and living in St. Lucia, Tropical Storm Debby hit the island. We prepared by stocking up on nonperishable food and filling bathtubs with water. The storm was slow and although not as strong as a hurricane, the sound of wind wrapping against itself and then against the house and trees was pervasive. The wind was loud, louder than the rain, which felt more like a constant thumping against windows and roofs. The storm's lashes rendered enclosure (both physically and mentally) difficult—its sounds, winds, and rains continually encroached. Even inside, I could feel everything. Daniel Glaser describes the complex sensations of experiencing hurricane winds by relating it to a tactile vibrational economy that is also highly reliant on emotion:

> Wind generates vibrations which are generally processed like touch, but it seems that for insects at least, it's the hearing circuits that are best placed to decode these signals. . . . Of course, the most basic response to these events is fear and awe. Our brain generates the fear and that triggers the gut, which feeds back to the brain. The sensation is really part of an indi-

rect loop. If the hurricane struck your body directly that would be a very different story.[1]

It was noisy—noisy in the way that Marina Peterson describes as "waiver[ing] between vibration and pressure."[2] Pressure, here, is both that which comes from the storm and the bodily response it elicits—what does one do when faced with the immensity of nature? Our rented house in Cap Estate was constructed from designs originally meant for the Arizona desert, which meant that there was no local specificity; the house had poor natural ventilation and required air conditioning. When the power cut out, then, there was a stagnant, humid heat that sat on me. We were in the dark, somewhat huddled together without any reassuring sonic hums, only the loud punctuation of destruction. The air felt dank and scarce because of the proximity of other people and its inability to circulate. During such storms, the churning funnel lifts fresh (warmer) air and only leaves what has already been breathed below. I was soaked, not from a breached exterior, but from my own sweat, although it was unclear if the moisture was coming from my own body or the humid air. Sweat, in this context, indexed the waves of fear, awe, heat, and humidity.

When I saw Teresita Fernández's *Puerto Rico (Burned) 6* (2018), in a Chelsea gallery on my birthday, I was returned to the sensations of the storm. The work of art looks like the weather-beaten remnants—fronds askew and broken—of palm trees. The displacement of this piece is profound, it is unclear if one is looking up at the destruction from the ground or looking down at its reflection in water. This gaze from above (or below) mimics the disorientation of a hurricane. Fernández produces this approximation of a storm by precisely cutting paper so that a black underlayer shows and then burns the edges. There are several works of art in this series, but it is this one that allows me to suture past and present through the worldmaking captured by the preposition "like." In thinking about race and representation, the work of drawing things together often threatens to evacuate specificity, producing an undifferentiated mass, something that Kyla Schuller and Jules Gill-Peterson, drawing on Kyla Wazana Tompkins's framework of the gelatinous, describe as "fungible surplus populations whose labor is extractable for profit, where individual bodies dissolve into a volatile, threatening mass."[3] Here, I work to draw out the embodied work underlying approximation—What are the politics of *like*?—so that it might emerge as a representational strategy that emphasizes a promiscuity of attachments, plurality, and difference (see plate 12).

Applying the framework of approximation to Fernández's work means holding my own knowledge of the storm beside the specificity of *Puerto Rico (Burned) 6*, whose title explicitly alludes to the devastation of Puerto Rico from the 2017 hurricane season. Hurricanes Irma and Maria hit Puerto Rico within several weeks of each other in September 2017. While Irma primarily wreaked havoc on the electrical grid, Maria, a slow-moving Category 5 storm, produced a direct hit, leveling buildings, ripping up trees, and wiping out roads and other infrastructure. Many people died, some during the storm, but most in the aftermath which made supplies (including food, clean water, and medical supplies) scarce.[4] Though technically a "natural" disaster everything about Maria can only be examined through the lens of colonialism and white supremacy. The adjective "burned" refers not only to Fernández's process but the effects of climate change as well as the failure of the federal government to provide meaningful federal relief to recover from the hurricanes, a morass that Yarimar Bonilla describes as "the coloniality of disaster."[5]

That a storm could become that large (and slow moving) is a testament to the impact of climate change, which itself is exacerbated by the extraction of raw materials, as well as the manufacturing and transportation of goods (predominately) from the global south to the global north.[6] In a hurricane, warm ocean air rises, meets cooler air, and coalesces into a storm with an eye and arms of violent rains and winds. As the burning of fossil fuels produces more carbon dioxide, the warm gases surrounding the earth become trapped closer to its surface, heating everything up. The ice caps melt, the sea temperatures rise, and hurricanes (and rains and tornadoes) become stronger and more frequent. Tropical islands are especially vulnerable to these extreme storms.[7] The entwinement of the colonial and corporate also manifests in the deforested landscape, a requirement for monoculture, but which exacerbates the effects of heavy rain by reducing the presence of tree roots, which help mountains hold their shape during storms. Mimi Sheller notes the collision of multiple temporalities of violence at work in these types of disaster: "In addition to the slow violence of deforestation, coral reef death, bauxite and gold mining, and coastal development for tourism, and to the sudden violence of earthquakes and hurricanes, we might also add the ongoing violence of debt extraction, foreign military intervention, and the repeated effects of crises associated with ongoing neocoloniality, racial capitalism, neoliberalism, and structural adjustment policies."[8]

Further, the devastation of infrastructure, including and especially the electrical grid, was facilitated by the fact that Puerto Rico has not had the money for more than mere upkeep because of its "debt burden" to the United States' federal government.[9] This debt is the product of years of borrowing combined with declining investment in the islands. This math is also complicated because Puerto Rico's status as a US territory makes it ineligible to file for bankruptcy or to default on its loans, producing an economic "death spiral."[10] Additionally, Puerto Rico's constitution itself is structured so as to prioritize US business interests over those of Puerto Rico. All of these factors combined to weaken Puerto Rico's ability to respond to disaster. As Bonilla writes: "The debt crisis thus paved the way for infrastructural vulnerability and social abandonment long before hurricane María."[11]

In her analysis, Bonilla examines multiple aspects of this racialized formation of coloniality. First, she highlights continuities between the US government's abdication of responsibility in Puerto Rico to its similar treatment of other nonwhite citizens: "One of the first things María revealed is precisely the place of Puerto Rico within a broad US archipelago of racialized neglect. This ties it to sites of climatic disaster like New Orleans, but also to places of urban ruin and social neglect like Detroit."[12] Second, she argues that this pattern is part of the aftermath of the way specific histories of slavery has shaped these islands' populations, infrastructures, economies, and cultures, profoundly determining the ways that disasters unfold: "I argue that disaster capitalism needs to be understood as foundationally a form of *racio-colonial* capitalism, that emerges directly out of the capitalism incubator of plantation slavery."[13] By foregrounding the racial and colonial dimensions of the disaster, Bonilla also helps us think expansively about the "temporality of disaster" and its entanglement with the racialized temporality of "always already." In the case of Irma and Maria, this racialized and colonial temporality of disaster manifested in the aftermath of the hurricanes as "a state of suspension." Bonilla elaborates:

> For weeks on end, there was no school, no work, no electricity, no phone service, no internet, no television, and no public services. With hospitals closed or only able to treat the most critically ill, sick patients were sent home unable to receive services such as cancer treatments or dialysis. Without electricity, funeral homes were unable to embalm the dead. (Although given the impassable roads, some are said to have buried the dead in their own backyards.) For weeks on end, roads remained blocked; food, water, and gasoline were scarce, and cell phone towers were down rendering most phones inoperable.[14]

Summarizing the affective impact of this cessation of normal life, especially amid the spectacular failure of governmental aid, Bonilla writes, "what characterized life after [María] thus was not progress but delay, deterioration, degradation, and the forced act of waiting."[15] This space between, this space that recognizes the violences of coloniality and the romanticism of resilience and yet still engages the possibility of something else, is what Sandra Ruiz calls "permanent endurance."[16]

What Bonilla and Ruiz do not say, but what I feel in Fernández's work, is just how disorienting this temporality is. In describing *Puerto Rico (Burned) 6*, I wrote that Fernández's work provides a view from above or below. In this uncertainty the image oscillates between felt polarities of power. The view from above is associated with the panopticon and visual dominance. As Ronak Kapadia reminds us, US militarism (and processes of colonialism) are central forces by which "those aerial views are conceived, framed, disavowed, and implicated in the fundamental destruction and reconstitution of populations, infrastructures, and social geographies."[17] In addition to evoking Puerto Rico's structures of colonialism, Fernández's view from above also calls to mind the processes of surveillance that are part of both disaster porn, a form of visuality that uses the sight of wretchedness to mobilize sympathy, and disaster capitalism, in which investors propose "repair," but actually siphon money away from the area through extractive contracts. By contrast, the view from below is seemingly more romantic in that it suggests an individualized possibility of resistance. We might wish to sense resilience in these broken trees, but as Caren Kaplan argues, "If the cultural history of aerial views conveys any lesson at all, it may be the recognition of the violence always already inherent in pursuing both [panoptic and subversive] desires."[18] Both Kapadia and Caplan move us to think with the violence of these perspectival gazes and their embeddedness in the landscape of the sensorial. In this way, I can feel the disorientation of Fernández's image as residue of colonialism and neoliberalism while also becoming immersed in my own sense memories of hurricanes and tropical forests.

By soliciting the affective attachments that enable approximation, Fernández makes manifest *Puerto Rico (Burned) 6*'s movement between representing the actualities of colonial violence and the multimodal attachments of memory—I cannot see the image without thinking of the landslides Tropical Storm Debby caused, remembering my family's fear and anticipation, or reflecting on other calmer moments under palm trees—by deploying the aesthetics of burning, a technology in which fire consumes oxygen and object to leave a char of imprecision. The burnt halos around each of Fernández's objects makes them hazy, less sharp, less tangible. The sepia tones reinforce the aura of nostalgia. Are we seeing these images float by a flooded river or street or merely in the mind's eye? The image feels like a memory in that it eschews objectivity while summoning unseen affective connections.

To produce approximation is difficult. In describing some of the embodied thinking underlying the task, Sonya Posmentier cites Barbadian poet Kamau Brathwaite's struggles to induce sensation given the constraints of language: "How do you get a rhythm which approximates the *natural* experience, the *environmental* experience?" and, evocatively, "The hurricane does not roar in pentameter."[19] Posmentier argues that Brathwaite's use of the verb "approximates" is important, as it signals "this action of bringing near that which is far, of bringing disparate entities close to but not into union—describes both the relationship between nature and culture in diasporic poetry and the ask of poetic form in articulating that relationship."[20] What Posmentier articulates is the tension between the political possibilities produced by invoking a sense in common while also acknowledging the gradations of opacity inherent in communication, which asks different perspectives to attempt to build something of a world together. It is, however, important—even ethical—to preserve this gap between entities, to make sure that approximation does not lose the "like" and flatten itself into "is."

On the other side of this effort is a perceiver, whose role Ocean Vuong describes in his unpacking of metaphor. Vuong argues that the preposition allows for a sensory connection to make the "detour" "lead to discoveries that alter / amplify the meaning of what is already there, so that a reader sees you as a servant of possibility."[21] This is to say that *like* opens worlds of imagination within the perceiver by providing a hinge into multiplicity and difference. In this way, Vuong argues, "the metaphor acts as a virtual medium, ejecting the text's optical realism into an 'elsewhere' / But this elsewhere should inform the original upon our return."[22] Metaphors function by showing sensory similarity despite difference—illuminating what Vuong calls "the 'DNA of seeing.' That is, a strong metaphor (Greek for 'to carry over') can enact the autobiography of sight." In this way they offer insight into the writer—Why were these choices made? What are the sensory connections at work?—while also requiring the reader to approach with an open mind and their own experience and knowledge. Vuong writes: "You have to look deeply and find lasting relationships between things in a disparate world. In this sense, the practice of metaphor is also, I believe, the practice of compassion. How do

I study a thing so that I might add to its life by introducing it to something else? . . . This calls that you see your life and your work as inexhaustible sites of discovery, and that you tend to them with care."[23] The conjoining of care and observation that metaphor harnesses is especially important for minoritarian artists, as it enables freedom of thought away from established paradigms of thinking and doing and, Vuong argues, "advocates for an anti-colonial gaze of the world" because it offers that finite truth does not exist and, following the Tibetan philosophy of Lojong, that everything one knows about the world is produced by and inextricable from our own perceptions. "We are in a 'simulation' and because there is no true gain in acquiring something that is only an illusion, it is better to observe and learn from phenomena as guests passing through this world with respect to things—rather than to possess them."[24] What Vuong draws out of Lojong are the central tenets that undergird my theorization of approximation as a representational framework through which to ethically consider difference—the impossibility of transparency, strategic laterality, and the valuation of multiplicity.

Cadastre, Surrealism, and Figurations of the Anticolonial

I wasn't intending to go inside, but I was struck by the juxtaposition between the gallery's gleaming concrete floors and the mess of its edges—a mass of yellow flowers and the display of a long fuzzy line running along several of the gallery walls. Inside, the large room was cool, dark, and slightly damp. I felt surrounded by the sounds of walking in a forest and my body remembered those sensations. *Cadastre* (2019), an installation by Puerto-Rican based artists Allora & Calzadilla (Jennifer Allora and Guillermo Calzadilla), conjured the smells of the interior of tropical forests and the shade of lush canopies. I was transported back to Monteverde, a large rain forest in Costa Rica whose trails I had walked as a preteen. I remembered hearing birds and monkeys (although I could never quite see them) and feeling the deep coolness of the tree shadows. I also remembered looking up and feeling dwarfed. I was not experiencing the forest only in my ear but feeling it along my whole body. This sense of deep embodied familiarity contrasted sharply with the industrial setting of the gallery space; a division between facticity and memory echoed by the plethora of yellow guayacán flowers on the ground and the smudges of the blurred line. Although technically they are individual components, the sound (*Penumbra*), flowers (*Graft*), and line (*Cadastre*) combine into an unfolding exploration that stretches the work of perceiving approximation into the imaginative realm of surrealism and anticolonialism (see plates 13 and 14).

When I looked more closely, I could see the smudged line take the form of a graph representing the erratic workings of Puerto Rico's electrical grid. Allora & Calzadilla connected the canvas to copper wires and used iron filings to show when the power was turned on and off in their studio in San Juan, Puerto Rico. By foregrounding change over time, the durative qualities of Puerto Rico's infrastructural precarity—products of its colonial and neoliberal past and present—emerge. The varying amplitudes add texture to the graph's volatility, each spike perhaps indicating the presence of a new patch for the grid and each lull, its failure. The underfunding of PREPA, the Puerto Rico Electric Power Authority, is on full display, as is Puerto Rico's reliance on imported and highly tariffed fossil fuels.[25] It is not just the irregularity of electricity that we feel; it is the (post- and neo-)colonial parable behind this inconsistency. This is a story that emerges by understanding one's personal embeddedness in these multiple ecologies and narratives. As Julie Livingston writes, "Parables reveal urgent and sometimes uncomfortable truths that are hiding in plain sight. They conjoin the listener (and in this case the teller as well!) to recognize herself within the story."[26] *Cadastre*, I argue, illuminates the multiple forms of colonial extraction at work in Puerto Rico—the failing electrical grid, the debt burden, the high tariffs—as well as the increasing pressure on these structures due to climate change. It also shows Allora & Calzadilla's embeddedness in the system; this is not an abstracted portrait of the electrical grid, but something that highlights their own reliance on electricity—it is important that the breaker is located in their studio. Further, viewing the installation in an air-conditioned Chelsea gallery adds additional layers of complicity to these (and other) forms of colonialism and extraction. However, by invoking the electrical grid but leaving the space of the sensory open, we move toward the "What else?" that I locate in the plethora of attachments that the piece produces. Though these attachments do not diminish the pernicious violence of colonialism and capitalism, they offer insight into experiences otherwise—especially the freedoms suggested by *Cadastre*'s invocation of Aimé Césaire—hailed by the openness of approximation.[27]

Cadastre does not mark the first time that Allora & Calzadilla turn toward PREPA and Puerto Rico's electrical grid to explore relations between disaster capitalism, debt, and neocolonialism. In *Blackout*, a 2017 sculpture, the artists presented a mangled portion of an electromagnetic power transformer that exploded during the infamous blackouts of 2016. In writing about the decomposition that the sculpture's "frayed, mangled, and corroded body" makes tangible, T. J. Demos argues that Allora & Calzadilla "express this depraved politicofinancial and socio-environmental situation, precisely embodying these unjust economic distortions, structural disfigurements, and legal maladjustments, revealing them for the massive failure they are."[28] Demos further offers that the sculpture makes evident Achille Mbembe's argument regarding the "Becoming Black of the world": "In joining energy production with financial debt servitude, Allora & Calzadilla's *Blackout* identifies the key neocolonial logic of extraction, which is, as we have seen, operative in the environment of finance capital that has itself become globalized."[29] Through Demos we sense Allora & Calzadilla's investment in theorizing the precarity produced by the histories and presents of global finance chains; the question of becoming Black, however, allows us to complicate their citation of Césaire. While Mbembe's "Becoming Black" asks us to consider the pervasive epistemological structures of anti-Blackness and their imbrications with capitalism, invoking Césaire moves us between his own theorizations of Blackness as an abstracted (and fungible) position and the material reality of him as a Black man.

In *Cadastre*, Césaire circulates as disembodied presence, explicitly cited and materialized obliquely through sound. This is enough, however, to invite a juxtaposition between the specific histories of Martinique, the location from which Césaire writes, and Puerto Rico. Although both Puerto Rico and Martinique are entangled in neocolonial formations with the United States and France, respectively, such that the impulse to link them together to critique imperialism is strong, the nature of these relationships and their histories differs. Puerto Rico was a Spanish colony that became a commonwealth of the United States and Martinique is a "department d'outre mer" of France, which is to say, it is considered its own region of France.[30] While Allora & Calzadilla call attention to debt and extraction, Césaire's preoccupation is with rejecting categories imposed by colonialism and capitalism such as property. Reading between the two activates a temporal and material difference into which we might register racial inflection—how does a mortgaged future compare to a foreclosed one? Moreover, how do we attend to this disembodiment in concert with an anti-Blackness that would prefer to produce affinity with Césaire's anticolonialism and distance from his attachment to Africa and Blackness as manifest in the philosophy and aesthetics of Negritude.[31] These tensions bring us toward questions not only about how Blackness signifies, but also about the legibility of Black theorizing. As a viewer, however, I offer myself: I am inserting my being and my situation into the hailing of Césaire in order to make manifest some of the possibilities enabled by his affiliation with Allora & Calzadilla's work.

Not only is *Cadastre* named after one of Césaire's volumes of poetry, but *Penumbra*, a violin composition by David Lang, is meant to explicitly reference the hikes that Césaire and his wife, Suzanne, led through the Absalon Valley in Fort-de-France, Martinique's capital, for a group of European refugees fleeing Vichy France in April 1941. When the refugees arrived, Aimé and Suzanne had just produced the first edition of *Tropiques*, their surrealist literary journal, which was published (amid much political difficulty from the Vichy government) between 1941 and 1945. In describing the journal and their mission, Robin D. G. Kelley writes that "Theirs was a conception of freedom that drew on modernism and a deep appreciation for precolonial African modes of thought and practice; it drew on surrealism as the strategy of revolution of the mind and Marxism as revolution of the productive forces."[32] The journal was able to survive as long as it did because the writers "had to camouflage their boldness, passing the publication off as a journal of West Indian folklore."[33] After *Tropiques* ceased publication, Césaire continued to publish volumes of poetry—including *Soleil cou coupé* (1948) and *Corps perdu* (1950)—before branching out into nonfiction and pivoting to politics. While *Cadastre* was published in 1961, the poems inside the volume were written around the same time as *A Discourse on Colonialism* (1950), his most famous essay, which argues that colonialism is a pathology of domination that seeks to negate original cultures in order to bolster its own, thereby turning people into "things" and preventing genuine interaction by creating racialized hierarchies of power: "My turn to state an equation: colonization = 'thingification.' I hear the storm."[34] Césaire was especially critical of colonialism's introduction of capitalism and concepts of property, describing the distortion on human interactions that this ideology imposed.

Notably, *cadastre* is the French word for the "official register of the quantity, value, and ownership of real estate used in apportioning taxes" and the volume offers a critique of colonialism shot through with surrealism.[35] Describing his surrealism as "a call to Africa," Césaire emphasizes surrealism's ability—like Vuong's metaphor—to break with French thought and customs, declaring, "if we plumb the depths, then what we will find is fundamentally black."[36] The first half of *Cadastre* is "Soleil cou coupé" (selected and edited poems from the eponymous 1948 volume), which translates roughly to "neck cut by the sun," or "Solar Throat Slashed," as the unexpurgated 2011 version published by Wesleyan University Press is titled. The Wesleyan edition describes the poems as "animalitically dense, charged with eroticism and blasphemy, and imbued with African and Vodun spirituality."[37] Tracing the line to Guillaume Apollinaire, a protosurrealist, Eric Sellin argues that both Césaire and Apollinaire move the "like" of the simile and the "is" of being into the ellipses, enabling a plethora of possible relations (and translations). In this space of sensorial approximation, I prefer to think of the title as invoking the sensation when "the sun beats down and whips the neck as though to cut it or that it refers to a sun truncated by the horizon."[38] I like this conjecture because the poems in this half collectively not only evoke feelings of attachment to a (mythical and flattened, yes) homeland in Africa, but they ask readers to feel for these African contours through sense memories—producing a diaspora based on sensation. Césaire is, after all, famous for being one of the founders of the Negritude movement, which celebrates African cultural heritage. "Soleil cou coupé" draws on Afro-diasporic myths and symbols in order to emphasize non-European epistemologies and imaginaries. In "Le griffon," for example Césaire writes: "Le ciel lingual a pris sa neuve consistence de crème de noix fraiche ouverte du coco" (The lingual sky took on a new consistency of a freshly opened coconut's cream).[39] The possibility of communicating experience and meaning through tropical sensations—fresh coconut cream—makes evident the broadening of imagination that Césaire's surrealism makes possible. This juxtaposition renews one's perspective on the coconut while broadening the sensory orbit of the lingual (taste, tongue, and language expand), allowing the reader to attach in any number of ways.

The second half of *Cadastre*, "Corps perdu," emphasizes the racialized violence of colonialism. Excerpted from *Corps perdu* (1950)—which can be translated literally as "lost body," or more colloquially ("á corps perdu") as "impetuously," we can feel the force of Césaire's critique, which Kelley describes as "a declaration of war . . . a polemic against the old order bereft of the kind of propositions and proposals that accompany manifestos."[40] Perhaps this is the storm he references in *Discourse on Colonialism*? Like that essay, these poems emphasize the brutality of colonialism—this lost body seems to me to directly reference its multiple displacements and the devaluation of certain people and epistemologies over others. The lost body also, however, reveals the dependence of Europe on the production of the colonized Other, a dynamic of submerged dependence that Césaire attempted to reveal and sever as a politician. We see these dynamics explicitly in the first poem of

"Corps perdu," "Mot" (Word), which reads like a semiotic deconstruction of Blackness by illustrating the complex gaps between *blackness* as word and Blackness as lived set of experiences.

> Le mot nègre
> tout pouacre de parasites
>
> The word negro
> stinking all over with parasites[41]

In addition to laying bare the violence of abstraction, we can also sense the extractive nature of colonialism in Césaire's use of the term *parasite*. Condensed in these lines, then, is also a reference to the multiple forms of labor that Blackness and Black people perform in the colonial setup. But, hovering behind the word, there is also the material entity, which cannot be wholly captured. Here, again we are in the oscillation between the view from above (projection) and lived experience; we are in the sensations of endurance.

In his poetry, Césaire employs surrealism to enact the otherwise representational possibilities of anticolonialism. Kelley argues that "The surrealist movement began as a spontaneous association, based on elective affinities, and that is what it has always been and still is. Abjuring, on principle, all proselytizing and recruitment, it has never entertained the aim of being a mass movement."[42] I am less interested in the temporal aspects of surrealism—its spontaneity—and more in its enactment of these "elective affinities." These affinities, in turn, being produced by the specificity of one's perception, lead to what Kelley describes as "an *open* realism [that] signifies *more* reality, and an expanded *awareness* of reality, including aspects and elements of the real that are ordinarily overlooked, dismissed, excluded, hidden, shunned, suppressed, ignored, forgotten, or otherwise neglected."[43] Through Kelley, we can parse surrealism as a representational and political strategy that augments perception, opening one toward what might be present but undervalued or repressed, and—making felt what was in the shadows—performing many of the same functions that Vuong attributes to metaphor.

Allora & Calzadilla also make Césaire's arguments felt in the sound piece *Penumbra*. In *Penumbra*, the violins are audible, but not decipherable, which is to say that what one imagines hearing is a bird, the sound of leaves rustling, and maybe light rain or a waterfall. A friend with training in the violin noted also that the experience of such tonal music depends entirely on where one is standing; experientially, it is impervious to recording. It is a geography of sound rather than a flat recording from one place.[44] In its spatialization, *Penumbra* requires us to think with shadow tones, a psychoacoustic phenomenon in which the listener uses their own experience to augment the soundscape—hearing sounds that are not explicitly played. Like Vuong's metaphor and Césaire's surrealism, this form of nonrepresentation requires personal perception. It is yet another way that we experience approximation. Tellingly, the piece's name—*Penumbra*—references the outer edges of a shadow or the type of eclipse that produces strawberry moons, evoking an excess that works outside of static representation.[45]

In addition to feeling the forest, *Penumbra* also allows us to sense, through a sort of shadow choreography, the 1941 hikes that Suzanne and Aimé led. Although Martinique was but a stopover for the group of artists and intellectuals escaping Fascist persecution, André Breton (often hailed as a founder of surrealism because of his 1924 manifesto) came across the first issue of *Tropiques* while exploring Fort-de-France on a day pass from the refugee camp, was introduced to the Césaires, and the hikes began.[46] Suzanne and Aimé led the group around the three-hour loop of forested mountains and valleys of Absalon. Though a popular recreational destination, much of the forest, dark and humid, has remained—aside from some hiking and swimming infrastructure—undeveloped. In a description from Helena Holzer, Wifredo Lam's then-wife, we feel the shock of abundance that the forest provides:

> Trees with enormous leaves . . . palm trees of many different types, including the Voyager palm with its fan. Wide open; ferns grown to tall, thin, elegant trees; orchids, lianas, the gigantic leaves of the yautica plant. Abounded. All were vibrant with color, striving for light and shimmering in countless shades of green where the sun penetrated the canopy of foliage.[47]

Holzer's attention to difference contrasts with the sameness of the yellow guayacán blooms in *Graft*. Though the trees shed their flowers annually during the dry season, set against the gray concrete, they are bereft of context, registering as mournful ode to the ravages of climate change.[48] Importantly, we can also register these processes of violent displacement—climate change, colonialism, enslavement—as shifting spatial relations. Often, as Césaire notes in an April 1942 letter to Breton, this shift is toward the register of loss: "We see the admirable Absalon valley only with you and through you: it is one of the few parts of this land that is still bearable to me physically."[49] In Césaire's anticolonial longing, he argues for relations untouched by capitalism and objectification, idealizing these social structures as communal, anticapitalist, democratic, and cooperative.[50] In his words, we can imagine that these are the dynamics that he sees embedded in the Absalon forest. These words find an echo with a difference in Suzanne Césaire's stirring words in her essay "Surrealism and Us: 1943": "Our surrealism will enable us to finally transcend the sordid antinomies of the present: whites/Blacks, Europeans/Africans, civilized/savages—at last rediscovering the magic power of the mahoulis, drawn directly from living sources."[51] In Suzanne's words, we hear the emphasis on the value of difference for Caribbean practices of endurance. As Emily Eyestone writes, "Suzanne Césaire dispels the utopian/dystopian dialectic entirely, and instead proposes adaptability as a defining feature of Caribbean history. She articulates an organic, locally emergent ontology of Caribbean human and spatial identity, in which climatic and geophysical instability preclude the reification of tropical islands as utopian paradises ripe for colonial consumption, or as dystopian hotspots in need of technological rationalization."[52] By emphasizing the flexibility of this specifically Caribbean form of amalgamation, Suzanne adds an element of futurity to the promiscuous affiliations that surrealism affords. In contrast to Aimé, it is not the potential of recovery or return that is compelling, but the valuation of abundance that inheres in these ecosystems of frictive survivance. This shift moves us away from Negritude toward something else—what Kara Rabbitt identifies as "antillanité" or "créolité."[53]

In the space between Allora & Calzadilla's *Penumbra* and *Graft*, I can feel the anticolonial possibilities of the tropical forest both as they are marked by Aimé and Suzanne's words and as I experienced my hikes in Monteverde. The first time I went to the rain forest, it was with my family, and we were taking advantage of Costa Rica's then nascent ecotourism industry—being in the rainforest offered an opportunity to visit "difference" and to witness its acclaimed biodiversity *before* . . . before development, before deforestation, before climate change. My other trips to these forests came under similar auspices: a school trip designed to foster appreciation for Costa Rica's natural beauty and participation in a documentary meant to convey youthful anxiety about climate change as well what would be lost without the rainforests.[54] Beyond the sense memories of this space, I carry with me the feeling of borrowed and vanishing time, a sentiment I cannot help but collapse onto Aimé Césaire's anticolonial fervor and the melancholy that haunts Allora & Calzadilla's *Cadastre*. The experiences commingle different facets of an apocalyptic century felt in the damp aftermath of a storm.

Interlocking Apocalypses: The Politics of Affinity

The fallen flowers of *Graft* (plate 14) suggest an ending—most benignly of the dry season, but in ways that our bodies know, they also speak of our increasingly erratic climate and its shifted worlds. Caribbean islands are particularly vulnerable to climate change, which erodes land on coasts, alters rainy seasons, and creates more frequent and stronger hurricanes. Moreover, it is not difficult to draw a line between the apocalypse that people are naming the Anthropocene and colonialism. Macarena Gómez-Barris makes explicit this dimension of colonial damage by employing the term *colonial Anthropocene* in order to emphasize the expansive and durational destruction wrought forth by colonialism. For Gómez-Barris, colonialism highlights the biopolitical dimensions of this exploitation, enabling one to see continuities between colonial projects of domination and contemporary manifestations of extraction. She writes, "we must continually make evident how industrial environmental damage was first organized by colonialism, its extractive project, and its desire to rapaciously rule over and decimate specific territories and peoples it constituted through difference."[55] Central to these power dynamics is the production of hierarchical forms of difference and the entity that Sylvia Wynter has described as "Man," our much-discussed and critiqued liberal subject.[56] To this point and drawing on the work of Zoe Todd and Heather Davis, Kim Tallbear emphasizes the appropriateness of the term *Anthropocene* precisely because it implicates Man while also allowing possibilities for other genres of being.[57]

Moreover, it is not a coincidence that scholars, including Kyla Schuller, connect climate change to higher prevalence of zoonotic diseases like COVID-19. Schuller writes, "Lyme disease has been called the first epidemic of climate change. . . . Humans now live in closer proximity to other animals than we used to, and our illnesses have become 'zoonotic'; three out of every four new infectious diseases spread from wildlife and livestock to people, including COVID-19, Ebola, and SARS."[58] With COVID-19, we also face the bitter irony of yet another mode of choking off air supply circulating within Black communities that makes "I can't breathe" resonate in multiple ways. Breath has become an important frame for thinking about the possibility of Black life, particularly in the aftermath of Eric Garner's 2014 death at the hands of police. His last words, "I can't breathe," famously reference the chokehold being used to restrain him. Since then, and especially after a grand jury refused to bring criminal charges against the white officer who killed him, the refrain has become a way to describe anti-Blackness. In *Blackpentecostal Breath*, Ashon Crawley draws on what happened to Garner to elucidate the multiple types of violence that engulf Blackness: it is not *just* the (endlessly repeating) legacy to which he refers, but a logic that continues to attempt to suffocate and eradicate in multiple permutations. Thus, this statement becomes a call for abolition and a way to approach breathing anew: "'I can't breathe' charges us to do something, to perform, to produce otherwise than what we have. We are charged to end, to produce abolition against, the episteme that produced for us current iterations of categorical designations of racial hierarchies, class stratifications, gender binaries, mind-body splits."[59] Christina Sharpe, too, references Eric Garner's death as but one of an endlessly repeating series of incidents that accumulate as an oppressive atmosphere, what she calls the weather: "In my text, the weather is the totality of our environments; the weather is the total climate; and that climate is antiblack."[60] Later, Sharpe works through the term *aspiration*, another synonym of sorts, in order to ponder the possibility of survival for Black people under these conditions. Survival means allowing for the intake of air; in part it means caring through the multigenerational trauma of the transatlantic slave trade, but it also means fusing breath with something else: "Aspiration here, doubles. . . . To the necessity of breath, to breathing space, to the breathtaking spaces in the wake in which we live; and to the ways we respond."[61] What Sharpe points toward is the affective excess that accompanies survival. It is the place where one might begin to see beyond the mere conditions of being toward joy, beauty, and thriving.

In October 2020, I participated in a zoom roundtable hosted by the Center for Gender and Sexuality Studies at New York University titled "How to Have Sex in a Pandemic." There, I used Leo Bersani's argument in "Is the Rectum a Grave?" as a jumping off point for working through some of the intimacies of the moment. Bersani, writing about gay men in relation to HIV and AIDS, argued that sex could provide a suicidal ecstasy—a self-shattering jouissance—that ruptured ideologies of masculinity and individuality through an embrace of penetration.[62] It was this abnegation of self that I found interesting because of the ways that the pandemic profoundly disrupted my own sense of self and opened me to difference on multiple levels, not so much from orgasm as by the virus's announcement of our profound lack of sovereignty. Most immediately, COVID-19 (and also HIV) offers a literal confrontation with difference that the RNA virus affords—one immediately understands that the body is a porous entity comprised of multiple forms of DNA and multiple different organisms. While this is always true—think of mitochondria and the microbiome—a pandemic makes one more intensely aware of the fallacy of the individual. However, I experience this realization as a profound form of connection in and through difference that involves extensions of being, not abnegation.

Kevin Quashie might describe this extension as aliveness. He writes, "In a black world imaginary, there is aliveness, blackness that gushes with existence, the *knowing* that Audre Lorde theorizes as embodied consciousness."[63] For Quashie, this abundance of being is signaled by the use of the pronoun "one" because it allows for capaciousness and specificity: "The person speaking through 'one' makes herself into an object of specificity and breadth—she multiplies through this imaginary praxis. This is oneness, which is not synonymous with terms of individuality; oneness where the subject is always relational."[64] Likewise, Jayna Brown's concept of Black utopias is also resonant because of its emphasis on porosity and sensation. Brown writes, "The body, the self, is porous, receptive, impressionable, and not so easily individuated. . . . The senses therefore make the self both coherent and porous, both unitary and multiple. Moments of utopia happen through the gratification of sensual desires; we open up and let ourselves go."[65] Both Brown and Quashie emphasize the blurriness that extension enables, but we lose sight of the politics of affiliation if we merely focus on what is undifferentiated rather than the work of self-reflexivity, attention, and criticality that bring us to that point. This labor is embedded in Quashie's invocation of a praxis of breadth and in Brown's reference to a capacity for receptivity and impressionability.

Central to the critical expansiveness that approximation permits, moreover, is an ethical relation to difference. Learning to exist in difference is what enables the emergence of new ways of being. It is notable that Audre Lorde, for example, finds power in friction. The position of a "sister outsider" refers to the specific forms of outsiderness that being a Black queer feminist entails in which dominant forms of feminism center white heterosexual women and dominant strains of the civil rights organizations still uphold Black patriarchy; as such, difference is actually the ontological condition of being a "sister outsider." These tensions add strength to the collective and enable the work of survival. We see the work that the embrace of difference does in "The Master's Tools Will Never Dismantle the Master's House." Lorde writes:

> Advocating the mere tolerance of a difference between women is the grossest reformism. It is a total denial of the creative function of difference in our lives. Difference must not be merely tolerated, but seen as a fund of necessary polarities between which our creativity can spark like a dialectic. Only then does the necessity for interdependency become unthreatening. Only within that interdependency of different strengths, acknowledged and equal, can the power to seek out new ways of being in the world generate, as well as the courage and sustenance to act where there are no charters.[66]

Lorde's theorization of friction also returns us to the embodied work that I described vis-à-vis approximation; friction requires an openness to approximation and an exploration that begins from one's perspective. In words that resonate with Vuong's description of metaphor, Quashie argues that "the ethics of black aliveness remains open, ushers an invocation toward (more) awareness, an invitation for the one to inhabit self-regard. I know that our social worlds probably can't withstand such openness, but I also don't want to be limited by the world we live in."[67] The difficulty to which Quashie refers requires not only the capacity for porosity but also the labor of avoiding the imaginative seductions of "Man."

To keep alive other modes of being is vital work; it is a labor of love. I think here especially with Jennifer Nash's argument that a Black feminist politics of love demands "a significant call for ordering the self and transcending the self, a strategy for remaking the self and for moving beyond the limitations of selfhood."[68] This movement beyond the self takes *work*, requiring what Nash describes as "ethical management of the self": "pushing the self to be configured in new ways that might be challenging or difficult."[69] For me, these lessons are compelled in deep sensual ways by approximation, which I understand as beginning with a situation and the choice to expand outward, to align politically, to align through joy, to value difference and the possibility of its friction.

5

Tamarind, Metabolism, and Rest

Making Racialized Labor Visible

IN TITUS KAPHAR'S *A Pillow for Fragile Fictions* (2016) a clear glass vessel rests on a slab of white marble streaked with gray and black. Inside is dark brown liquid, a mixture of rum, tamarind, lime, and molasses, which rests in the glass's uneven pockets. The whole apparatus sits atop a low pedestal (see plate 15). Kaphar's work often reveals elements of history that have been repressed (the shadow side, shall we say?) in favor of a particular historical narrative, leaving us with much to decipher.[1] When we begin with George Washington, whose glass-blown bust has been made into a vessel—shaped literally from hot air—we can begin to sense the ways that Kaphar turns the myth of Washington as upstanding founding father on its side (look closely to see his features in the glass). While Kaphar uses rum, tamarind, molasses, and lime to represent a colonial-era system of commodifying Black life as well as Washington's involvement with the slave trade, the mixture also offers a stand-in for Tom, a man who was in bondage to Washington at Mt. Vernon. Although Kaphar does not mention Tom by name, the specific echo between the sculpture and the terms Washington set for Tom's exchange are unmistakable. Here are Washington's instructions, delivered in a letter of July 2, 1766, to sea captain John Thompson, about to sail to the West Indies:

> With this letter comes a negro (Tom) which I beg the favor of you to sell in any of the islands you may go to, for whatever he will fetch, and bring me in return for him:
>
> 1 hhd. Best molasses
> 1 ditto best rum
> 1 barrel Lymes if good
> 1 pot Tamarind containing about 10 libs.[2]

By summoning Tom within this portrait of Washington, Kaphar complicates conventions that surround the representation of race. Like the notorious story of Washington's dentures and rotting teeth, Kaphar's figuration of Washington emphasizes the fictive quality of white masculine individualism in presenting us with a vulnerable and fragile man.[3] Likewise, by keeping Tom as a shadow presence, evoked by market goods but not necessarily represented by them, Kaphar invites us to think about the relationship between commodification and racialized labor, the theme of this chapter.

In Kaphar's sculpture, the heft and definition of the marble pillow accentuates the delicateness of the glass that comprises Washington's head. Since marble is usually used as a symbol of immortality and monumentality, it lends permanence to Washington's position of repose, granting the sculpture an aura of the funereal. Perhaps the sculpture is a tribute to his (and his reputation's) demise? The glass, meanwhile, positions Washington as fragile, especially in comparison to the marble. And, as container for liquid, the glass invites us to consider what it might mean to theorize Washington as vessel, a feminized object that tends to connote receptivity, openness, and emptiness.[4] Rendering the boundaries of Washington's person transparent, Kaphar emphasizes their instability as well as the work that maintaining them requires. In describing the effort behind bounded masculinity, Cynthia Barounis writes, "We require male bodies to be invulnerable, impenetrable, and impervious to injury.... In addition to maintaining the boundaries of his physical body, he must also control and contain his emotional response to the world, and particularly to other men."[5] However, the Washington we are presented with is both fragile and multiply penetrated—by the cork and by the liquid in his head. In this way, one of the "fragile fictions" to which

Kaphar refers is not only Washington or historical memory, but also the liberal (bounded) subject. I think specifically of Lisa Lowe's description of "a colonial division of intimacy, which charts the historically differentiated access to the domains of liberal personhood, from interiority and individual will, to the possession of property and domesticity."[6] Lowe allows us to make connections between the naturalization of the idea of liberal subjectivity with possession, enclosure, and whiteness through notions of property, domesticity, and desire. Further, Lowe points to the ways that this set of relations is part of an unmarked universalization of an idea of subjectivity that suppresses affects designated as nonwhite.

The vessel might also remind us of the role of greenhouses, made of glass, in cultivating a European and American (colonial) taste for tropical goods especially because its contents are an amalgamation of West Indian commodities.[7] Nested within Washington's head, their presence invites us, I argue, not exactly to make Washington Black, but to read the content of his whiteness through its dependence on Black labor and Black people. In this way, this portrait of Washington makes transparent the network of "exteriorities" that permitted Washington's interiority in the first place. Notably, history does explicitly place Washington in the Caribbean. At nineteen, he accompanied his brother to Barbados, one of England's most prized colonies owing to its robust sugar production. Washington spent several months on the island in late 1751. There, he met with British military men, learned a great deal about military tactics, and sampled local fruits.[8] He also, importantly, caught smallpox, which ended up providing useful inoculation against the disease when, later, in 1775, it ravaged the rest of the colonial army.[9] These complex exchanges of sensorial, military, and immunological knowledge suggest that not only Washington, but the United States, owes a great debt to Barbados.

While rum, lime, tamarind, and molasses offer a proxy for Tom, whose person Washington wanted to exchange, we must turn to the archives of Washington's Mount Vernon estate to learn more about him and his life. Tom, it emerges, was a foreman at the River Farm for twelve years before attempting to run away in 1766. As punishment, Washington sent him to the West Indies on the *Swift*. In his note to the captain of the ship, Washington described Tom as a "rogue and a runaway" who was "exceedingly healthy, strong, and good at the Hoe," and "he may . . . sell well, if kept clean and trim'd up a little."[10] Tom was sold in St. Kitts for "£40 local currency. In return, Washington received 66 gallons of spirits and 10 pounds of sweetmeats (candied fruit), as well as 'two half-joes, 1 pistole,' and 'small silver' (Portuguese and

Spanish currency used in the colonies)."[11] A straightforward reading would see the rum, lime, tamarind, and molasses as interchangeable with Tom's person, marking the violence of what Zakiyyah Iman Jackson terms plasticization: "the fundamental violation of enslavement . . . coerced formlessness as a mode of domination and the unheimlich existence that is its result."[12] What Jackson isolates is the ways that this malleability—signaled by various regimes of fungibility as well as the explicit commodification of the marketplace—evacuates possibilities for personhood.

This existential threat helps us identify the fears that Phillip Brian Harper associates with Black abstraction, which, in turn, allows us to speculate that the possibility of recreating this absenting of personhood prevents Kaphar from naming Tom despite clearly invoking him.[13] But Tom hovers. We might attempt to recuperate his personhood by arguing that the presence of rum, tamarind, lime, and molasses gestures toward what Monique Allewaert describes as "ecological personhood," which is a "para-human" formation that emerged among Afro-Caribbean people in the colonial era of plantations and Maroons.[14] For Allewaert, ecological personhood exists alongside other emergent forms of personhood such as the subject and citizen, but it is marked by expansiveness in its encompassing of organic and inorganic matter along with spiritual and vegetative forces. These porous bodies, Allewaert writes, "evince an imbrication with their outsides that registers a terrifying vulnerability to the events and forces on its outsides."[15] For Allewaert, it is important to connect ecological personhood to African-based onto-epistemologies where people and objects are not so strictly separate, describing this expansive formation as a way to distribute interiority—it is not confined to one specific body.[16] A person is not an insular being distinct from "external" entities and forces, but, instead, an ecological being, whose components are diffuse and not self-same. On the one hand, Allewaert's formulation gives us a way to resignify Black plasticity into personhood, so that the bounded self is (again) exposed as fictive and the abundance of attachments and intimacies of these exteriorities are privileged. However, I cannot move beyond the glass enclosure. It limits the breadth of how we can imagine Tom's expansiveness. In contrast to the possibilities of escape that inhere in the swamps, forests, or spiritual icons that Allewaert presents, the substance denoting Tom is encircled by Washington, an echo of Tom's situation of servitude. Moreover, sugar, rum, and molasses are items that connote Black bondage rather than freedom since they are embedded in the marketplace. And this commercial framework of exchange, as Max Hantel argues, inaugurates the commodification of Black labor and exploitative systems of global capitalism more broadly. In Hantel's argument, what Sylvia Wynter names the pieza, or "the standard unit of measurement created by Portuguese slave traders in the sixteenth century for African slaves," made tangible the ways that "the exchangeable, standardized Black body becomes 'the general equivalent of physical labor value against which all the others could be measured.'"[17] As such, personhood might not be the appropriate métier to apprehend Tom.

Kaphar's entwinement of Tom and Washington is profound—both are decoupled from conventional representational regimes and personhood; yet, in their entanglement, we also gain a sense of more than their shared history. We can, I argue, sense the extracted racialized labor that lies at the heart of their relationship through a representational regime that I term "the metabolic" because of its ability to make visible what is usually unseen: the temporal and energetic economies attached to Black life. The metabolic offers some trace of Tom in addition to possibilities (still recoverable to my mind) for thinking otherwise.

The first of these possibilities is the effect of combination. When we think of tamarind, rum, lime, and sugar together they make a version of a tamarind sour.[18] In the sour category of drink, defined by the presence of "base spirit, water, sugar, and a citrus element, usually lemon," the flavor of the spirit dominates, but the juice helps dissolve the sugar and balance its sweetness.[19] Describing the origin story of sours, Brian Petro notes the genius of repurposing items brought on board to combat scurvy and malnutrition into a drink: "Sailors had a ration of various things, like limes and lemons to prevent scurvy, and liquor for something safe to drink. To prevent a ship full of intoxicated shipmates, the liquor, usually rum once it was discovered, was watered down and lemon or lime juice was added to mask the flavor of the rum."[20] In this set of chemical reactions, atoms meet, exchange electrons, and produce bonds, either consuming or releasing energy to become a different compound—a sour. While this is not the usual way of thinking about cocktails, it offers an inroad into what I am calling the metabolic because it allows us to parse questions of temporality and energetics. The aesthetics of the metabolic, then, involve thinking about how to make these unseen qualities felt. In parsing what it means to think about the coming together of lime, tamarind, rum, and molasses in relation to Tom, I see Tom's labor as the energy that is used to turn these goods into something else. Further, since the reaction is bounded by the glass enclosure—which we might think of in relation to white supremacy's attachment to and demand for transparency—especially from those racialized as nonwhite, the reaction will only last until the individual components are exhausted, that is to say, when there is no more energy.[21]

When I saw Kaphar's *A Pillow for Fragile Fictions* as part of an exhibit, *On Whiteness*, put on in New York by Claudia Rankine's Racial Imaginary Institute and The Kitchen in summer 2018, the corked vessel had droplets of liquid streaming down the side—the result of condensation (see plate 16). Since the liquid is enclosed, any reaction between substances that releases energy activates some molecules enough so that they assume gaseous form and evaporate, only to become liquid again when they hit the glass. To me, this condensation (a change of state rather than chemical reaction) offers a perceptible trace of Tom in its visibilization of his emplacement within these energetic exchanges. Clearly Tom is more than the sum of these reactions, but there is a representational politics to connecting Tom to these reactions. In lieu of representing Blackness as coalesced into a body, we are given to understand racial formations as complex interrelations that actually evade objectified representation. This sculpture, however, illuminates the conditionality of process and personhood. Just as it matters that Tom haunts, but is not named, we also see that there are moments when his trace might be apprehended (if only briefly) through temperature and exposure to light. That this is shaky ground on which to stake personhood is important: it speaks directly to Tom's own complex access to personhood. But instead of dwelling in the morass of whether Tom can or cannot be figured or can or cannot be a person, I prefer to go where Kaphar's sculpture leads us—toward the complex entanglement between work, exhaustion, and rest in which Black life, then, as now, is mired.

Sugar's Extractive Economies and Tamarind's Taste of Rest

As indicated by Washington's letter, rum and molasses were sent to the mid-Atlantic and northeastern colonies, but the most profitable plantation export of the British Caribbean was sugar. While there is debate about who actually introduced sugar to Barbados in the 1600s, by 1750, the flat island was awash with sugar plantations and laborers for those fields.[22] This was a deadly industry—Tom, notably, does not resurface in the archive—that was highly dependent on an intricate network of land and labor management.[23] Justin Roberts describes, for example, several teams of workers sorted according to ability: those who were physically able cut the cane and others tended to other crops, ran the house, tended to children, managed the sick or injured, built barrels, watched the cane to prevent theft, managed the waste, using some material for roofs or walls, burning some, and made rum. I dwell on these diverse forms of labor to make clear the expansive imprint of the sugar industry on Black life, not only with regard to the dangers inherent in its cultivation but as an invasive and extractive form of time and energy management.

While sugar cultivation controlled the parameters of Black life in the Caribbean, its consumption also dramatically altered life and labor for many in Europe and North America. Sidney Mintz famously links the increased use of sugar and rum (among other things) to the desire for speed. Sugar itself provided a caloric boost, but it also became an important way to cloak the bitterness of popular caffeinated drinks like tea, coffee, and chocolate, which provided their own pep. This impetus toward a faster pace of life was especially important in an industrializing world: "Sugar was taken up just as work schedules were quickening, as the movement from countryside to city was accelerating, and as the factory system was taking shape and spreading."[24] Embedded in Mintz's note about the quickening pace of life is the looming dominance of an ethos of productivity that spreads beyond the factory toward other parts of life (even leisure pursuits), making speed (and sugar) increasingly important parts of modern life. Further, this increasing reliance on speed and sugar served to underscore the deep imbrication of capitalism, slavery, and empire, or, as he writes, "the slave trade, the plantation system, slavery itself, and, soon enough, the spread of factory industry in the metropolis."[25] Importantly, this twinning of the desire for sugar and productivity with Black labor and the shortening of Black lives is inseparable from legacies of anti-Black violence and corporeal discipline.[26]

Time management, Elizabeth Freeman argues, is a central aspect of the modern episteme and its practices of extraction. She writes, "In Foucault's eye, what distinguished modern institutions of power from their medieval counterparts was that precision of time was met by precision of bodily movement, such that even gestures came under the control of 'collective and obligatory rhythm[s].'"[27] By drawing attention to the role of temporality in disciplining the body, Freeman's overall project is to bring forward the imbrication of the social and the temporal, such that being in sync is the mark of embodying a particular modern norm. Importantly, one of the primary ways that the racialization of different temporalities and of being out of sync manifested was through enslavement's shortening of Black life via multiple forms of violence. As Freeman writes, "Slave owners had absolute power to wrest enslaved people from genealogical time, and to shorten or terminate slaves' lives—to effect what Orlando Patterson calls the 'social death' of enslaved people as a prelude to and rehearsal of an actual death imposed from without as a matter of murder or enforced deterioration."[28] There is also, however, the lost time of leisure and rest—a temporality that invites us to think outside of productivity, labor, and being in sync.[29]

First, I want to be clear that the affective economy and temporality of rest is separate from the conjoining of Black pain with the spectacle of enjoyment, which Saidiya Hartman has argued produced racist stereotypes of "Negro nature as carefree, infantile, hedonistic, and indifferent to suffering and to an interested misreading of the interdependence of labor and song common among the enslaved."[30] Further, Hartman argues, the idea of enjoyment itself, within the context of enslavement, serves to further reveal enslaved people's estrangement from liberal subjectivity and the depth of enslavement's invasive forms of possession. Hartman writes, "The seemingly casual observations about black fun and frolic obscure this wanton usage and the incorporation of the captive body in realizing the extensive and sentient capacities of the master subject."[31] This is to say that enjoyment attempts to occlude servility by highlighting moments of nonwork, but these moments are still structured by the extraction of labor—a relation that is similar to that of rum and sugar. Rum might provide enjoyment—in all the ways that I have described—but it also cannot be severed from the sugar's forms of discipline.

Second, the temporality of rest is also distinct from extractive capitalism's production of waste and wasted time. Conjoining the racialized implications of waste to sugar and rum, Kyla Wazana Tompkins argues that one should also consider the ways that waste is figured temporally through the undervaluation of Black labor: "Within the representational logics of Western racism, both sugar and alcohol (in the shape of rum, sugar's accomplice) came to be associated with the necropolitical economy of disposable Black labor, and the various waves of narcotics-based carcerality that reentrenched enslaved unrecompensed labor within the prison-industrial complex."[32] In Tompkins's statement we see that the fungibility of Black flesh is also tethered to the criminalization of time spent unproductively (especially by Black people). Through Tompkins, then, we can sense how augmented speeds and productivity have been directly stolen from Black workers even as Black time is spent negotiating these forms of devaluation—not only disposability, but also the slow (and fast) violences of racism.

Rest is important. Its politics align, I think, more closely with what Tina Campt describes as refusal or "striving to create possibility in the face of negation."[33] For her, refusal is a way to combat the persistent precarity of Blackness. These practices of refusal are not exactly nonengagement, but they suggest a way of being in the world that is not governed by the logic of extraction. In the words of the Nap Ministry, "Rest is a form of resistance because it disrupts and pushes back against capitalism and white supremacy."[34] Physiologically, too, rest is critical. It allows the body to do away with the embodied excesses of productivity—stress. When stressed, the brain signals the release of adrenaline to boost your energy and heart rate; cortisol is released slightly later and works to depress nonessential bodily activity—like digestion and reproduction—so that threat is the primary focus. When the body has been under duress for long periods of time, cortisol is no longer effective and the body goes back to producing adrenaline to stay in fight or flight mode, but the long-term effects of this include inflammation and fatigue as multiple bodily systems work to stay activated. Rest, however, allows the body to curtail its active stress response by activating the parasympathetic nervous system. The heart can return to its slower rhythms, breathing can slow, muscles can unclench, digestion can begin properly, and the body can then eliminate excess stress hormones like cortisol and adrenaline through the liver.

Rest—a combination of physical and mental calm—activates a different sensory compass than sugar; it moves us toward tamarind and sourness. No, not the aforementioned tamarind sour, but the sour taste of acid on the tongue, a taste we might consider to be the shadow of sweetness. As Tompkins writes, "In the Western history of the senses, sourness is sweetness gone bad; sourness is sweetness rendered unprofitable."[35] In contrast to sweetness, sour is related to fermentation and rot; it is the flavor of excess time and, as Tompkins remarks, "the unprofitable." I use Tompkins's invocation of the market to think beyond the disciplinary mandates of productivity and being in sync as embedded within monoculture (sugar) toward various disfigurements that tree crops—like tamarind—provide. Not commodifiable in the same way as sugar, tamarind—one of the surprising fruits in Kaphar's sculpture—invites us to think about alternatives to economies of extraction.

The tamarind tree is tropical, native to Africa, and made its way, like sugarcane, to the Caribbean in the 1600s, presumably aboard ships carrying enslaved Africans.[36] Like sugarcane, which is grown from cuttings, tamarind is easily made portable; its fruit pods have a hard shell and the interior fruit has seeds that can last up to three months under the appropriate (cool, dry) conditions. This explains its presence in Asia, where it has been found long enough to be described as native and in Central and South America. In addition to a bounty of recipes, this expansiveness affords south-south intimacies, solidarities, and ecologies, giving us a different diasporic perspective on Blackness.[37] In seventeenth-century British colonies in the Caribbean, like Barbados, the main crops were cotton, tobacco, sugarcane, yam, and cassava; cotton, tobacco, and sugarcane were grown for export while the root crops were grown for local use. One might also find a few scattered trees, which produce much fruit. In this context, tamarind would act as a flavoring agent, adding a little punctuation to those starches, or it would be used to make a version of *aqua fresca*—a refreshing fruit and water-based beverage that is good on a hot day.

It is likely, then, that tamarind was grown alongside sugar in a formation that Wynter calls the "plot" as a way to designate parts of the plantation that were used by enslaved people to farm their own food. While this arrangement was economically beneficial to those who ran the plantations—it cost them nothing—as Wynter argues, it also contains possibilities of resistance: "The planters gave the slaves plots of land on which to grow food to feed themselves in order to maximize profits. We suggest that this plot system, was . . . the focus of resistance to the market system and market values."[38] While the plot is inextricable from relations of property and capitalism because it is part of the plantation, it alludes to an alternate structure of relation that is not based on extraction: "For African peasants transplanted to the plot all the structure of values that had been created by traditional societies of Africa, the land remained the Earth—and the Earth was a goddess. . . . Around the growing of the yam, of food for survival, he created on the plot a folk culture—the basis of a social order—in three hundred years."[39] Interestingly, Wynter also describes the plot in relation to the folk—folk knowledge and stories—and against the novel's consolidation of heroic individualism into narrative. The novel and presumably the liberal subject on which it relies is coextensive with the capitalism's forms of extraction: "Now, the novel form itself . . . came into being with the extension and dominance of the market economy, and it 'appears to us to be in effect, the transposition on the literary plane, of the daily life within an individualistic society, born of production for the market.'"[40] The plantation is structured by "the rights of property" while the plot speaks to a reliance on community and people. While Wynter notes the impossibility of return to an existence before the plantation, this does not diminish the importance of the folk as a contravening force. Wynter's analysis lets us explicitly connect Washington's bounded individualism and elevated status as "founding father" with the colonial emphasis on sugar as a profitable monoculture while highlighting folk modes of being embedded in the plot where diverse plants offered sustenance on multiple levels. These plants connected people to African traditions, cultures, and food ways while also offering a modicum of nutritional and medicinal independence, giving us insight into the difference between community-based rather than property-based systems.[41]

Grown within the plot, tamarind occupies a specific place within the folk economy to which Wynter alludes. (It feels important to note at this point that Washington did *not* receive tamarind in exchange for Tom—perhaps he was thwarted by its resistive possibilities?[42]) Tamarind does not occupy the tier of commodity (like sugarcane) or staple (like yams), nor is it a luxury item. It circulates among those who *know*, a particular type of folk knowledge generally passed down orally from tropical cook to tropical cook. One of my joys in the hot weather season is drinking Jarritos Tamarindo. The soda's gentle bubbles multiply the sweet and sour tang and augment tamarind's jaw-tingling earthiness. I did not, however, understand what tamarind could really do until Moon Charania taught me how to cook. These sessions, during the early months of New York City's pandemic lockdown, assembled six or seven of us over Zoom. Everyone attempted to follow along as we cooked in our own kitchens with our own materials. The first time we used tamarind was for Burmese stew. While noodles and toppings—hardboiled eggs and peanuts—were kept separate, meat, garlic, ginger, and chilis commingled. We added broth along with turmeric, salt, chili powder, ketchup, lemon juice, and fried onions before siphoning off the meat and adding coconut milk and tamarind to the remaining liquid. Once the liquid thickened and we were satisfied that the tamarind had done its work—a few minutes is all it took to see the oil atop the broth—we assembled everything into a large bowl. The tamarind adds a dash of tartness and depth, brightening the dish so that each flavor stands out.

This flavor augmentation is what happens when one cooks with sour ingredients. Their acid, in the words of the Cook's Country chefs, "competes with bitter flavor compounds in foods, reducing our perception of them and brightening other flavors."[43] The addition of tamarind, in other words, "balance[s] a dish and tease[s] out other flavors without calling attention to itself."[44] This is because sour, like sweetness, is often described as a taste rather than a flavor. In describing the difference, food writer Ligaya Mishan argues that taste is located primarily in the mouth while flavor is something that mingles with smell and texture. Citing Gabriel Valentin, a nineteenth-century German physiologist, Mishan writes, "Sour was a matter of touch, not taste, since its effect was to 'chiefly excite the sensitive, and not the proper gustatory nerves.'"[45] This culinary effect also has physiological benefits. Herbalist Guido Masé argues that this "excitation," this touch, is a mild chemical irritation, which tells us a lot about how the acid in sour foods is metabolized by the body.[46] The sour taste produces the effect of "cleansing tissues in the body and increasing your body's ability to absorb minerals. . . . These foods aid in digestion, circulation and waste elimination."[47] To return to the framework of temporality, we might say that the acid in sour foods helps the body initiate its relaxation response, increasing activity in the digestive system and slowing heart rate and breathing.

In addition to letting the body know that it can relax, plants that herbalists describe as tonics, such as tamarind, accelerate this process by actively metabolizing stress hormones.[48] Parsing why tonics work, Jim McDonald hypothesizes that they bring people into their bodies, not just because they aid in digestion, "but because they instilled a sense of 'grounding,' helping to strengthen one's connection to the instinct. They helped to shift people from intellectual 'brain' energy (which looks at things, takes them apart, and sees the pieces) to gut energy (which reacts to things instinctually, independent of intellectual consideration)."[49] McDonald also emphasizes the ways that this grounding is temporal, situating being present with favoring the gut over living in one's head.

Overall, given its sour taste and tonic properties, tamarind points us toward the beneficial properties that accrue from excess time. In contrast to the "heady" adrenal speed that sugar harnesses, tamarind stimulates an altogether different compass—that of "rest and digest." Tellingly, Masé likens this state of rest to what psychologists have described as "flow state," when one "experience[s] deep appreciation and satisfaction, highly creative and adaptive thinking, and feelings of strong connection to their environment."[50] While it might seem incongruous to theorize flow, which has been co-opted by a neoliberal lean toward productivity, with rest, I bring flow into the conversation in order to gesture toward how we might think outside of the binary between rest and productivity entirely.[51] For me, this is the imaginary attached to tamarind and its activation of the feeling of being *in* time (and its multiple temporalities) rather than subject to its discipline. In the context of the labor demanded during enslavement, tamarind offers, perhaps, a glimpse of an energetic economy that might evade cooptation by the plantation system. Within Kaphar's sculpture, I see tamarind's presence as gesturing toward this potential while also conjoining it to a method of conceptualizing racialization (the metabolic) without the forms of capture and projection that figural representation often entails.

Cravings, Abundance, and the Microbiome

While the experiences of discipline and overwork that enslaved people faced are largely unavailable to me—unknowable in ways that Darieck Scott astutely describes—I have my own (relatively privileged) experience of the temporal and physical pressures of racialized labor.[52] In spring of 2018, for example, I felt the effects of the university's entanglements with capitalism and white supremacy acutely—in my gut. There were so many meetings and so much travel and so much exhaustion, part of a pattern of overwork—the labor of "diversity" and scarcity—that Black and Brown people (femmes especially) undertake institutionally. I have written about these pressures elsewhere, but Grace Kyungwon Hong contextualizes this work within the post–civil rights neoliberal university's investment in making difference marketable while disavowing the labor (and laborers) that it requires, often actually endangering these workers' health.[53] Underpinning Hong's analysis is the centrality of neoliberalism's attachment to "color blindness," a post–civil rights ideology that imagines a horizon of equality such that race no longer matters except as commodifiable difference. Color blindness invisibilizes the effects of racialization because discrimination is assumed to be illegal even as structural inequalities persist. In her elaboration of the dynamics of expression and repression that characterize this perspective, Hong draws particular attention to "the racialization of ideologies as well as the racialization of bodies; the establishment of white liberalism alongside white supremacy; and the commodification and affirmation of minority difference alongside its repression."[54] What Hong emphasizes is the way that what color blindness attempts to disavow—the effects of racialization—becomes affixed to bodies and naturalized. From this perspective, we might also contextualize Kaphar's invocation (but not figuration) of Tom as a rejoinder to contemporary demands that racialization conjoin with the figural in the name of diverse representation. However, while the labor of racial representation is often "unseen," its effects can certainly be felt.[55] We might, for example, situate the emergence of women of color feminisms and critical race theory in the academy in the 1970s and 1980s as attempts to make visible the effects of racialization under this regime of "blindness."[56] Again, I turn to the metabolic as one way of making this racialized labor apprehensible.

When I say I felt the effects of capitalism and white supremacy in my gut, I am being literal. I felt bloated and tired and had an intense craving for sour. I wanted that tamarind soda or kimchi or kombucha. As it turned out, my craving for sour was an attempt to compensate for my lack of digestive potency due to stress and overwork. These acids were their own forms of excess time which helped my gut "rest and digest." Craving sour turned out to be an indication that my gut was overrun by excess microbes, which had migrated from large to small intestine because of stress. Eventually, I was diagnosed with SIBO (Small Intestine Bacterial Overgrowth), a condition in which digestion is slowed and archaea (an ancient class of bacteria), which thrive in harsh conditions, move from the large intestine, where they keep hydrogen levels low by metabolizing indigestible foods, to the small intestine, which is less equipped to handle their production of methane. Since most humans do not in fact produce this gas, its presence in the breath serves as diagnosis. The shift in location, in turn, leads to bloating, physical discomfort, and, in severe cases, the inhibition of the absorption of nutrients.[57]

In the larger scheme of ailments befalling Black female academics, SIBO is minor, but it speaks to the somatic impact of occupying multiple forms of marginality simultaneously—perhaps a different version of being constituted by multiple exteriorities. As Myisha Priest writes, "Death is becoming an occupational hazard of black female intellectual life."[58] Priest catalogs a long list of dead scholars—Barbara Christian, Audre Lorde, June Jordan, Toni Cade Bambara—to argue that they have succumbed to "progressive debilitation, a slow chipping away of power and energy that was a precise mirror of the slow destruction of progress she saw around her."[59] The problem for Priest is the lack of valuation of Black intellectual labor in the form of defunded programs and reduced tenure lines in the context of dismantling affirmative action programs and academia's perpetual "crisis of the humanities." Compounding these pressures are the political and economic effects of these deaths which reduce the overall profile of Black female intellectuals. Priest writes, "Their silencing is the destruction of historical and cultural continuity, the failure of a dream of community. Without them, who will create the brilliant works that force us to move forward by thundering into our minds, bringing change like rain—nourishing, overwhelming, necessary—and startling us into action?"[60]

While Priest theorizes recognition of these women and this crisis as a form of salvation, I am flagging these deaths and this slow violence to ask what it means to live in scarcity. These deaths and the accumulated other ailments (metabolic and otherwise) are ways that make visible the very real costs of the labor of working for structural change in a regime of color blindness. As Priest describes, these labors include administrative work trying to establish and maintain departments that are often marginalized; becoming an institutional representative for diversity (often attempts to include minoritized perspectives renders these perspectives synonymous with minoritized people, making racialized people bear the brunt of this labor); trying to support other scholars who are often isolated intellectually, professionally, and socially through mentorship, friendship and letters of assessment; performing similar labor for students; working with organizations to focus attention on people who have been marginalized; as well as imagining and implementing visions of other possibilities. Since this work is technically representational, it often preys on people's political investments and yet is often hidden by the logics of neoliberalism—more perniciously, it is often actually disavowed—until it emerges as stress. In Priest's analysis we can see how the chronic stress of this racism, scarcity, demand for labor, and desire for a different present and future can get stuck in the body—legacies of the cumulative effects of the slow violences of racism.

While craving sour does not obliterate violence, it offers a reorientation toward rest and release. To me, it suggests that even in the absence of structural change, the body-place knows another way; here, the idea of "self-care" hovers. But I refer to the version of self-care articulated by Jina Kim and Sami Schalk, who elaborate on Audre Lorde's use of the phrase in "A Burst of Light" in reference to determining what cancer treatment looks like for her. Lorde, they argue, "must take time for self-care consistently, demonstrating that care cannot occur outside of time or only during what capitalism would consider 'personal time' but, rather, is an ongoing engagement that cannot necessarily be adapted to a forty-hour work week or a nine-to-five job."[61] This version of self-care functions not as cure, but as a mode of making living palatable, like the reorientations provided by cravings. Most important for Kim and Schalk is that this version of self-care is political because this care emerges in relation to a hostile environment. The structural elements of harm, moreover, render "the self" metonymic in relation to care—this is to say that one might be performing self-care, but a community benefits. As Kim and Schalk write, "When you live in a world that seeks to do you harm or one that neglects you in such a way that your death is allowable, even necessary, both how you live and how you die are political."[62] This expansive, communal self might also help us understand the ways that cravings, themselves, are deeply situated within the social. For example, we might think of Beyoncé noting that she carries "hot sauce in [her] bag" as offering a balm against numerous types of violence.[63]

Kim and Schalk also make clear, however, that Lorde is also responding specifically to neoliberalism's "erosion of state and federal supports and protections for various marginalized groups" and that self-care is also about labor.[64] The consequence of the evacuation of social programs has been to shift the burden of social reproduction onto individuals, who have ever-vanishing personal time within this economic framework. Kim and Schalk thus frame the demolition of the welfare state as "a crisis of time, in which the unforgiving temporalities of capitalism increasingly disappear the slivers of time available for replenishment and renewal."[65] In the context of the neoliberal university, we might register the work of diversifying the academy through the lens of social reproduction in that it involves labor and time that are usually uncompensated for by official job titles, infringing on one's personal time even as they may speak to one's politics. We might similarly consider the additional labor scholars of color are often tasked with producing so as to maintain the "blindness" of color blindness alongside its accompanying affective (and other) negotiations, of which Moya Bailey writes, "This extra work, the additional work of having to do twice as much to be in the same standing as white peers, can produce an unrelenting self-flagellation."[66] What Bailey draws our attention toward is the way that the neoliberal university debilitates by normalizing a fast pace, an acceleration that cannot be separated from contemporary representational politics, but which impacts marginalized people more intensely.

In the face of these pressures, Bailey offers an ethics of pace, a personalization of temporality to make time for organic connection and knowledge production. This turn to personalization returns me to the question of the "I," which I argued Kaphar undoes in his contemplation of racialized labor and commodification, but which I think can be further decomposed by turning to the matter of cravings: What exactly are they? Who or what are their agents? And, finally, can I really say that *I* was craving sour?

In *Habeas Viscus*, Alex Weheliye ponders the relationship between cravings and survival. He asks, "How can CLR James's hunger strike while he is detained on Ellis Island and the Muselmänner's apparitions of food teach us to mouth 'I craves' in a tongue as of yet nonexistent in the world of Man?"[67] James, who had overstayed his tourist visa from Jamaica, was detained on Ellis Island during his trial and before his deportation. Faced with bland institutional food, James could barely eat enough to stay alive. What Weheliye is pointing us to is the way that craving is political. It moves us away from the question of bare life toward thinking about what shapes the conditions of enfleshment, sustenance, and pleasure. If the "world of Man" is focused on pragmatic ways to stay alive, cravings are full of want and infused with sociality. As an appetite in excess of the minimal requirement for survival, cravings add thickness and point us toward the noisiness of the body. Compared to desires, they are rawer, more opaque, and less tangible. They are governed by smells, textures, flavors, memory, and opportunity; all of which are subject to multiple circuits of power. Cravings are also deeply embedded in the viscera, which themselves can be understood as occupying temporalities and forces of the geopolitical—think of tamarind—and the microbial, which the gut microbiome points us toward.

The microbiome of the digestive system consists of thousands of bacteria, fungi, archaea, viruses, protozoa, and helminths; it is a noisy ecology whose diversity is literally unquantifiable. Originally imagined as invaders and studied in relation to disease or allergy, these microorganisms have more recently been connected to many behavioral elements including immunity, mood, and hormonal balance. Bacteria begin to migrate into the gut in utero, but their composition shifts after birth and with the introduction of solid food—changes which illustrate the different levels of relation embedded within the flesh. If my previous discussion of attuning to the gut focused on invigorating it as a site of bodily intelligence such that it could act as a microcosm for the emotions of the larger entity that we call selfhood, this version emphasizes the gut as multigenomic, multispecies, and wholly relational. What is appealing about the microbiome is that it offers a way to theorize the porosity of the human and to simultaneously grapple with the movement of power at multiple scales. The gut is still embedded in sociality, but of a dramatically different sort; the gut's micro dimensions expand its domains of knowledge in profound ways. In an analysis of the shift toward the micro in queer theory, Kyla Schuller argues that the micro offers a different perspective on biopower, emphasizing the micro's location "adjacent to and within the administrative vectors of the individual and the population, circulating throughout a milieu independently, accumulating within and as persons, and forming links among matter that forge bodies and populations."[68] The micro, in other words, is potent—producing relations that circulate at multiple scales, each of which displaces the "I" by admitting the sensual orientations that occur beyond individuality's conventional boundaries.

The gut microbiome is not only vast, but its sociality means that its components shift in response to external conditions. Eating an abundance of sugar, for example, prevents the production of Roc, a protein on which bacteria who are useful for breaking down vegetables rely. In the absence of these bacteria, those that prefer sucrose and fructose proliferate, producing a craving for more sugar and, eventually, a bacterial imbalance where the gut's barriers are impaired and the balance of the entire body shifts.[69] During my bout with SIBO, for example, the unexpected archae in the small intestine inflamed the liver impairing its production of bile and its regulation of blood sugar. I experienced this as hanger—intense and sudden hunger and anger that felt overwhelming and uncontrollable. Instinctively, I relate this to the feeling of performing racialized labor, where ways that the problem of diversity has been structured demands an unending supply of labor and time without actually producing a therapeutics of community, but forever dangling it as promise. The craving for sour increased the amount of bile in my system, offering some modicum of emotional regulation as well as facilitating digestion. In this second turn toward "rest and digest," the emphasis here is on digestion and its relationship to processing emotions that get stuck in the body.[70] This form of release is also about the creation of excess time. This means acknowledging these desires (cravings?) for community, but perhaps letting go of rigidity and form, to allow its energies and compositions to happen in ways untethered and ungoverned by institutional time.

Conclusion

Inflammation

Notes from the Front

IN THIS BOOK, I have fleshed out sensualities anchored in description in order to reach a place between shadows and noise, which is to say, outside of monolithic representation, so as to marinate in the unruliness of being. In turn, each of these stories offers insight into ways that bodies know and feel. More specifically, they implicate specific contours of my own being, as critic and as person in the world. Criticism is, after all, produced through extension; it happens when critic meets object and renders contemplation, description, comparison, analysis, and interpretation. This is to say that these moments of criticism can also be read as a shadowy and noisy narrative of my being. Quite deliberately, they do not coalesce into autobiography, which would privilege the production of self. Instead, they have focused on sensations: the dull ache of a spinal knot, the sharper pain of tight hip flexors, the bloat of SIBO, the suffocation of COVID-19, the unfurling afforded by rest, abundance in movement, the immersive quality of imagination, and the stillness of attending to the present in order to illuminate peril and possibility as they ricochet between critic and object.

To conclude this book, I focus primarily on the sensations that hew toward discomfort because they lead me toward where I am now: in the middle of treatment for acute myeloid leukemia (AML). While the temptation to retroactively construct a narrative of causality from these other incidents—moments that arc along the contours of unbelonging with varying intensity—is great, I bring them together under the rubric of inflammation in order to gain another perspective on shadows and noise. Inflammation helps me understand what happens when there is no triangulation through art, when the extension of being is directed internally instead of externally, and when one brings an analytic of sensation and description to experience in order to feel one's way to theory.

Inflammation is a form of embodied holding that can be productive or curdle into something pernicious; it occurs when the body sends blood cells to deal with threat. Usually, the issue is resolved quickly, but occasionally, the defense mechanism goes awry and stagnates, keeping the area primed for attack, upending the balance of the body and creating other systemic issues, including, but not limited to cardiovascular disease, Crohn's disease, long COVID, and many forms of cancer. Inflammation, then, both helps and hinders, which is to say it has its own shadows and noise. I borrow that list of inflammatory related disorders from *Inflamed! Deep Medicine and the Anatomy of Social Justice*, a recent book by medical journalists Rupa Marya and Raj Patel. In addition to arguing that inflammation is the causal mechanism behind these somatic disruptions, Marya and Patel draw attention to inflammation's sociocultural causes. They weave together systemic narratives of inflammation with social, cultural, and geographic context allowing us to sense what happens when threat actually forms the condition of living. They focus, in particular, on structural racism's somatic effects (a constant grind), corporations' greed (when profits govern instead of well-being), capitalism's relentless pace and propensity toward producing debt, sexism's persistent devaluation of feminized labor, tokenism's toll, and Western medicine's refusal to attend to forms of care that are not rooted in its epistemologies of objectivity and scientification.[1] Ultimately, Marya and Patel argue for a decolonial deep medicine that, like the body-place I describe, does not abide by a separation of humans from environment and attends to multiple modalities of care and being.

Marya and Patel are not alone in making this connection between discomfort and disease and structural violence. In addition to his description of the affective and sensational impacts of racism (and colonialism) in *Black Skin, White Masks*, Frantz Fanon elucidates the psychiatric disorders occasioned by colonialism among Algerians in *The Wretched of the Earth*.[2] More recently, work in Black studies has emphasized how the crossings between anti-Blackness and disability have been used to understand configurations of the color line as well as racialized formations of gender and sexuality.[3] Likewise, Audre Lorde's insistence on marking the myriad connections between racism, environmental and industrial harms, and access to health and health care puts her discussions of cancer into conversation with theorists working on debility or crip of color critique who examine impairment as the result of extractive state, capitalist, and racist epistemologies.[4] Each of these theorizations deepens our ability to grapple with the complex relationship between racialization and experience. Taken together, they allow me to register uncomfortable sensations as providing their own form of insight into how racism, colonialism, sexism, tokenism, objectification, and other forces seek to diminish and discipline the potentiality and unruliness of being.

An analytic of inflammation foregrounds the stakes of these sensations—their difference as productive of multiple temporalities and body-places—as they announce the competing and complex modes of being unfolding in the wildness of my present. As is the case with most cancers, doctors cannot tell me when or why exactly things started. At some point years and years ago, there was a mutation in my FLT3 gene, which signaled the body to overproduce immature blood cells (blasts). At a more recent moment—months ago?—there was a tipping point and these immature cells were, predictably, doing nothing in the manner of repair; instead, they enabled an unbridled inflammation to demand more of them and, in turn, produce fewer red blood cells, which provide oxygen to organs, and platelets, which control bleeding. At an even more recent moment, I experienced physical symptoms of this leukemia as forms of inflammation—namely as fevers, chills, swollen lymph nodes, and an inexplicable rash all over my body. This is to say that my cancer is inextricably bound up with inflammation's messy "present."

As this book suggests, there have been many sources and types of inflammation—each with its own relationship to temporality. I think of my spinal knot, an inflammation of the fascia technically caused by scoliosis, but rooted, I think, in the residues of colonialism and diaspora—a reminder of the way those forces shape the ever-folding now. In understanding this temporality, I am drawn to Christina Sharpe's use of "the weather" as a temporal descriptor because it describes a fully immersive epistemological quality.[5] While this ache subtends all, there are other durational forms of inflammation—the stress of performing representation, for example, or the existential dread occasioned by climate change—that I classify as chronic, as (also) grinding and unending temporalities, which come to the fore in relation to what might be otherwise (un-injured, perhaps?).[6] There is also the extended temporality of the ancestral, which, although related to the residues of colonialism and diaspora, operates through narrower specifics of matter and circumstance. Some might describe this as the realm of the epigenetic, although I want to heed Zakiyyah Iman Jackson's caution about the epigenetic's potential to pathologize the Black maternal instead of understanding the ways that individuals are positioned within various structures of debilitation and violence.[7] Still, the stress and difficulty experienced by my progenitors forms the conditions of my matter—does my premature birth, for example, render my cells more reactive to inflammation or produce a smaller bandwidth for error? What about the inflammation incurred by being a Black queer woman in the world? Or, that caused by COVID-19, long COVID, or merely living through a pandemic? Even as these more transient instances of inflammation might appear to reinforce liberal subjectivity, they cannot be thought of separately from these extended temporalities of inflammation, which complexify any notions of "when."

Although my discussion of the inflammatory is not usually where theories of Black temporalities begin, its polytemporality finds resonance with the ways that these theorists mobilize the complexity of temporality to find under- (or non-)represented possibilities for being, reinforcing the dynamic potential of shadow and noise.[8] For example, one of the key elements of Tavia Nyong'o's theorization of afro-fabulation is that the practice "deconstruct[s] the relation between story and plot" and rearranges temporality toward what he calls "tenseless time."[9] Tenseless time, Nyong'o argues, allows minoritarian subjects a glimpse of possibilities that are often foreclosed by diverting linear temporality and rational causation. He writes, "Such a sense of tenseless time is of particular importance to black and minoritarian subjects, for whom the gap opened out between the possible and the potential, no matter how slight, remains crucial."[10] While Nyong'o stresses the fleeting nature of these moments, he argues that "black art and performance can aid this process of critical fabulation in a variety of ways . . . especially insofar as they bring into co-presence a sense of the incompossible, mingling what was with what might have been."[11] In Nyong'o's emphasis on bringing together what was and what might have been, he gestures toward the "then and there of queer futurity" summoned by José Esteban Muñoz's notion of utopia, as well as theorizations by Malik Gaines and Joshua Chambers-Letson that build on Muñoz to articulate a performance theory of the "not yet."[12] In this framework, we can see that afro-fabulation works the complex grammar of the conditional, the verb tense of contingency that allows for multiple possible grounds and numerous futures by highlighting what might enable possibility. This is to say that the conditional summons the thickness of temporality—what could have happened, what has to have happened, what might still happen—into the now. As Michelle Wright argues, "The only spatiotemporal moment that can accommodate all these dimensions is the current moment—not the present—so to speak, but the moment of now, in which the present and the future are conflated and as many past and present moments exist as we can currently discuss, actively linked to blackness."[13] Likewise in *Black Futures*, Kara Keeling argues for the political importance of the unruliness of the now because of the possibilities that it carries: "The ungovernable, anarchic here and now harbors Black futures."[14] In Keeling's formulation, we see the fullness (noisiness) of the present—which contains not only what could have happened, but what might happen. Inflammation holds multitudes; in addition to cancer, I have found the noise of chimerism and shadow structures of care.

Chimerism, Hematopoiesis, and Noise

My AML diagnosis has meant that I have spent a lot of time thinking about hematopoiesis, the process of making blood. I find hematopoiesis intriguingly complex; signals from the lymph nodes, kidneys, and liver prompt lymphoid or myeloid stem cells to develop into specific blood cells depending on bodily need. Myeloid cells develop into blasts, which, in turn, can develop into multiple types of blood cells—platelets, red blood cells, and an array of granulocytes—basophils, eosinophils, and neutrophils, each of which offers a first line of defense for fighting infection. Lymphoid stem cells, meanwhile, produce lymphocytes, including B cells and T cells, which "remember" pathogens and confer acquired immunity.[15] The distortions of AML happen with the myeloid cells—encouraging them to overproduce blasts—so the other label that I was given for my cancer was acute myelogenous leukemia. I like this terminology because it emphasizes the hyperfecundity at work in this cell line, which also aligns this cancer with those that produce solid state tumors—excessive and overabundant growths. This emphasis on reproduction run amok also reoriented my thinking about blood and the circulatory system. Most people think of the heart as its central player, but really without the marrow and its production of cells, the heart would have nothing to pump and the body would be left vulnerable to infection. The marrow is, thus, nurturing and protective matter, or "mother."

My marrow went awry—tipping so far into the activity of defense that it became an engine of overall depletion—bad mother, indeed. And so, I underwent a bone marrow transplant. First, my untrustworthy marrow was killed off with chemotherapy and then it was replaced with stem cells harvested from my brother, which became the marrow that resides inside my bones. This means that my blood now bears his DNA, rendering me a chimera, someone with multiple lineages of DNA in their body—more noise. Chimerism also happens as a result of pregnancy—placentas enable this type of cellular exchange, the in utero absorption of a sibling, or when two different sperm cells fertilize an egg simultaneously.[16] Both the bone marrow transplant and the resultant chimerism, however, are intriguing beyond the possibility generated by modern science (though I am grateful for its miracles even as I am mindful of its harms), because they point us toward the noise of coexistence and make literal the nonindividuality that this book has been describing. Again, cancer does away with the triangulations of representation.

In thinking with approximation, doubleness, myth, or possession, we also come toward nonsingularity, but chimerism emphasizes not only plurality but the functionality of the aggregate and the importance of cooperation. For my transplant, for example, it was deeply important to have a donor whose HLA (human leukocyte antigen—a protein that the body uses to determine what is self and what is other) markers matched my own, but it was equally important for my body to be receptive so that both components could actually work together to create new blood that did not make my tissue, which still has my own DNA, react and reject the other. This is a working together outside of competition, toward mutual survival. I was deeply fortunate that my brother, Thomas, was an exact match with the same blood type, but many transplants are conducted with unrelated donors and half matches and different blood types—each difference amplifying the potential for complications. And, interestingly, vertical transplants (between parents and children) tend to have more complications because they activate dynamics of competition that horizontal ones do not—whither sibling rivalry?[17]

Symbiosis, like chimerism, is another place where cooperation and horizontality are privileged; however, Lynn Margulis faced backlash from the scientific community for hypothesizing that eukaryotic cells—cells that contain organelles and can develop into multicellular organisms—evolved through endosymbiosis. Margulis focused on mitochrondria, which reproduce independently of the rest of the cell and are complex organelles comprised of an outer membrane encasing an inner matrix with DNA and proteins.[18] Though now a widely accepted fact, this hypothesis was controversial in 1967 when Margulis published her now seminal paper, "On the Origin of Mitosing Cells." Though others had put forth some of the basic frames for the argument, Margulis was the first to incorporate data from biochemistry and fossils to make her argument. Protomitochondria, which could derive energy from oxygen, became engulfed by other cells early in the evolutionary process and became important to the development of eukaryotic cells and more complex multicellular organisms. Margulis narrates: "It is suggested that the first step in the origin of eukaryotes from prokaryotes was related to survival in the new oxygen-containing atmosphere: an aerobic prokaryotic microbe (i.e., the protomitochondrion) was ingested into the cytoplasm of a heterotrophic anaerobe. This endosymbiosis became obligate and resulted in the evolution of the first aerobic amitotic amoeboid organisms."[19] In this quick story, there are several details of note. First, we see that the introduction of an atmosphere of oxygen was actually a trauma of sorts. As more organisms began using the sun's energy to convert carbon dioxide into oxygen, other organisms had to adapt to this highly oxygenated atmosphere. Given their ability to convert oxygen into energy, protomitochondria thrived, producing endosymbiotic (engulfed) relationships with other organisms and leading to the production of more complex organisms, which eventually led to multicellular life. In this scenario, mitochondria offered the key to surviving the event of oxygenation.

Resistance to Margulis's theory, however, is instructive, because it tells us a lot about the valuation of individuality, competition, and vertical evolution, all of which come under scrutiny when we think with mitochondria and endosymbiosis. First, Antonio Lazcano and Juli Peretó describe the context in which Margulis was writing, a context in which evolutionary biology in the United States was invested in assessing the relationship between dominant and recessive traits. This framework, which drew on Gregor Mendel's nineteenth-century research on pea plants, meant that scientists were focusing on vertical inheritance (genetic material being transmitted from parents to offspring) and revealing the means through which certain traits were expressed. This also meant that DNA from each parent was imagined to be in competition with the other and that the cell's nucleus was of primary importance for understanding how inheritance worked.[20] Margulis's focus on mitochondria was eccentric to these goals; thinking with endosymbiosis challenges the primacy of the nucleus and the valuation of competition in evolution. Instead, it introduces the possibility of cooperative relations and horizontal forms of evolution. This view of the eukaryotic cell also shifted evolutionary interest in the 1960s toward microbes, whose "evolutionary history and classification . . . were shaped by their relationship to medicine, agriculture and industry. The pervasive influence of Pasteur and his followers had reinforced the clinical perspective that perceived microbes as pathogens and not as ancestors of extant life forms."[21] Margulis's hypothesis also explicitly redrew phylogenetic connections such that plants and animals—both eukaryotic cells with mitochondria—were more similar to each other than to prokaryotic cells. This meant that they could be studied together, which the historical separation of botany from zoology was ill-equipped to grapple with, thus challenging extant modes of categorization.

Instead of a version of multiplicity in which entities compete, chimerism and symbiosis speak to modes of coexistence with difference, which, although more complex than idealistic mutualisms, trouble individuality by introducing noise at the scalar level.[22] This is noise produced by multiple temporalities, modes of transmission, and functions. I need healthy marrow in order to make the blood to help me move, breathe, and ward off infection and the marrow in my bones produces that blood, encoded with Thomas's DNA, in response to signals from my tissues. This marrow reproduces not quite independently, but it is sort of its own hematopoietic system encased in the larger systems of my body-place. Between these differences in scale and motivation, a version of "me" is allowed to thrive.

Everything I've told you about chimerism so far is at the level of the molecular, perhaps because we understand it to occupy the realm of facts, but there are also things that operate at the level of sensation. While chimerism gives me a way to think of the positive dimensions of nonsingularity, there have also been aspects of my experience of AML that speak to the difficulty of this position. In this, I found that Audre Lorde's *Cancer Journals* capture much of this anxiety surrounding the loss of self that cancer, breast cancer in her case, occasions—both because of medicine's emphasis on isolating specific parts of the body and the overwhelm caused by confronting one's mortality.[23] Like Lorde, I have kept a journal—well, a blog—to keep my loved ones informed and to process this experience. The first entry, written three weeks into my first hospital stay, gives a brief overview of my transition from person who was not feeling well to person with a diagnosis. Since everything happened so quickly, I wanted to let the friends and family who were reading know what was going on since I had spent much of December and January in isolation trying to tend to myself. The March 4 entry was written during my first week at home following the first round of chemotherapy and remission when I was still bewildered by just how much of my life I had to give over to the medical-industrial complex and I was struggling with ideas of the self. By March 31, I had completed the second round of intense chemotherapy which necessitated an unexpected hospitalization because of a fever, so I was focused on resilience. The first April entry was written at the beginning of my hospitalization for the transplant and the other one was written in its aftermath. Together, they show a slow acceptance of the various dissolutions of self that were happening. There was resistance to being a patient; a diagnosis and then a reframing; a curiosity about these processes of transformation and what they meant; and a desire to hold this noise, this multiplicity, together. In them, I describe the difficulty of registering what happens when individuality is not available—one of the persistent themes of this book—and find insight into what embracing this multiplicity might feel like. In my case, the plurality of me(s) plus brother plus, plus, plus, plus has felt like a strength, a multiplication of interiorities and an enlargement of sensory possibilities.

February 14, 2022

I realize many of you don't know the story of how I got here. It started in early December when I got the COVID-19 booster shot and I started feeling bad. I had had a bad reaction to the second dose, so I didn't really think anything of it, but it went on and on—fevers, chills, mysterious illness with swollen glands, limited appetite, and fatigue. I thought I had turned a corner around New Year's but then I got a full body rash—no itching but lots of red spots and the fatigue got worse. I got a throat infection where I couldn't eat or talk for a week and as I was recovering from that, I thought that maybe the shot had retriggered my long COVID or induced mono. So, I had a telehealth visit and followed that up with blood work the following Monday morning (January 24).

Well, the blood told a different story—it said I was severely anemic. My doctor called like eight times that night and told me to go to the emergency room for a blood transfusion. I didn't get the message until the morning because I was so tired that I turned off my ringer in order to get more sleep. I woke up, panicked, spoke to Carrie who said she would drive me to the ER, but I should pack a bag and make sure they took my insurance and also that we should go to NYU in case I needed to get transferred to another department. We arrived around 10 a.m. and they did more of their own blood work and the questions began.

The transfusion—two units because my hemoglobin levels were at four and normal people's are eleven and acceptable is seven—started at 2 p.m. and felt so good and then I just had to wait. The hematology team would meet me in the morning for a bone marrow biopsy and I would be transferred there, but there were no beds available. So they wheeled me into a "quieter" part of the ER, which was actually not quieter—it was next to the nurses' bay so there was talking and bright lights all night where I just hung out. I had my vitals taken, got food, and waited for a bed to open up. I spent two nights in that space and almost cried with frustration. It was disgusting. I thought it was my lowest point. I still thought I'd just be going home soon. Carrie and Michael took turns visiting me. Carrie and I talked and played gin rummy and she brought me my computer, granola bars, a water bottle, and some clothes and Michael held my hand while I slept off the bone marrow biopsy.

A bed opened up around 2 p.m. on Thursday and I was brought up to hematology—my own gorgeous room with a view of the East River and a tentative leukemia diagnosis. There was a moment when maybe it was going to be a bone marrow injury, but no—AML with FLT3 mutation. So, they put in the PICC [peripherally inserted central catheter] line that night (I made Carrie wait with me because I was petrified) and started seven intense days of chemo that Friday, which is what they count as day one. And now, here we are two weeks later after a stomach infection and pneumonia, and after another bone marrow biopsy and I'm in remission waiting for my white blood cell count to increase. My marrow is clean and now we just have to keep it that way through the transplant.

March 4, 2022

One thing that I keep relearning in this process is how impossible it is to maintain any borders. I've surrendered myself to the pharmaceutical-medical complex for survival. For their help and expertise I am eternally grateful, but there's a constant battle between my emotional desire to barricade myself against everything by cocooning and the actual impossibility of that. I have to be completely transparent about my food intake, body movements, and so on, in order for treatment to have the best chance of success. I have to literally surrender tissue and blood CONSTANTLY. I have to pick up every single phone call because it might be a doctor telling me that they have scheduled me for X or Y appointment and I just make time. Or, it is the insurance company telling me that they have authorized X or Y or that they just want to check in. It is jarring to suddenly be blasted open and feel as though you have nothing—not even time—to yourself. I know Buddhism teaches you to surrender to this and flexibility is part of resilience, but it is also hard to constantly feel intruded upon even when you know it's good for you. It gives the lie to the myths of property and individuality, but since they are so engrained, feeling this falseness doesn't feel liberating.

March 31, 2022

Bodies are amazing. I'm still trying to sort out for myself my feelings about my body. On the one hand, I'm a little pissed that it glitched and produced this cancer. On the other hand, I wonder if I was pushing too hard and asking too much and then, well, mistakes happen. I think because I don't have a tumor, I can't quite produce a separation between me and the cancer. I mean cancer is always one's cells going awry, but it's still me. I'm kind of amazed that my marrow was able to absorb the chemo and then produce normal cells and then get beaten back again and then rebound. That is so much work—so much protein going into all of this rebuilding—and I feel proud of its capacity for regeneration even though generation is what got me (us) into this mess. So we're at an impasse. I'm grateful for what my body has been able to do—its ability to heal is insane. And I'm not sure I totally trust what is going on in there, hence my reliance on the numbers. How do you feel? Well, what's my hemoglobin count?

I have a whole PhD in history of science so there is a lot I can say about what this turn in medicine means, but it is weird to experience one's body through this type of numerical triangulation. I'm not someone, for example, who has ever lived with a scale. Reliance on external metrics to grapple with my body is weird. I mean, I do Tarot every morning and meditate to palpate my inner self, but that's a different inner self and I'm not entirely sure how to reconcile these interiors and how they circulate in the world as me, all these versions that I don't even actually have access to.

April 10, 2022

As I was doing my sun salutations with my new chest catheter I noticed that its three external points of entry—lumens—interfere with me being able to lower my upper body to the floor comfortably and it made me think about how many different ways I've had to learn to relearn my body. In December, it was the transition from well person to sick person—though how sick, I had no idea—but I gradually got used to staying inside because I was tired and trying to take care of myself as best I thought I knew. Then, when I started getting the throat infections, it was all about trying to get enough protein in liquid form to maintain body mass. In the hospital with chemo—the first time—it was trying to survive. I wasn't really thinking about my body too much except to note its inflation and deflation and working to regain some mobility that I lost when I was fighting infection and the total lack of conditioning that occurred in December and January. Going home with the PICC line introduced new body challenges since I couldn't lift more than ten pounds with my right side and I had to learn how to shower with it. So, no downward dog and lots of help from friends with moving things around. I had ten days without it which is when I started with the sun salutations and upper body workout. Carrie has already noted that I am starting to get a little muscle tone—like a green banana, as my grandfather used to say. So here with the chest catheter, there are fewer mobility restrictions, but the lumen brush against my right nipple, so it makes some poses challenging and means I expose myself whenever I get blood taken or an infusion of any sort. I'm on a constant learning curve with my body and its changing needs and that will continue. It's necessary and I guess sort of what happens in all stages of life, but you notice it more when the changes feel more extreme. So, I'm getting to know all of these different Ambers and appreciate them and then let them go and welcome the new bodies and shapes to come.

April 19, 2022

This time being neutropenic (having no immune system), at least today, feels different. I mean my nose is still a little runny, but I actually don't feel like I'm vibrating out of focus. I feel calm and stable—no small feat on like three hours of sleep and no real blood components to speak of. I'm feeling, however cheesy, like the difference is Thomas. It feels like I'm in the embrace of his many millions of stem cells. My doctor stopped by yesterday afternoon and told me that because Thomas had generated so many stem cells he was able to give me a bit more than they usually do. My mother asked my brother if it was love that allowed him to produce so much and he nodded affirmatively. I cried when she relayed the story. I mean I know if cures were a matter of love, no one would die of cancer, but still I do actually feel like I'm in my brother's embrace and it is nice and it feels like hope and like maybe those some of those cells are ready to start engrafting and getting real cozy.

I feel a new vitality coursing through my veins and I can feel my body relax into feeling some of the stability it has lacked since at least December—though who knows when that first mutation happened. I have been so parched for this deep internal groundedness and just been buzzing and buzzing and now I'm exhaling into being, just being. In addition to the obvious amazingness of Thomas's cells, I've been feeling like so much of this stability is being unleashed from an inner reserve of community and ancestry that holds so much strength. It feels like it vibrates through my matter—biological and spiritual and whatever else.

In the Shadow of the Empress

It is easy to think of cancer in relation to shadows; by the time one is diagnosed, mutated cells have been growing undetected for a while—weeks, months, or even years. Receiving a cancer diagnosis means that one can no longer ignore the knowledge that more pernicious cell growth is possible, perhaps even more likely. It is difficult to live with the wholeness of that reality, which is really mortality. And, although it is often easier to ignore, mortality provides the context for living. Moments gain meaning because we know that they are ephemeral. The prognosis for untreated AML is dire—at best, a few months, but usually weeks. The hope for bone marrow transplant is that it goes beyond remission toward a cure. In this space of waiting, my time feels borrowed, making me more attuned toward the shimmer of the present, which vibrates with possibilities as I bear witness to its unfolding. All because of the shadow.

I think often of Frantz Fanon, who died of AML in December 1961. From our contemporary vantage point, his death has acquired a mysterious aura, partially because the CIA helped him receive treatment in Washington, DC, after treatments in Moscow did not produce remission and partially because of speculation that he delayed treatment to complete writing *The Wretched of the Earth*, which was published as he lay dying.[24] In his introduction to the 2005 reprint of *The Wretched of the Earth*, Homi Bhabha furthers this association, writing, "Perhaps it was the writing of *The Wretched of the Earth* in a feverish spurt between April and July of 1961 that contributed to this fatal delay" between becoming ill and seeking treatment in the United States; "when his wife, Josie Fanon, read him the enthusiastic early reviews of the book, he could only say, 'That won't give me back my bone marrow.'"[25] Further, Fanon's emphasis on the efficacy of violence to combat colonialism has been read as symptomatic of the nihilism brought forth by his own poor prognosis, and his illness and death itself have registered as manifestations of Fanon's own theoretical investments in the different ways that violence is embodied.[26]

But to read *The Wretched of the Earth* as the chronicle of a death foretold ignores the ways that it might help us make sense of what it is like to live with illness and to invest in futurity despite, or at least in the face of, fatigue. Here, I am thinking of Fanon's use of gardening as a therapeutic and what it tells us about a reoriented future. Stephanie Clare performs such a reading in *Earthly Encounters*, arguing that Fanon's theorization of decolonization also takes the form of appropriation, which is "an engagement with the organic and inorganic world that leaves traces of life even when life is no longer there . . . the drive to appropriate is entangled with a form of perpetuity: as life appropriates parts of the earth, it transforms this earth so that it exists in reference to this life form, even when the living creature is no longer present."[27] Clare's theorization of appropriation allows us to register how meaning, understood in this context in relation to futurity, emerges through a revitalization of being with land. She writes, "His writing develops an account of human subjectivity where the subject emerges in part through appropriation, giving shape to part of the earth and recognizing that shape as one's own."[28] Though neither uses the language of body-places, I think that this is what is at stake, although appropriation's emphasis on futurity reveals yet another one of its modalities while also underscoring the importance of the shimmering present that I have described.

For me, what emerges now, perhaps unsurprisingly, is care. I spent roughly two months (during the span of three months) in the hospital, where I was cared for by teams of doctors, nurse practitioners, nurses, physical therapists, patient technicians, and custodial personnel. Each of these people held me in mind, monitored me, inquired into my well-being, buoyed my mood, and performed various forms of labor for me—providing medication and food, taking my vitals, making my bed, and keeping my room clean. Out of the hospital, this labor has shifted onto me and my home caregivers, but I still have frequent communication and in-person appointments that comprise the care of close monitoring. Embedded in the conjunction of care and work are not only the various forms of labor (affective and physical) that "hold things together," but also the ease with which it veers into the territory of coercion; a mandatory component of employment.[29] Here, we delve into the racialized and gendered hierarchies within what is labeled service work, but which we might consider a waged extension of the work of social reproduction.[30] It is impossible for me to not notice, for example, that most of the patient technicians and porters who I encountered on my daily perambulations on the hospital floor bade me good morning in lilting Caribbean accents—giving me a history of migration and a taste of nostalgia all at once.

Still, there were moments in the hospital that feel as though they exceed the parameters of logistics and work that make up some of this care: nightly discussions about HGTV with Greg, who emptied my trash; Danielle rushing in to tell me that my blood counts had risen enough so that I could finally be released from the hospital; Jay stopping by to chat about the Deana Lawson's exhibit at MoMA PS1. There are other innumerable kindnesses that people in the hospital offered, to say nothing of those proffered by my friends and family. After accompanying me through the disorientation of being admitted to the hospital, getting diagnosed, and beginning treatment options, Carrie kept me supplied with chocolate chip cookies, laughter, and visions of a future. Ankur remade each hospital room into homey (and hygienic) cocoons in addition to picking me up from outpatient procedures and ordering takeout when I couldn't get off the floor. Kandice helped me clear my teaching and service schedule, brought me pastries and sheet masks, and gave me sage advice. Friends visited, went on masked walks with me, and sent encouraging messages along with food, sweatpants, and scarves. Jasbir and Carrie set up a GoFundMe to which people gave generously. Friends cleaned and packed up one apartment and moved me into another one. Thomas donated his stem cells—its own complicated medical procedure. People—Ankur, Kadji, and my parents—stayed with me to cook and clean and keep me company after the transplant. Kadji even mastered the virgin piña colada, massaged my scalp with black castor oil to stimulate hair growth, and produced a menu of well-cooked, delicious food. All of this care has been a balm and source of strength throughout my experience with AML even as my access to it is embedded in my own forms of privilege: a loving and supportive partner, best friend, and family of origin, stable employment with good insurance, and good friends with emotional and financial resources and the ability to make their own schedules flexible.[31]

In each of these actions, I feel held with tenderness and hope. This labor and love has been an enactment of care that Sandy Grande might describe as "a praxis of relationality and kinship critical to the development of just and liberatory futures."[32] Notably, Hil Malatino describes his postsurgical queer and trans "care web" in similar terms. These care webs, he argues, have been forged through "the force of traumas psychic and physical . . . dispersed through its filigree of filaments" and work to refuse the centrifugal forces of the nuclear family in order to enact kinship more broadly.[33] Throughout *Trans Care*, Malatino elaborates on the different forms of societal exclusion that produce queer and trans care webs while also describing the negotiations of exhaustion and consistent work of self-reflection required to keep these networks vibrant. He writes, "A resilient care web coheres through consistently foregrounding the realities of burnout and the gendered, raced, and classed dynamics that result in the differential distribution of care—for those receiving it as well as those giving it. A care web works when the work that composes it isn't exploitative, appropriative, or alienated."[34] I also see an overlap between the grammar of conditionality that Tina Campt describes as a Black feminist praxis and the various forms of care that Malatino describes and that I received: "The challenge of black feminist futurity is the constant and perpetual need to remain committed to the political necessity of *what will have* ***had to*** *happen*, because it is tethered to a different kind of 'must.' It is not a 'must' of historical certainty or Marxist teleology. It is a responsibility to create one's own future as a practice of survival."[35] In Campt's unpacking of the conditional, we see an orientation toward survival, process, and an ethics. The future is not a given, but a collaborative enactment *toward*. In meeting my needs in the now, my caregivers are investing not only in a future that we could share but also an orientation to the world that prioritizes being with and thinking with another.[36] Temporally and otherwise, I find resonance with the way that Clare connects Fanon's decolonization efforts with forms of land appropriation—each tilts the polytemporal present toward a future entwined with justice.

In many ways, I am living in an orientation toward the world that I have been working toward—one that pivots around prioritizing care as a way of being. Grande positions this understanding of care as "a *politics of refusal*, one that rejects the exploitative relations of racial capitalism and settler colonialism."[37] Care, framed in this context, forms a shadow structure to the privileging of individualism and autonomy. In the coda to *Sensual Excess*, I use Melanie Klein to move away from Oedipal forms of recognition toward relations that might privilege care. I write:

> Through this we can see that grappling with the mother produces a rich world where the presumed goals of subjectivity—individuality and

omnipotence—are undermined. Not only is individuality revealed to be the product of violence, but it is also shown to be impossible: one is always in a state of coexistence and immersed in violence. Vulnerability is the underside of fantasies of omnipotence, and love and hate must be woven together in order to provide a path toward existing ethically as a self in the world. Opacity and sensuality come together in this work of producing a self in relation to the mother.[38]

One of the things that have been surprising, then, is my own difficulty receiving so much care and generosity. Although being part of a care web, Malatino writes, "challenges us to be deliberate, to communicate capacity, to unlearn the shame that has become attached to asking for, offering, and accepting help when we've been full-body soaked and steeped in the mythos of neoliberal, entrepreneurial self-making," it has felt easier to theorize caregiving than to grapple with the profound asymmetries involved in receiving care.[39] Some of this has to do with the overwhelming nature of my needs and their suddenness. It has been difficult to distill what I want—to be better, to feel better—into any type of request. Some of this also has to do the fact that so many theories of care (including Klein's) position the recipient as an infant. Although my posttransplant self is often described as having the immune system of a newborn (which is to say, immune to nothing), I find myself chafing at the comparison because of the ways that it implies a lack of knowledge about the world coincident with a lack of self-determination. Moreover, the position of dependence feels freighted with debt, both affective and material.[40] The questions running through my mind: how could I even begin to repay these kindnesses and how was I worthy of such attention? Although thinking of care as praxis felt urgent and compelling, I still had to unlearn a latent ableism that understood my value in relation to exchange and productivity rather than being.

One way that I have tried to understand this work is through Tarot, and the card I had the most difficulty connecting with: the Empress or Divine Feminine. In the Rider Waite deck, which is one of the most popular decks, the card depicts a blonde woman with a heavy crown seated on a throne in the middle of a forest, holding a scepter aloft in her right hand. The throne is covered in pillows and blankets and the gown's embroidery and heavy folds allow it to be read as regal. The Empress is the third numbered card of the Major Arcana and associated with the element of Earth and the astrological sign of Taurus. I had been taught that the card symbolized a welcoming of abundance. Generally, people enjoy receiving this card because it is assumed to correlate with reveling in pleasure, in moreness.

Faced with this onslaught of generosity, I have had to learn how to receive. I first started to understand the Empress card and the beauty of receptivity a few years ago when Samita invited me to visit her at the beach. The water was nice and cool and the pebbles and larger boulders on the beach were hot. Swimming and then drying off by lying on a big rock was how one passed time delighting in the sun, really soaking in its bounty of energy and light. This, I thought, is Empress behavior. This is receiving outside of exchange, but as part of the enjoyment of being. I could fill myself with the sun's gift of warmth and hold on to it and its memory for another day. In this way, the Empress suggests a durative temporality, a quality of holding, outside of an economy of depletion—it invites one to nurture being now so that one can be later. Now, I am living in Empress mode. I am engorging myself on the care that others are extending as part of the realization that surrendering to these regimens of care isn't about giving autonomy, but about enlarging a vision of self to encompass others. Being embedded in these circles of care provides necessary sources of strength, not only for me, but for my communities; it reveals the deep plurality of being.

Of Inflammation . . . and Flamingos

Both chimerism and care, as I have described them, play with the additive and temporal aspects of inflammation. Chimerism emphasizes the importance of different temporalities and modes of being within a larger aggregate. Likewise, thinking with care works with the conditional aspect of futurity and the enlargement that comes with receptivity. Both destabilize the conventional idea that inflammation consolidates the singularity of self through defense.[41] Both also provide alternate vantage points to consider modalities of nonsingularity and polytemporality—two of the themes that this book has explored repeatedly in its engagement with art in order to produce a theory of sitting with difference that emphasizes sensual knowledge.

And so, Ming Smith's *Flamingo Fandango (West Berlin) (painted),* again (see plate 1). Returning to this photograph now I am struck by the flamingos' grouping as a flamboyance. In iconography, especially lawn decorations, flamingos often appear as featured soloists on one leg, but in Smith's photograph, we see a crowd, which more accurately depicts the way flamingos live both in the wild and in captivity. In these groupings, these long-living birds find both lovers and friends, suggesting systems of care and multiple forms of relation.[42] The flamboyance is also notably different from the collectivity of the swarm that Hypatia Vourloumis and Sandra Ruiz theorize and which they describe as "movement in large numbers," emphasizing the importance of nonverbal cues, such as vibration, for coordination.[43] While the flamboyance asks us to pay heed to the overarching noise of the group, we can also bring our attention to the specific and different types of intragroup dynamics at work—melodramas of care and neglect that form their own type of noise. I am also struck by the specific distance from which Smith has invited us to consider the birds. They occupy the lower half of the image and are surrounded by shadows of trees, by enclosure, and by water. To me, this perspective activates a sense of dread; it feels as though anything could happen at any given time. This is the shadow side of anticipation; this is the residue of living in and through diagnosis. There is probably more to say, there will always be more to say, but I will leave that for another time.

Notes

Introduction. Body Work

1. Ozkan, "Thousands of Flamingos Die."

2. Greenberger, "Ming Smith Shook Up Photography in the '70s."

3. Chuh, "It's Not About Anything," 127.

4. See Rancière, *Ignorant Schoolmaster*, for more on the production of this common sense. My use is also indebted to Kandice Chuh's reading of Rancière in Chuh, *Difference Aesthetics Makes*.

5. Nicola Vassell has been instrumental in bringing attention to Ming Smith's post-Kamoinge photography work through hosting an exhibition at the Nicola Vassell Gallery in May 2021 and working to put together *Ming Smith: An Aperture Monograph*, among other efforts. See also, Vassell, "On Ming Smith." For more on Ming Smith and her relationship to the Kamoinge collective, see Brooks, "Vision & Justice Online."

6. The blurriness of the image, like Fred Moten's blur, refuses individuation and argues for an embrace of multiplicity and enmeshment. Flamingos and background appear to bounce between perspectives, dismissing a prioritization of a singular view, which is expected to emerge from the bounded individual. Rebecca Wanzo situates Moten's blur as existing between the racialized objectification experienced by Black people and the possibility that this invisibility enables, writing that "The 'blur' shaped by this intersubjectivity between the subject and the object might also dissolve that binary and create conditions of intimacy and dissolution of individualism for different political and social ends." Thinking with Wanzo and Moten, then, allows us to grapple with the onto-epistemological implications of Smith's subversion of racialized representational norms. Moten, *Black and Blur*, 246; Wanzo, "Moten's Magical Meditations"; Greg Tate and Arthur Jafa also make this connection between Moten's blur and Smith's photographs in "Sound She Saw," 217–26.

7. Talbert and Smith, "Portrait of the Artist," 15.

8. Talbert and Smith, "Portrait of the Artist," 15.

9. Serpell, "Shimmering Go-Between," 58.

10. Tate and Jafa, "Sound She Saw," 221.

11. Tate and Jafa, "Sound She Saw," 225.

12. Casid, *Scenes of Projection*, 7.

13. Raengo, *On the Sleeve of the Visual*, 166.

14. See Stoever, *Sonic Color Line*; Chion, *Sound*; Hainge, *Noise Matters*; Attali, *Noise*.

15. Stoever, *Sonic Color Line*, 13.

16. The claims of toxicity stem from environmental discourses, which frame these cities as out of sync with the present. Though begrudgingly acknowledged as modern, the timing and speed of urbanization and industrialization is deemed suspect. They are "late" entries into industrialization—an orientalist assignation of backwardness (Buckley and Wu, "In China, the 'Noisiest Park in the World'").

In *Animacies*, Mel Chen traces this sneering tone through a panic about lead paint, which Chen argues is "a highly selective [narrative] dependent on a resiliently exceptionalist victimization of the United States" (165). The United States (and "the environment"/ "the west") becomes the targets of Chinese toxicity and backwardness—thereby ignoring the environmental changes that urbanization and industrialization have already wrought and blaming the Chinese factory workers, while ignoring the fact that the vast majority of Chinese residents are more impacted by these toxins than those abroad. This narrative also forgets the ways in which much of this impulse toward modernization is driven by particular histories of international intervention through warfare and capitalism, which David Harvey identifies as a "race to the bottom" in which governments overlook unjust labor practices in order to participate in the global economy (Harvey, *A Brief History of Neoliberalism*). What we see in the analysis that Chen provides is that the individual bodies of consumers (those with capital) are privileged over those of the workers in factories, rendering them faceless masses vulnerable to exploitation, but, most importantly, imagined in the aggregate. We can also consider (thinking with Anne Cheng and Rachel Lee) how this orientalist discourse coheres with those of Asian inhumanity and automaticity, which renders the city more visible than the people.

17. Bradley, "SANDRA BLAND."

18. As William Cheng writes, "Altogether, stereotypes of black physical excess and black sonic excess implicate the threatening physicalities of black sound and, in turn, the threatening sounds of black physicality" (119). What we see in all these examples, but especially in Davis's murder, is the conflation of noise with the Black body. Davis is perceived to be the source of noise, to embody all of its unwanted excesses.

19. In the dossier that Gluibizzi compiles, artist Laura Libson argues that edges are about "negotiations and divisions between internal and external edges (to and from the world)." This is to say that they demarcate concepts of interior and exterior through questioning "the limits of the social, political, and personal." Edges are how

we "recognize where objects and subjects intersect, begin and end, separate and join." Gluibizzi, "On Edge(s)"; Libson, "Edges/Limits. Edges/Tableau."

20. Jacques Attali's treatise on noise is most famous for his embrace of noise, but a narrative of full embrace negates some of the deadly consequences of being designated noise, which we see in the Jordan Davis case. We might also consider that noise has been designated a pollutant by the Environmental Protection Agency as part of their Clean Air Act since 1972. In *Sound, Space, and City*, Marina Peterson argues that noise's effects are also physiological in that excessive noise can lead to physiological stress, loss of productivity, and diminished hearing capacity. This tendency toward idealization, however, is a staple in academia. We can locate it in narratives of queer theory, for example, as traced by Kadji Amin in *Disturbing Attachments*, who argues for de-idealization. Here, I am arguing for a similar approach to noise.

21. McKittrick, *Dear Science*, 36.

22. Zakariya, *A Final Story*, 5.

23. Here, we might turn to Sylvia Wynter, Kandice Chuh, Roderick Ferguson, Zakiyyah Iman Jackson, and others for elaborations on this list of disciplining forces.

24. Chuh, *Difference Aesthetics Makes*, 5.

25. Rusert, *Fugitive Science*, 20.

26. Rusert, *Fugitive Science*, 20.

27. Kapadia, *Insurgent Aesthetics*, 10.

28. Musser, *Sensual Excess*.

29. Kim, dir., *[Closer Captions]*. For more on the history and politics and ideas of audio captioning and "deaf gain" see Holmes, "Expert Listening"; Mills, "Do Signals Have Politics?"

30. In *To Describe a Life*, Darby English works through several objects of art that utilize description as a way to pierce representational schemas that might presume subjective transparency. In this project, English follows Eve Kosofsky Sedgwick, who argues that "the commitment to description that is not in a predetermined relationship to theoretical questions, even though it would ideally be open to them at every point, is a really important practice." Sedgwick shows that although description is not neutral, when practiced with curiosity, it may endeavor to present complications and nuance without preconceived judgment. Sedgwick in conversation with Gavin Butt, "Art, Writing, Performativity," 129.

31. Simone de Beauvoir, *Second Sex*, Toril Moi, *What Is a Woman?* and Judith Butler, "Sex and Gender in Simone de Beauvoir," have elaborated on this aspect of Beauvoir's philosophy.

32. Haraway, "Situated Knowledges," 579.

33. Ahmed, *Queer Phenomenology*, 2.

34. Ahmed, *Queer Phenomenology*, 1.

35. Mecca Jamilah Sullivan, for example, describes various strategies of embodying difference through poetics as a particular strategy of Black queer femininity in Sullivan, *Poetics of Difference*.

36. Hong, *Death beyond Disavowal*, 7.

37. Puar, *Right to Maim*, 60. Such specificity takes seriously Michael Gillespie's argument in *Film Blackness* that "the discursivity of *black* demands greater rigor than speculations of universal blackness" (6).

38. Muñoz, "Brown Commons," 7.

39. Glissant, *Poetics of Relation*.

40. English, *To Describe a Life*, 5.

41. English, *To Describe a Life*, 5.

42. I first heard this fused land acknowledgment through the *Brooklyn Rail*'s "New Social Environment," a daily virtual lecture series that started in March 2020 when New York City began its lockdown. Throughout the year, their statement would add the names of specific individuals killed by state and state-sanctioned violence. Their land acknowledgment, in turn, is publicly indebted to the Indigenous Kinship Collective, https://indigenouskinshipcollective.com/take-action.

43. Leroy, "Black History in Occupied Territory."

44. King, *Black Shoals*, x.

45. Kim, "Caribs of St. Vincent."

46. Kim, "Caribs of St. Vincent"; rumors are reported by my mother.

47. Kim, "Caribs of St. Vincent," 119, 120.

48. This theory might be bolstered by David Reich's discovery of an abundance of Taíno DNA in contemporary Caribbean populations, which suggested much travel and relatedness between island populations. Patterson and Reich, "Ancient DNA."

49. Alexander, *Pedagogies of Crossing*, 3–4.

50. Carby, *Imperial Intimacies: A Tale of Two Islands*.

51. Nadia Owusu writes movingly of these sets of contradictions of growing up in a "biracial" family in *Aftershocks*. She specifically describes being seen a symbol of multicultural integration as well as being seen as someone who should not be. I put "biracial" in quotation marks because I think the use of this term perpetuates the idea that Blackness is unassimilable and that race is straightforward.

52. Although there is more scholarship on United Fruit Company, which became Chiquita in 1984, because of its extractive labor practices and collusion with the US government to overthrow governments in Central America, Standard Fruit Company is not above reproach in these matters. Standard Fruit Company was founded by the Vaccaro brothers, who began importing bananas from Honduras to New Orleans in 1924; it was acquired by Castle and Cooke corporation in the 1960s, at the same time as the Hawaiian Pineapple Company, which was started by James Dole. In 1991, Castle and Cooke changed its name to Dole Food Company. For a brief timeline, see https://www.unitedfruit.org/chron.htm.

53. Tongson, *Why Karen Carpenter Matters*, 22, 23.

54. See Stoler, *Race and the Education of Desire*.

55. Kincaid, *Small Place*, 3–4.

56. Now, my parents, brother, and I live in northeastern cities in the United States, but the entanglement continues. My father now has his own company (working with

my sister-in-law, Ashley) importing organic fair-trade produce, including mangoes from Haiti; my mother runs an arts organization in St. Vincent (Youlou) and spends several months a year there. I, however, am an occasional visitor. Sheller, *Island Futures*, 42. See also, Sheller, *Mobility Justice*.

57. Alexander, *Pedagogies of Crossing*, 22–23.

58. Gill, *Erotic Islands*, xxvii. Gill, in turn, cites Mimi Sheller and M. Jacqui Alexander.

59. Gill, *Erotic Islands*, 11.

60. Gill, *Erotic Islands*, 28.

61. Agard-Jones, "What the Sands Remember," 339.

62. Agard-Jones, "What the Sands Remember," 326.

63. Gill, *Erotic Islands*, 209.

64. Tinsley, "Black Atlantic, Queer Atlantic," 193.

65. Tinsley, "Black Atlantic, Queer Atlantic," 199.

66. Tinsley, "Black Atlantic, Queer Atlantic," 199.

67. Tinsley, "Black Atlantic, Queer Atlantic, 194.

68. Tinsley, "Black Atlantic, Queer Atlantic," 194.

69. Tinsley, *Ezili's Mirrors*, 144.

70. Tinsley, *Ezili's Mirrors*, 144.

71. Spillers, "Interstices," 153.

72. Gumbs, "End Capitalism."

Chapter One. *Us*, the Uncanny, and the Threat of Black Femininity

1. Freud, "Uncanny."

2. Hartman, *Scenes of Subjection*, 102.

3. Hartman, *Scenes of Subjection*, 103.

4. Owens, "Yes Means Yes."

5. Those without access to subjectivity and desire are, in turn, designated as other, a framework that Denise Ferreira da Silva reminds us occupies the space of projection and opacity. While the subject is assumed to occupy "the stage of interiority, where universal reason plays its sovereign role as *universal poesis*," the other is assigned to the realm of the external as an "affectable I." This means that the properties of the other are determined from the outside and are therefore deeply constrained. This also means that recognition and desire are impossible in this framework; they are blocked by the workings of projection and the omission of interiority. Silva, *Toward a Global Idea of Race*, 31.

6. Redmond, "*Us* Liner Notes."

7. Bradley, "How *Men in Black*."

8. Bradley, "How *Men in Black*."

9. In the ballet, the Sugar Plum Fairy welcomes the children into the land of sweets and provides delightful (though possible deadly) entertainment. Her solo consists of small, precise movements that build into larger more expansive motions, by way of leg-extending arabesques and stage-crossing pirouettes. Dance historian Roland John Wiley describes the dance as having "a sense of dynamic build up: from delicate

angularity . . . to circular shapes, to plainer but more virtuoso movements—*pirouettes* to *rounds de jambe*—near the end." As her duet partner, the Cavalier's task is largely to escort her across the stage and provide support during lifts; in a separate short solo, the Cavalier spins in the air before finishing with a series of fouettes (turns in which the lifted leg cycles between being straightened and bent). Wiley, *Tchaikovsky's Ballets*, 219.

10. Bradley, "How Men in Black."

11. Jean-Paul Sartre describes vertigo in this way in *Being and Nothingness*. I elaborate on this sense of vertigo in *Sensational Flesh*.

12. Harrison, "Us and Them."

13. In "Us and Them," Harrison also writes,

> *Us* is similarly about labor. It's also about work, home ownership, and aspirations of class ascent in an economic environment where such mobility and property acquisition are competitive, dehumanizing, and nearly impossible for those who didn't begin their lives with wealth in the first place. The film's callbacks to the 1986 Hands Across America campaign and N.W.A.'s 1988 track "Fuck tha Police" tether its action to the passage between 1984 and 1990. In those years, the growth rate of US GDP fell from a high of 7.2 percent to 1.9 percent. If Hands Across America registered increasing poverty, as marked by hunger and homelessness, "Fuck tha Police"—which begins to play in the film when a voice-operated home entertainment system mishears a dying command to "call the police"—marks the moment when this decline is registered in California and the rest of the United States as a racial crisis. That this economic context manifests in the film through a grainy commercial and music played wirelessly on voice command renders it uncannily ambient. It haunts the present, like the mysterious figures who appear as spectral doubles of the film's main characters.

14. For a longer elaboration on property and liberalism, see Walcott's *On Property*, in which he connects the abolition of property with Black liberation. For more on liberalism and the ascendency to whiteness, see Eng, *Feeling of Kinship*.

15. King, "In the Clearing," 206.

16. Harrison, "Us and Them."

17. I put American in quotation marks because it is a reference to Red's response to the query of who they are: "We're Americans." It also speaks more broadly to the United States as settler-colonial nation. Indeed, settler colonialism might be said to be operating as the film's collective unconscious. Noting that the horror starts inside the Native American–themed "Vision Quest" attraction, film critic Emmy Scott writes, "From that point on, *Us* . . . became a story about Native appropriation for me." Scott, "Native Imagery of Jordan Peele's *Us*."

18. I am grateful to Julia Willms for pointing out this aspect of Peele's filmography.

19. In addition to the home invasion genre that I described, we can also think of the genre of film like the *Stepford Wives*, *Demonseed*, or *Rosemary's Baby* where domesticity itself is the trap.

20. The "Black Privacy" issue of the *Black Scholar*, edited by Shoniqua Roach and Samantha Pinto, has many essays theorizing creative impulses enabled by privacy.

21. Davis, "Reflections."

22. Davis, "Reflections," 49.

23. In color film, red and cyan are negatives of each other, so I am hypothesizing that the name Red implies some relation of inverse relation.

24. Kyla Schuller's *The Trouble with White Women* provides a history and theory of how white feminists have worked to uphold white supremacy by focusing on the rights of individuals rather than collective forms of justice.

25. Lacan, "Subversion of the Subject."

26. Fanon, *Black Skin, White Masks.*

27. Aviva Briefel describes the rarity of the Wilsons' initial display of Black leisure, arguing that the ability to take a break is what marks them as members of bourgeois society even as "*Us* exposes the violent aspects of this forced rupture, reconfiguring the capitalist 'break' as a breakdown." Briefel, "'We Want to Take Our Time.'"

28. Ginsberg, *Passing and the Fictions of Identity*. Ginsberg uses the example of Harriet Beecher Stowe's anxiety that white children would be inappropriately sold as octoroons in *Uncle Tom's Cabin*.

29. Wald, *Crossing the Line*, 24.

30. Smith, "Reading the Intersection of Race and Gender." While women are more likely to be punished for passing, she argues that narratives like Julie Dash's *Illusions* (1982) and Charles Lane's *True Identity* (1991) complicate the passing narrative, making it less reactionary and more in service of exposing the constructedness of race and the class implications of boundary crossing.

31. Wald, *Crossing the Line*, 151.

32. Gaines, "Racing Work and Working Race in Buppie Horror," 152.

33. Gillespie, *Film Blackness*, 53–54.

34. Gillespie, *Film Blackness*, 60.

35. James, "Womb of Western Theory," 255.

36. James, "Womb of Western Theory," 256, 258.

37. Notably, Edwards makes explicit reference to the uncanny, titling a section that speaks specifically to the cooptation of Black achievement for the war on terror "Uncanny Collisions."

38. Edwards, *Other Side of Terror*, 39.

39. See Edwards's elaboration in *Other Side of Terror*, 58.

40. Edwards, *Other Side of Terror*, 142. Emphasis in original.

41. Edwards, *Other Side of Terror*, 147. Emphasis in original.

42. Aviva Briefel produces a different reading of *Us,* which centers the vacation setting. She reads the film within the genre of terrifying vacation film, which might allow us to register Peele as making a critique of the racial dimensions of leisure. Briefel, "'We Want to Take Our Time.'"

43. There is ambivalence about these collectivist impulses throughout the film. They are not connected to economic structures, so are difficult to connect to a broader economic critique, and the film ends with an image of people in jumpsuits clasping hands—evoking the stance of those participating in the Hands Across

America fundraising event, which is also described by Gabe (perhaps as critique) as "performance art." However, one might also argue that the 1986 event, whose aim was to have people across the United States join hands in an unbroken chain for fifteen minutes in order to raise money to fight poverty, was similarly performative rather than structural in its intervention. I am grateful to Sailaja V. Krishnamurti for bringing this to my attention.

44. We might, however, critique *Get Out* for making a TSA agent a hero of the narrative, producing similar intimacies with (and valorizations of) imperialism.

45. Cox, *Shapeshifters*, vii.

46. Wright, *Black Girlhood in the Nineteenth Century*.

47. Cox, *Shapeshifters*, 12.

48. For more details on how this disciplining happens, Savannah Shange's *Progressive Dystopia* offers ethnographic accounts of the specific ways that Black girls are disciplined within the so-called progressive educational system.

49. McMillan, *Embodied Avatars*; Brooks, *Liner Notes for the Revolution*.

50. Ibrahim, *Black Age*, 36.

51. Ibrahim, *Black Age*, 14.

52. Ibrahim, *Black Age*, 20, 35.

53. Stephens, "Skin, Stain and Lamella" 322.

54. Stephens, "Skin, Stain and Lamella," 322.

55. Ibrahim, *Black Age*, 37.

56. Thanks to Caetlin Benson-Allot for bringing forth my own lack of attention to Zora. Benson-Allot suggests an analysis through Samantha Shepard's *Sporting Blackness*, especially in connection with the interest in Black female runners in the 1980s, which would amplify Peele's attention to this era.

57. Here, we might find an echo with Robin Coste Lewis's identification of objects that were described as Black girls in *Voyage of the Sable Venus*.

58. Sharpe, *In the Wake*, 44–45.

59. Sharpe, *In the Wake*, 51.

60. Hartman, "Venus in Two Acts," 3.

61. Hartman writes extensively about this narrative of overdetermination and the archival silence of possibilities otherwise: "And the stories that exist are not about them, but rather about the violence, excess, mendacity, and reason that seized hold of their lives, transformed them into commodities and corpses, and identified them with names tossed off as insults and crass jokes. The archive is, in this case, a death sentence, a tomb, a display of the violated body, an inventory of property, a medical treatise on gonorrhea, a few lines about a whore's life, an asterisk in the grand narrative of history. Given this, 'it is doubtless impossible to ever grasp [these lives] again in themselves, as they might have been "in a free state."'" "Venus in Two Acts," 3.

62. Hartman, *Wayward Lives*, 10.

63. Ibrahim, *Black Age*, 107.

64. I am grateful to Michael Gillespie for this insight into the importance of the cinematic for this other layer of analysis.

65. Hillel, "Spasmodic Dysfonia."
66. Belyk, Johnson, and Kotz, "Science Explains."
67. McKittrick, *Demonic Grounds,* 121.
68. The lyrics to "Brown Girl in the Ring," as sung by Boney M.:

Show me your motion
Tra la la la la
Come on show me your motion
Tra la la la la la
Show me your motion
Tra la la la la
She looks like a sugar in a plum
Plum plum.

69. Sharpe, *In the Wake*, 85. Emphasis in original.
70. Owens, "Reading Sideways"; Simmons, *Crescent City Girls*.
71. Ellis, *Territories of the Soul*, 6.

Chapter Two. Inside Out: *Shango* and the Spectacles of the Spirit

1. Barzel, *Shango*.

2. I was conducting this research for an essay on Trajal Harrell's relationship to butoh, which evolved into an examination of the flamenco dancer La Argentina and Katherine Dunham. That essay, "Racialized Femininity and Representation's Ambivalences in Trajal Harrell's *The Return of La Argentina*," is the germ for this chapter.

3. *Carib Song* was a musical play that ran at the Adelphi Theater in New York for a month (September 27–October 27) in 1945. Nichols, "'Carib Song' with Katherine Dunham and Avon Long."

4. Summary of *Shango* performance: Barzel, *Shango*; and Das, "Choreographing a New World."

5. The US invasion of Trinidad began when Winston Churchill and Franklin Roosevelt agreed that Trinidad (then a British colony) would accommodate US naval and air bases in exchange for fifty old American destroyers because the specter of the US military was considered a key aspect of defending the Caribbean (and British and US interests) from German forces during World War II. While Trinidadian governance continued as before (tethered to Great Britain), the cultural impact of the occupation, as Harvey Neptune notes, was profound, especially impacting Trinidad's gender and race relations. Neptune, *Caliban and the Yankees*, 2.

6. Das, "Choreographing a New World," 173.

7. See also the first hit from Trinidadian Mighty Sparrow, the 1956 song "Jean and Dinah," whose lyrics read:

Jean and Dinah, Rosita and Clemontina
Round de corner posin'
Bet your life is something dey sellin'

But when you catch them broken you could get dem for nuttin'
Doh make no row
De Yankee gone and Sparrow take over now.

8. "Carib Song," *Playbill.*

9. Her training in anthropology took place at the University of Chicago—she earned her bachelor's degree in 1936 and wrote a master's thesis (though she did not complete the required coursework or examinations). She was awarded grants from the Guggenheim Foundation and Julius Rosenwald Foundation, which primarily supported Black educational endeavors and research into Black history and culture for this research. At the University of Chicago, she was influenced by Robert Redfield, who specialized in Mexican folk cultures (and the idea of the folk more broadly), and Bronisław Malinowski, who emphasized participant-observation in ethnography. In parsing these influences more specifically, Joyce Aschenbremmer argues that "Redfield greatly influenced Dunham with his view of folk society as exhibiting cohesive social organization and a sacred worldview; these ideas later helped her to see the sacred dance of the voudun in Haiti as an intrinsic part of peasant social and cultural life," while Malinowski's "work set the precedent of the 'mythic charter' of anthropology, of the ethnographer as her, and of the 'ethnographer's magic' in translating inexplicable actions into meaningful behavior through a process of identification that can only come with complete involvement in an alien culture." Aschenbremmer, "Katherine Dunham," 140, 142.

10. The US military occupied Haiti from 1915 to 1934. Bolstered by paternalism and racism, the US invasion of Haiti was more hostile than the occupation of Trinidad; the military installed a puppet government and attempted various social reforms. These invasive actions provoked vigorous resistance on the part of Haitians and retaliatory violence from the troops—leading to a US characterization of Haiti as a place of "sexual excess, gender disorder, and primitive savagery; it was a land characterized by the effective absence of the family as a basis for social order." Renda, *Taking Haiti*, 174.

11. Das, *Katherine Dunham*, 38.

12. The early part of the twentieth century brought renewed Black interest in the Haitian Revolution, as evidenced by Jacob Lawrence's painting series about the life of Toussaint L'Ouverture (1936–38) and C. L. R. James's publication of *The Black Jacobins* (1938).

13. Dunham, *Dances of Haiti*, 52.

14. Dunham, *Dances of Haiti*, 32.

15. Dunham, *Dances of Haiti*, 32.

16. Dunham, *Dances of Haiti*, 21.

17. Dunham, *Islands Possessed*, 123.

18. Dunham, *Islands Possessed*, 127.

19. Dunham, *Islands Possessed*, 132.

20. Dunham, *Dances of Haiti*, 51.

21. Cervenak, *Wandering.*

22. Magloire, "Ethics of Discomfort," 12.

23. Magloire, "Ethics of Discomfort," 12; Brown, *Mama Lola.*

24. Magloire, "Ethics of Discomfort," 12.

25. Dunham, *Islands Possessed*, 136.

26. I am bracketing the particularities of Dunham's relationship to this philosophy because it is couched both in modern dance's early twentieth-century orientalism and the orientalism of the United States in the 1960s.

27. Alessandra Benedicty-Kokken argues that the discipline of anthropology was especially keen to exceptionalize practices of Haitian Vodou even as forms of possession exist worldwide. Benedicty-Kokken, *Spirit Possession*.

28. See Kate Ramsey for how and why Vodou was legislated around ideas of possession and also how possession was a threat for twentieth-century French philosophy, which was arguing for a subjectivity attached to an integrated mind-body. In *Spirit Possession*, Alessandra Benedicty-Kokken writes:

> On the one hand, subjectivity is the phenomenon of constituting one's sense of unity of being, one that integrates the body, the psyche, the metaphysical, the spiritual, and/or the scientifically unexplainable. On the other hand, possession is an experience that integrates all of the above, not just for one individual "self," but as an amalgamate of various "selves," with separate psyches and even bodies, into one consciousness of being. In a sense, the constitution of human subjectivity and the event of possession operate in similar ways, only subjectivity is reflective of a cosmology that privileges the category of the individual as an analytical category to study "being," while possession is reflective of an ontological order that, in addition to using the individual as an analytical category, also integrates fragmented subjectivities. (28)

29. Osumare, "Dancing the Black Atlantic"; Kraut, "Between Primitivism and Diaspora," 447.

30. Likewise, in her description of Zora Neale Hurston's representation of Vodou, Roshanak Kheshti argues that Hurston instantiates the "'feather-bed resistance' discussed in *Mules and Men* (1990), which is Hurston's thesis on black resistance to the white gaze." Kheshti, "Toward a Rupture in the Sensus Communis."

31. Das, "Choreographing a New World," 174.

32. Waddington, "Katherine Dunham Raises Primitive Dance," 303.

33. Clark, "Performing the Memory of Difference," 323.

34. Clark, "Performing the Memory of Difference," 324.

35. This is Clark's schema for appreciating dance, in "Performing the Memory of Difference":

> 1. Historiography of a researcher's individual memory of regional dances; 2. Representations of African-American and Caribbean milieu de memoire on stage; 3. Style and mood conveyed to the audience through characteristic movements memorized as it were; 4. Allusions in the text to which the audience might respond differently as a company tours; 5. Subtle differences in performance over the period of a company's history as principal dancers are replaced; 6. Responses to cultural differences on the part of the mainstream critics whose literacy of black dance varies; 7. Class and gender difference that challenge an audience to recognize variations in black culture. (327–28)

36. Manning, "Watching Dunham's Dances," 264.

37. Das, *Katherine Dunham*, 5.

38. Dunham added *Shango* to her *Bal Negre* revue, where it was one of the most popular dances, underscoring the ways that the dance occupies an uneasy tension between ritual and spectacle. Citing John Martin's assessment that Dunham's work "is not designed to delve into philosophy or psychology, but to externalize the impulses of a high spirited, rhythmic, and gracious race," Marina Magloire argues that "many white critical reviews of African American concert dance of the interwar period relegate black dance efforts to the ethnographic, that is to say, to an expression of ancestral racial characteristics rather than a concerted intellectual effort to define and articulate identity out of the inconsistencies of diasporic cultures." Magloire, "Ethics of Discomfort," 4.

39. Arimitsu, "From Voodoo to Butoh," 3.

40. Arimitsu, "From Voodoo to Butoh," 3.

41. Vogel, *Stolen Time*, 8; 4.

42. Tobias, "Some Like It Hot."

43. Clark, "On Stage with the Dunham Company," 281.

44. We were not necessarily dancing to Becket's "I Want Soca," the road march for St. Vincent in 1986, but it is a song whose rhythms and lyrics resonated through my childhood.

45. Magloire, "Ethics of Discomfort," 10, quoting Dunham.

46. For more on carnival in St. Vincent, see "History of Carnival," Ministry of Tourism, Government of Saint Vincent and the Grenadines, n.d., https://tourism.gov.vc/tourism/index.php/history-of-carnival.

47. Dunham, "Negro Dance," 221.

48. Juhan, *Job's Body*, 66.

49. Juhan, *Job's Body*, 81.

50. Juhan, *Job's Body*, 268. Emphasis in original.

51. Juhan, *Job's Body*, 274.

52. Muñoz, *Cruising Utopia*, 67.

53. Rodríguez, *Sexual Futures*.

54. Muñoz, *Cruising Utopia*, 80.

55. Servera, "José E. Muñoz's Queer Gestures," 148.

56. Servera, "José E. Muñoz's Queer Gestures," 148.

57. Elizabeth Anker's *Ugly Freedoms* argues that these contradictions are embedded in the very idea of freedom itself.

58. Dunham, *Dances of Haiti*, 41. Although Dunham uses *loa*, I prefer to use *lwa* as it is the term I see used more frequently in current-day writing on Vodou.

59. Cosmologically speaking, the union of snakes was protective and fortuitous: "Two snakes together, Dambala and his wife Ayida Wedo, make an alliance and, in an arch, cover and protect the world; their typical movements reference copulation and life." Daniel, *Dancing Wisdom*, 77.

60. Daniel, *Dancing Wisdom*, 77.

61. Dunham, *Islands Possessed*, 32.

62. Dunham, *Islands Possessed*, 138.

63. Benedicty-Kokken, *Spirit Possession*, 36.

64. Strongman, "Transcorporeality in Vodou," 14.

65. Daniel, *Dancing Wisdom*, 12.

66. Daniel, *Dancing Wisdom*, 2. Emphasis in original.

67. Chapman, "The Diasporic Re-membering Space," 55, 58. Chapman writes, "Due to entrenched class and race-based bias against Vodou and the Haitian peasantry, Haitian folkloric dance is socially undervalued, at best recognized rhetorically as cultural heritage. Dance pedagogy, in turn, often instills a disjuncture between folklore and Vodou in order to elide negative associations: movement is offered with neither context nor explicit connections to the dance forms' Vodou depth" (57).

68. Daniel, *Dancing Wisdom*, 111–12.

69. Daniel, *Dancing Wisdom*, 52.

70. Gilles and Gilles, *Remembrance*.

71. Daniel, *Dancing Wisdom*, 229.

72. The word can be spelled either *yanvalou* or *yonvalou* or *yanvalu* or *yonvalu*. I have seen it spelled as *yanvalou* more recently, so that is the spelling that I use. Daniel, *Dancing Wisdom*, 229.

73. Dunham, *Islands Possessed*, 135.

74. Das understands Dunham to be fusing physiology and cosmology to emphasize the connection between the uterus and creation: "The creation of life literally began in the uterus. It thus made sense why movement about the unity and connectivity of life would emanate from that region of the body." Das, *Katherine Dunham*, 45 (in text); 46 (in note).

75. Kurt Leland provides an intriguing history of the ways that energy centers and endocrine glands became associated with specific chakras in Western adaptations of the system, largely as a result of the way that New Age ideology filtered through the United States. We can also contextualize Dunham's interest in chakras as part of a broader 1960s New Age movement in the United States. Leland, "Rainbow Body," 25–29.

76. Wyman, "Yanvalou."

77. Wyman, "Yanvalou."

78. Wyman, "Yanvalou."

79. These complications loom over Tobi Tobias's discomfort with *Shango*: "He is not having a religious experience, and, if he *were* having one, would that make us, the audience, no better than a pack of voyeurs?" Tobias, "Some Like It Hot."

80. Bambara, "Yanvalou's Elliptic Displacements," 291.

81. Bambara, "Yanvalou's Elliptic Displacements," 291.

Chapter Three. Noise and the Body-Place: *This ember state* and the Critical Encounter

This chapter draws on the essays Musser, "*Tear* and the Politics of Brown Feeling"; and Musser, "Infinity Folds."

1. Spillers, "Mama's Baby," 72. Emphasis in original.

2. Fanon, *Black Skin, White Masks*.

3. Fanon, *Black Skin, White Masks*, 109, 112, 113.

4. Calvin Warren offers the phrase "ontological terror" to describe the disintegration that the narrator experiences, writing that "the function of black(ness) is to give form to a terrifying formlessness (nothing)." In Warren's use of the phrase "formlessness," we recognize that one of the sensations associated with fungibility is terror. Warren, *Ontological Terror*, 5.

5. Scott, *Extravagant Abjection*, 61.

6. Scott, *Extravagant Abjection*, 68.

7. Clare, *Earthly Encounters*, 74.

8. Wynter, "Unsettling the Coloniality."

9. Alexander, *Pedagogies of Crossing*, 6.

10. I am grateful to Kyla Schuller, "Biopower," for this framing.

11. Goeman, *Mark My Words*, 3.

12. Goeman, *Mark My Words*, 2–3.

13. In a conversation with Eiko Otake on February 16, 2021, as part of Sinha's Breathing Room workshops conducted with Danspace, Otake referred to Sinha's nudity as reflective of Sinha's emotional nakedness and intense present-ness. Because Otake appears later in the chapter, I mark this comment here.

14. Asia Society, "This ember state."

15. Mathur et al. write, "Ragas are improvisational; their power comes not from fidelity to a pattern, but from their ability to draw out emotion. In fact, one of the primary ways that they have been discussed within a Western framework of music is in relation to their ability to elicit specific emotions in the listener regardless of whether or not the words are understood." Mathur et al., "Emotional Response to Hindustanti *Raga* Music."

16. A more extended version of the myth tells us that Sati is the incarnation of Adi-Parashakti, a goddess of matrimony who assumes mortal form as the daughter of Daksha and his wife Prasuti in order to marry Shiva. From her youth, she is devoted to him, but her father disapproves of her intention to marry Shiva. Eventually Sati prevails and wins over Shiva by embarking on a life of ascetism. Dismayed by this, her father refuses to invite the couple to an important sacrifice. Sati is reborn as Parvati, who finds Shiva, wins him over, and marries him. Kinsley, *Hindu Goddesses*.

17. Samita Sinha interview with *Sound American*.

18. Sinha's specific explorations of rage through Sati also brings us to the complications that surround the practice of sati or suttee—widow burning. While always fringe, the practice, especially during the colonial era, was singled out as a paradigmatic example of female oppression in South Asia. As Gayatri Chakravorty Spivak discusses, the example of sati was specifically used to justify British intervention as a form of saving women and yet was also used as nativist objections to colonialism: "The abolition of this rite by the British has been generally understood as a case of 'White men saving brown women from brown men.' While simultaneously being upheld as an Indian nativist tradition to be protected: 'The women actually wanted to die'" (297). As Spivak

argues, however, the practice also becomes important for us to see the difficulties that attend to the questions of representation. In her seminal essay "Can the Subaltern Speak?," Spivak traces these debates about sati to show the ways in which both positions erase the possibility of understanding what the women might actually want—this is to say that it is impossible to represent them. In part, this has to do with the fact that the scrutiny accorded to sati is part of an imperialism that makes public what had been private, thereby transforming sati from personal devotion to public symbol linked both to progress and to resistance to colonial norms.

In addition to parsing problematics of representation, Spivak reminds us of the impossibility of grappling with the myth of Sati in the present *without* also thinking through the British colonial encounter in India. And, now, we should add President Narenda Modi's oppressive mobilization of Hinduism under the guise of national unification in the postcolonial era, by which all non-Hindus have been declared foreign. In this way, it is impossible to separate the controversial (now virtually obsolete) practice from the myth of Sati. The politics that surround her are gendered, geographic, and religious. Spivak, "Can the Subaltern Speak?"; Ibrahim, "Modi's Slide Toward Autocracy."

19. Asia Society, "This ember state"; quoted lines from Roberto Calasso, *Ka: Stories of the Mind and Gods of India* (1999).

20. Felman, *Jacques Lacan and the Adventure of Insight*, 155.

21. Zakariya, *Final Story*, 11.

22. Nyong'o, *Afro-Fabulations*, 26. Emphasis in original.

23. Gopinath, *Unruly Desires*, 5.

24. Sinha, interview with *Sound American*.

25. Estés, *Women Who Run with the Wolves*, 33.

26. Estés, *Women Who Run with the Wolves*, 32.

27. Estés, *Women Who Run with the Wolves*, 4; 6.

28. Estés, *Women Who Run with the Wolves*, 36.

29. Sinha, interview with *Sound American*.

30. Of these tensions, Cheng writes, "On the one side, white American identity and its authority is secured through the melancholic introjections of racial others that it can neither fully relinquish nor accommodate and whose ghostly presence nonetheless guarantees its centrality." The other side of this, for the racial other, is melancholia produced by loss because "his or her racial identity is imaginatively reinforced through the introjections of a lost, never-possible perfection, an inarticulable loss that comes to inform the individual's sense of his or her own subjectivity." Cheng, *Melancholy of Race*, xi.

31. Cheng, *Melancholy of Race*.

32. Shimikawa, *National Abjection*, 3.

33. Shimikawa, *National Abjection*, 3.

34. Manring, "Review of *Contradictory Lives*," 330.

35. See Knight, *Contradictory Lives*: "In negotiating their social identity, Baul women engage in and manipulate the very structures and discourses that encumber them and jeopardize their social standing" (26).

36. Tagore, *Religion of Man*, 540.

37. Yin yoga teacher training, Corina Brenner, October 23–26, 2020, Integral Yoga Center, New York (over Zoom).

38. Though the meridians are named for organs, these names describe bodily functions and energies rather than solid-state organs. Each yin-and-yang pair of meridians correlates to an element, emotion, and bodily symptoms. Symptoms are caused by imbalances, but the imbalances themselves may be due to excess, deficiency, or stagnation. Here is a brief breakdown (yin element first):

> Liver/Gallbladder are wood and control decision making; imbalances can manifest as anger or indecision.
>
> Heart/Small Intestine are fire and govern the capacity for joy; imbalances can manifest as mania or apathy.
>
> Spleen/Stomach are earth and concern the processing of information; imbalances can manifest as worry or irritability.
>
> Lung/Large Intestine are metal and mediate relations to the external world; imbalances can manifest as grief, emotional stagnation, or constipation.
>
> Kidney/Bladder are water and deal with fear; imbalances can manifest as phobia, low libido, or paranoia.

Pericardium/*San Jiao* do not correlate with an element but work to protect organs from imbalances in other systems; they ease internal communication within the body. *San Jiao* governs the movement of water and Pericardium protects the heart energy.

39. For the fundamentals of Chinese Traditional Medicine, see *Sacred Lotus*, https://www.sacredlotus.com/go/foundations-chinese-medicine/get/jing-essence-vital-substance.

40. Deleuze, *Fold*, 7.

41. Spivak, “Can the Subaltern Speak?” 295.

42. Spivak, “Can the Subaltern Speak?” 308.

43. Nancy, *Listening*, 14.

44. Furlonge, *Race Sounds*, 2.

45. Stoever, *Sonic Color Line*, 7–8

46. Kheshti, *Modernity’s Ear*, 3.

47. James, *Sonic Episteme*.

48. Musser, *Sensual Excess*, 5.

49. Vazquez, *Listening in Detail*, 21.

50. Vazquez, *Listening in Detail*, 4.

51. Vazquez, *Listening in Detail*, 4.

52. Chambers-Letson, *After the Party*, 164–68.

53. Chambers-Letson, *After the Party*, 167.

54. We can also sense in Chambers-Letson’s description the importance of presentness for Otake and why her comments about *This ember state* were so important.

55. Díaz, “Silence.”

56. Feminisms, in particular, have worked to reclaim anger as an important component of recognizing injustice and finding ways toward solidarity. Audre Lorde, for

example, argues that anger has an important relationship with self-love and activism. In "Uses of Anger," she writes, "Anger is loaded with information and energy" (127). In this way, anger acts as a fuel for healing. Later, in "Eye to Eye," Lorde writes, "It is empowerment—our strengthening in the service of ourselves and each other, in the service of our work and our future—that will be the result of this pursuit. . . . I have to learn to love myself before I can love you or accept your loving" (174). Likewise, Brittney Cooper begins *Eloquent Rage* by arguing that anger "is a place where more women should begin—with the things that make us angry" (1). This version of anger correlates with an awareness of injustice and sets the stage for action. By way of showing how quickly this affect can be neutered, however, Cooper argues against sass, which she describes as anger's more palatable cousin. For Cooper, it is anger's uncontainability and power to disrupt that mark it as a potent emotion. Lorde, "Uses of Anger"; Lorde "Eye to Eye"; Cooper, *Eloquent Rage*; Chemaly, *Rage Becomes Her*.

57. Cooper, *Eloquent Rage*, 164.

58. I discuss this movement between masochism, depression, anger, and femininity further in *Sensual Excess*.

59. See Wilson, *Gut Feminism*.

60. King, *Black Shoals*, 48.

Chapter Four. On the Brink: Approximation, Difference, and Ongoing Storms

1. Glaser, "How to Describe What It Feels Like to Be in a Hurricane."

2. Peterson, *Atmospheric Noise*, 115.

3. Schuller and Gill-Peterson, "Race, the State, and the Malleable Body," 3.

4. Carla Minet describes the difficulty of assessing the true death toll from Maria in "María's Death Toll."

5. Bonilla, "Coloniality of Disaster."

6. This analysis has recently become more accepted. See Baldwin and Erickson, "Whiteness, Coloniality, and the Anthropocene."

7. See Barlow et al., "Future of Hyperdiverse Tropical Ecosystems."

8. Sheller, *Island Futures*, 12.

9. Bonilla's "Coloniality of Disaster" provides an incisive overview of the history of Puerto Rico's debt.

10. Walsh, "Puerto Rico's Governor Warns of Fiscal 'Death Spiral.'"

11. Bonilla, "Coloniality of Disaster."

12. Bonilla, "Coloniality of Disaster."

13. Bonilla, "Coloniality of Disaster."

14. Bonilla, "Coloniality of Disaster."

15. Bonilla, "Coloniality of Disaster."

16. The series of photographs by ADÁL, *Puerto Ricans Underwater/Los Ahogados* (2016), in which people are depicted holding objects of their choosing while submerged in a bathtub, is the first example Ruiz provides of this strategy of endurance. Ruiz writes:

In the aftermath of Hurricane Maria, one notices how ADÁL prefigures Rican endurance, each subject breathing against the national current of death, disease, and debt. These photographs leave the viewer in a state of suspension: in seeing this breathless subject, we, too, are left without breath. In capturing the quotidian life of Ricans struggling to stay afloat under imperial rule, the artist unveils the perceived "debris" of those unwanted lives given scant attention in dominant visual narratives. (5)

Puerto Ricans Underwater/Los Ahogados makes visible the physical and emotional strain of working to survive as well as the constant threat of possibly not. These subjects are in medias res without external aid, but the "something else" is figured as personal comfort manifest in the quotidian. Ruiz, *Ricanness*, 2.

17. Kapadia, *Insurgent Aesthetics*, 50.

18. Kaplan, *Aerial Aftermaths*, 3.

19. Postmentier, *Cultivation and Catastrophe*, 135, 211. Emphasis in original.

20. Postmentier, *Cultivation and Catastrophe*, 136.

21. Ocean Vuong @ocean_vuong, pinned Instagram story; posted November 18, 2020.

22. Ocean Vuong Instagram stories.

23. Ocean Vuong Instagram stories.

24. Ocean Vuong Instagram stories.

25. In an interview held eleven months after electricity returned to most of Puerto Rico, José Ortiz, the head of PREPA, bemoans the precarity of these fixes, which were meant to be temporary: "There are many patches—too many patches—developed just to bring power to the people." In their artist statement, Allora & Calzadilla make reference to these series of entanglements, explaining, "When the breaker is turned on, the electrical current causes the iron particles to self-organize into a composition of lines and shapes governed by the electromagnetic field. As the Latin title and full subtitle (Meter Number 18257262, Consumption Charge 36.9kWh × $0.02564, Rider FCA-Fuel Charge Adjusted 36.9 kWh × $0.053323, Rider PPCA-Purchase Power Charge Adjusted 36.9kWh × $0.016752, Rider CILTA-Municipalities Adjusted 36.9kWh × $0.002376, Rider SUBA Subsidies $1.084) suggest, the work probes the propriety politics of electricity and the power grid." Robles, "Puerto Rico Spent 11 Months Turning the Power Back On"; Gladstone Gallery, "Allora & Calzadilla."

26. In *Self-Devouring Growth*, Livingston explores the entwinement of cattle, rain, and sand in Botswana, revealing the specific ways that the enlargement of ecologies from local tribal networks to nation reliant on exporting beef creates roads (connection and traffic accidents), increased need for water (more drought), and a shifted diet enabling the emergence of epidemics of hypertension and diabetes. Livingston, *Self-Devouring Growth*, 2.

27. Though these are not the ways that I am attempting to read otherwise, I do want to highlight how others have seized on this possibility. Posmentier's *Cultivation and Catastrophe* explores the creativity that emerges in and through these types of catastrophe. In a similar vein, Ren Neyria vocalizes possibility amid Maria's upheaval:

"Miles of brown, uprooted, storm-felled trees daunt the eye looking for a familiar landscape. Wind-snapped canopies rot among bursts of growth. In the rains that continue to fall and flood the island after Hurricanes María and Irma, we are sure of nothing but that Puerto Rico is irrevocably changing. By changing, I mean that the invasive structure of U.S. colonialism and the everyday, racialized disparities between Puerto Ricans are extruding through the wreckage. I think that if Puerto Rico is changing, then the Caribbean is changing. I fantasize that global warming will contribute to uprisings." Neyria, "Towards an Un-American Solidarity."

28. Demos, "Blackout," 61.

29. Demos, "Blackout," 62; Mbembe, *Critique of Black Reason*.

30. For a general history of Puerto Rico, see Van Middeldyk, *History of Puerto Rico*. For more on Martinique and why it chose to remain entangled with France, see Childers, *Seeking Imperialism's Embrace*.

31. For more on Puerto Rico's anti-Blackness and its history, I am thinking with Rodriguez's *Sexual Futures*.

32. Kelley, *Freedom Dreams*, 168.

33. Kelley, *Freedom Dreams*, 168.

34. Césaire, *Discourse on Colonialism*, 42.

35. *Merriam-Webster*, s.v. "cadastre." Accessed June 21, 2023. https://www.merriam-webster.com/dictionary/cadastre.

36. Césaire in Kelley, *Freedom Dreams*, 169–70.

37. Césaire, *Solar Throat Slashed*, back matter.

38. Sellin, "Soleil cou coupé," 14.

39. Césaire, *Solar Throat Slashed*, 24–25; translation from this edition.

40. Kelley, *Freedom Dreams*, 173.

41. Matthews, "Singularity and Collision," 138.

42. Kelley, "Introduction," 1.

43. Kelley, "Introduction," 3.

44. I am grateful to Ankur Ghosh for pointing this out to me.

45. Other versions of *Penumbra* do, in fact, explicitly become connected to a performance of shadows produced by Allora & Calzadilla. See "Studio Visit: Artist Duo Allora and Calzadilla on Steering Installations Remotely and the Benefits of Eschewing Social Media," *Artnet News*, October 9, 2020, https://news.artnet.com/art-world/studio-visit-allora-calzadilla-1914209.

46. The group included Helena Benitez, André Breton, Wifredo Lam, Jacqueline Lamba, Claude Lévi-Strauss, André Masson, and Victor Serge, who were held in camps in Martinique (and viewed warily). They were, however, granted day passes into the city. Notably, Claude Lévi-Strauss was held at a different camp and was not part of these hikes as Jennings narrates them. Jennings, *Escape from Vichy*.

47. Jennings, *Escape from Vichy*, 202.

48. Allora & Caldazilla write: "Graft alludes to environmental changes set in motion through the interlocking forces of colonial exploitation and global climatic transformation." Gladstone, "Cadastre."

49. Gladstone, "Cadastre," 181.

50. In *Discourse on Colonialism*, Césaire writes:

> They were communal societies, never societies of the many for the few.
> They were societies that were not only ante-capitalist, as has been said, but also anti-capitalist.
> They were democratic societies, always.
> They were cooperative societies, fraternal societies.
> I make a systematic defense of the societies destroyed by imperialism. (44)

51. Césaire, "Surrealism and Us," qtd. in Kelley, *Freedom Dreams*, 171.

52. Eyestone, "Cannibalizing Paradise," 2.

53. Rabbitt, "In Search of the Missing Mother," 37.

54. Sadly, the documentary was never completed and so that footage is lost to a Midwestern archive.

55. Gómez-Barris, "Colonial Anthropocene."

56. Wynter, "Unsettling the Coloniality."

57. Tallbear, "Sharpening of the Already Present."

Other possibilities for orienting not around Man exist; in "On the Universal Right to Breathe," Achille Mbembe underscores the ethics of working against climate change by theorizing breath beyond the human to include everything that is alive. He writes, "This fundamental vulnerability is the very essence of humanity. But it is shared, to varying degrees, by every creature on this planet—a planet that powerful forces threaten to render inhospitable, if not uninhabitable, to the majority of living things and beings" (section 1). Mbembe is speaking most directly about the destruction of ecosystems due to industrialization and looking toward reembedding humans into the larger category of Earth-based life that relies on oxygen (and therefore breath) to survive: "With the increasing emission of greenhouse gases, the atmospheric concentration of ultra-fine dust, toxic emissions, invisible substances, tiny granules and all sorts of particulate matter, soon there will be more carbon and nitrous dioxide in the atmosphere than oxygen. Now is the time to expand our freedoms by instituting a universal right to breathe" (section 3).

58. Schuller, "Losing Paradise."

59. Crawley, *Blackpentecostal Breath*, 1.

60. Sharpe, *In the Wake*, 75.

61. Sharpe, *In the Wake*, 109.

62. Bersani, "Is the Rectum a Grave?" I have previous analyses of this essay in *Sensual Excess* and *Sensational Flesh*.

63. Quashie, *Black Aliveness*, 31.

64. Quashie, *Black Aliveness*, 31.

65. Brown, *Black Utopias*, 14.

66. Lorde, "Master's Tools," 111.

67. Quashie, *Black Aliveness*, 124.

68. Nash, "Practicing Love," 441.

69. Nash, "Practicing Love," 449.

Chapter Five. Tamarind, Metabolism, and Rest: Making Racialized Labor Visible

This chapter draws in part on my essay Musser, "Tamarind and the Politics of Rest."

1. In an interview with Jason Stanley, Kaphar describes the impetus behind his revisioning of monuments. He says, "Like so many others, I've been struggling with what to do in response to what is happening in this country; the act of painting itself becomes a fight to remember the names of all the young black men and women who were forgotten by history or taken too soon at the hands of unconscious bias. Every day is a fight to remember that when this issue disappears from the media, it's not permission to forget. It's a fight to remember that change is possible." Kaphar and Stanley, "Titus Kaphar." For more of an overview of Kaphar's projects, see Kaphar, "Fight for Remembrance."

2. Coulombe, *Rum*, 116.

3. For more on the evidence that Washington's dentures were made from teeth pulled from some people he enslaved, see Gehred, "George Washington's False Teeth?"

4. I have written more on the significance of vessels in a meditation on Simone Leigh's work. Musser, "Toward Mythic Feminist Theorizing."

5. Barounis, *Vulnerable Constitutions*, 3.

6. Lowe, *Intimacies of Four Continents*, 17–18.

7. As Kent Brinkley writes, "the presence of even a small greenhouse on one's plantation became a graphic symbol of horticultural power in the landscape that served the needs of politically powerful men by enabling them to display their mastery over nature; and by providing a visual reminder of the way society was structured and how the hierarchical, class-ridden world of that period was organized." Brinkley, "Historical Overview of Greenhouses," 124.

8. Warren, "Washington's Journey to Barbados."

9. Roos, "Crude Smallpox Inoculations."

10. MacLeod, "Tom."

11. MacLeod, "Tom."

12. Jackson, *Becoming Human*, 71.

13. Phillip Brian Harper outlines the discomfort with abstraction as associated with fears that racialization will slide into caricature or stereotype producing "bad" representations. Harper, *Abstractionist Aesthetics*.

14. Allewaert, *Ariel's Ecology*, 9.

15. Allewaert, *Ariel's Ecology*, 19.

16. In describing wooden objects used for spiritual practice, she writes, "Far from being wordless or mute, [these objects] could be conceived as dense interiorities or constellations of force that could store, process, and actualize information and that were also crucial to the production of the collectivities, or assemblages, through which personhood was articulated." Allewaert, *Ariel's Ecology*, 119.

17. Hantel, "Plasticity and Fungibility," 97.

18. Many thanks to Sean Brotherton for bringing this to my attention.

19. Petro, "Classic Cocktails in History."

20. Petro, "Classic Cocktails in History."

21. Jasmine Rault describes the way that transparency has become lauded, even as it is a mark of a settler colonial ethos, and what this has meant for architecture. Rault, "Window Walls and Other Tricks of Transparency."

22. Harris, "Confined Spaces, Constrained Bodies."

23. Roberts, "Working Between the Lines."

24. Mintz, *Sweetness and Power*, 174.

25. Mintz, *Sweetness and Power*, 174.

26. Within capitalism's valuation of sweetness and sugar, molasses occupied a lower tier, not only as a by-product, but through its invocation of less refined, more blackened economy. Molasses, the dark semisweet viscous liquid left after sugar paste has been boiled to extract as many crystals as possible, was copious and was used in cooking and in the production of beer and rum. Perhaps because of its ubiquity, molasses was considered inferior—but also perhaps because of its brown color and its literal lack of refinement. Erica Fretwell writes, "Bookended by its raw brown state and the dark dregs of its refinement (molasses), sugar production traffics not only in pleasure but also in *disgust*, a word that means 'bad taste.'" This repulsion also has to do with molasses's crudeness, what Kyla Wazana Tompkins describes as "the barbarism of base aesthetics: rough, rude, and blunt, lacking finish or maturity." Notably, in both Fretwell's and Tompkins's assessments of the undesirability of molasses, there is a temporal component. In describing molasses as "immature," and the unfinished remainder, we see the dominance of the temporal regime of productivity associated with sugar. Fretwell, *Sensory Experiments*, 212; Tompkins, "Crude Matter, Crude Form," 26. For more on the process of making rum, see *Encyclopedia Britannica*, "Rum," September 18, 2022, https://www.britannica.com/topic/rum-liquor.

27. Freeman, *Beside You in Time*, 2.

28. Freeman, *Beside You in Time*, 22.

29. Thanks to Elizabeth Dillon, who pointed me toward the "sleep has no master" narrative in Edwards, *History, Civil and Commercial, of British Colonies in the West Indies*, 2:85. The embedded narrative reads: "It was a servant who had brought me a letter, and, while I was preparing an answer, had, through weariness and fatigue, fallen asleep on the floor: as soon as the papers were ready, I directed him to be awakened; but this was no easy matter. When the Negro who attempted to awake him, exclaimed in the usual jargon, 'You no hear Massa call you?' that is, Don't you hear your Master call you? 'Sleep,' replied the poor fellow, looking up, and returning composedly to his slumbers, 'Sleep hab no Massa.' (Sleep has no Master.)."

30. Hartman, *Scenes of Subjection*, 22.

31. Hartman, *Scenes of Subjection*, 25.

32. Tompkins, "Sweetness, Capacity, Energy," 854.

33. Campt, "Black Visuality and the Practice of Refusal."

34. The Nap Ministry, "Resources from 'a Space to Rest' Virtual Experience."

35. Tompkins, "Sweetness, Capacity, Energy," 853.

36. Hulse, "Black History Month in the Adventure Garden."

37. For more work on these types of south-south intimacies in queer studies, see Powell, *Sounds from the Other Side*; and Gopinath, *Unruly Desires*.

38. Wynter, "Novel and History," 99.

39. Wynter, "Novel and History," 99.

40. Wynter, "Novel and History," 95.

41. Again, Elizabeth Dillon pointed me toward Makandal, an enslaved man in Saint-Domingue in the early eighteenth century who was known for both healing and poisoning people through his knowledge of plants and Vodou. His presence in the archive reminds us of the types of knowledge that circulated as well as its fusion with Afro-Caribbean religions. Simpkins, Johnson, and Brice, "Makandal Exhibit."

42. It is, however, striking that he asked for the fruit, which had moderate circulation during the colonial era. Michael Twitty, for example, has found records of Black people in Maryland buying tamarind at markets in Annapolis, returning to plantations with "red rice, coconuts, peanuts, white rice, tamarind, ginger, spices, and various tropical nuts" (Twitty, *Fighting Old Nep*, 40). In my fantasy narrative of Washington, his brush with smallpox introduced him to Bajan fruits, tamarind included, and medical practices, some of which may have overlapped with those in Virginia, and others of which may have been steeped in Obeah (Afro-Caribbean spiritual) traditions. There is no record of this, but this speculation speaks to what it is to think with the sensory life of tamarind.

43. Cook's Country, "All About Acid, Cooking's Most Versatile Ingredient."

44. Cook's Country, "All About Acid, Cooking's Most Versatile Ingredient."

45. Mishan, "How Sourness Has Come to Dominate Our Dining Habits."

46. Masé, *Wild Medicine*.

47. Voight, "Difference Between Sour and Bitter."

48. In Masé's words, tonics "potentiate the effects of our natural stress hormone, improving our ability to handle disruptive influences and sparing the adrenal glands." Masé, *Wild Medicine*, 220. In actuality, the entire tamarind plant has medicinal properties. When we cooked with tamarind, we were using the soft gelatinous paste inside the pods, which has historically been used as a digestive aid and a cooling tonic because it can reduce fevers and inflammation. The leaves and flowers can be made into a poultice to reduce swelling, and the bark, like the fruit, is said to be a tonic. Tadimalla, "7 Health Benefits of Tamarind."

49. Jim McDonald, *Foundational Herbcraft*, 94.

50. Masé, *Wild Medicine*, 50.

51. One might think, for example, of exhortations to tap into your flow state to maximize productivity. Cutruzzula, "Key to Productivity."

52. See Scott, *Extravagant Abjection*, for a beautiful elaboration on what it is and is not possible to know with regard to enslavement and its complication of categories such as subjectivity, agency, desire, and so forth.

53. Musser, "Specimen Days"; Hong, *Death beyond Disavowal*.

54. Hong, *Death beyond Disavowal*, 13.

55. Importantly, Hong describes the effect of these regimes of color blindness as manifesting an intense desire to control Black women's bodies through various forms of respectability. While this is not the avenue I pursue, Hong's analysis feels very apt.

56. We might also connect the contemporary backlash against critical race theory to a fervent (Republican) wish to make the effects of racism unseen.

57. Rene Wisely explains SIBO in "This Gaseous Culprit Could Be Causing Your Stomach Pain and Constipation."

58. Priest, "Salvation Is the Issue," 116.

59. Priest, "Salvation Is the Issue," 117.

60. Priest, "Salvation Is the Issue," 121.

61. Kim and Schalk, "Reclaiming the Radical Politics of Self-Care," 330.

62. Kim and Schalk, "Reclaiming the Radical Politics of Self-Care," 332.

63. Beyoncé, "Formation."

64. Kim and Schalk, "Reclaiming the Radical Politics of Self-Care," 332.

65. Kim and Schalk, "Reclaiming the Radical Politics of Self-Care," 333.

66. Bailey, "Ethics of Pace," 290.

67. Weheliye, *Habeaus Viscus*, 113.

68. Schuller, "Biopower Below and Before the Individual," 630.

69. Hathaway, "Sugar Targets Gut Microbe."

70. Jim McDonald argues that tonics, the most potent of which are described as bitter, can "help one let go of stuck energy—particularly anger and frustration—emotions often viewed in traditional medicine as being tied to stagnant/sluggish liver energy.... In addition to releasing bile, [bitters] also help people let go of the emotional energies housed in different organs." One of the ubiquitous tonics that McDonald describes is dandelion, the plant often considered a weed, but which is rich in vitamins and whose roots can be roasted and steeped in hot water for an energizing, bitter, and bile stimulating drink. Used by some as an alternative to coffee, its energy does not come from caffeine but through its stimulation of digestion to leave time for something else. McDonald, *Foundational Herbcraft*, 94.

Conclusion. Inflammation: Notes from the Front

1. Marya and Patel, *Inflamed*.

2. Fanon, *White Skin, Black Masks*; Fanon, *Wretched of the Earth*.

3. There is a plethora of work in this intersection, but I am thinking specifically of Dennis Tyler, *Disabilities of the Color Line*, who argues that ideas of what constituted Blackness cannot be thought without disability; C. Riley Snorton's *Black on Both Sides*, which positions Black gender in relation to transness and questions of ability; Cynthia Wu's analysis of Chang and Eng, which weaves together race, ability, and sexuality, *Chang and Eng Reconnected*; and Mel Chen's analysis of race and mattering, *Animacies*.

4. Lorde, *Cancer Journals*; Livingston, *Debility and the Moral Imagination*; Puar, *Right to Maim*; Kim, "Toward a Crip-of-Color Critique"; McRuer, *Crip Times*.

5. Sharpe, *In the Wake*.

6. I take this from a reading of Jonathan Sterne's description of chronic illness and its relationship to disability studies and crip of color critique in *Diminished Faculties*.

7. Jackson, *Becoming Human*.

8. In *Physics of Blackness*, Michelle Wright describes the tension between a prevailing Middle Passage epistemology and local, or what Wright terms epiphenomenal, narratives. According to Wright, this tether to the Middle Passage links "our cultural practices and expressions, our politics and social sensibilities, to the historical experiences of slavery in the Americas and the struggle to achieve full human suffrage in the West." In other words, it marks the Middle Passage and enslavement as "the defining moments of collective Blackness." However, this epistemology contends with specific narratives of other migrations, genders, sexualities, and ways of being that interrupt this fantasy of unity because they have been repressed, marginalized, or are unknown. Drawing on quantum physics, Wright argues that Blackness exists in multiple temporalities and geographies, always. In addition to thickening Blackness, Wright's analysis helps us complexify the experience of spacetime. Wright, *Physics of Blackness*, 8.

9. Nyong'o, *Afro-Fabulations*, 3.

10. Nyong'o, *Afro-Fabulations*, 10.

11. Nyong'o, *Afro-Fabulations*, 7.

12. Muñoz, *Cruising Utopia*; Gaines, *Black Performance*; Chambers-Letson, *After the Party*.

13. Wright, *Physics of Blackness*, 60.

14. Keeling, *Queer Times, Black Futures*, 32.

15. "Hematopoesis," ScienceDirect.

16. Cirino, "What Is Chimerism?"

17. Interestingly, David Haig, who served as advisor for my senior thesis, is best known for his research on maternal-fetal conflict and the theory of imprinting.

18. This separateness is the reason one can trace genetic lineage through mitochondrial DNA which come from the matter of the fertilized ovum.

19. Sagan [Margulis], "On the Origin of Mitosing Cells," 228.

20. Though, interestingly, these theories were part of Russian and Latin American readings of evolution: "In sharp contrast with most of their English and American colleagues, most Russian naturalists did not identify the theory of natural selection with an emphasis of competition between species or intraspecific struggle epitomized by Malthus' metaphors, but tended to see it as a 'theory of mutual aid.'" Lazcano and Peretó, "On the Origin of Mitosing Cells," 81.

21. Lazcano and Peretó, "On the Origin of Mitosing Cells," 82.

22. In their critique of the tendency to idealize symbiosis, Patrick Keeling and John McCutcheon describe mutualisms as "a way to manage the inherent conflicts of interests between organisms." They portray a process in which "the ecological context must change so that the benefits of the interaction outweigh the costs," writing that "endosymbiotic interactions are best thought of not as mutualistic "happily ever-after"

stories, but instead as "use it up and cast it off" situations that are stable for variable lengths of time." Keeling and McCutcheon, "Endosymbiosis," 76.

23. Lorde, *Cancer Journals*.

24. For more on Fanon's relationship with the CIA at this time in life, see Meaney, "History Unclassified."

25. Bhabha, "Framing Fanon," viii.

26. Gendzier, "Frantz Fanon"; Gordon, *What Fanon Said*.

27. Clare, *Earthly Encounters*, 79.

28. Clare, *Earthly Encounters*, 81.

29. As María Puig de la Bellacasa writes, "Nothing holds together without relations of care." She frames care as a matter of "labor/work, affect/affections, ethics/politics," "always situated, specific to, and embedded within a given context." Puig de la Bellacasa, *Matters of Care*, 67, 5, 1.

30. See, among others, Federici, "Wages against Housework."

31. I borrow this listing and framing of privilege from Hil Malatino's description of his postsurgery care web in *Trans Care*.

32. Grande, "Care," 46.

33. Malatino, *Trans Care*, 1.

34. Malatino, *Trans Care*, 2.

35. Campt, *Listening to Images*, 17, italicized and bolded in original.

36. Though there are many vantage points from which to consider "thinking with," I draw on James McMaster's elaboration because his framing emphasizes what happens when thought moves away from a subject-object binary. Specifically, McMaster describes "thinking with" as a threefold reconfiguration that extends beyond the confines of an individual act toward theorizing envelopment and engagement as ethical formations: "care-full thinking means 'thinking-with' (more than human) others; the affective life of care does not foreclose 'dissenting-within' collectivities; and a caring knowledge politics shifts feminist standpoint theory's imperative of 'thinking from' to one of 'thinking-for' marginalized others in a directional rather than a representational sense." This movement toward thinking broadly with difference, but not necessarily conformity, is what is at stake in grappling with shadow work. McMaster, review of *Matters of Care*, 352.

37. Grande, "Care," 46.

38. Musser, *Sensual Excess*, 169.

39. Malatino, *Trans Care*, 2.

40. For more on this version of a debt economy in relation to care and refugees, see Nguyen, *Gift of Freedom*.

41. For a history of this theory, see Cohen, *Body Worth Defending*.

42. Morell, "Like Humans, Flamingos Mate for Life."

43. Ruiz and Vourloumis, *Formless Formation*.

Bibliography

Agard-Jones, Vanessa. "What the Sands Remember." *GLQ* 18, nos. 2–3 (2012): 325–46.

Ahmed, Sara. *Queer Phenomenology: Orientations, Objects, Others*. Durham, NC: Duke University Press, 2006.

Alexander, M. Jacqui. *Pedagogies of Crossing: Meditations on Feminism, Sexual Politics, Memory, and the Sacred*. Durham, NC: Duke University Press, 2005.

Allewaert, Monique. *Ariel's Ecology: Plantations, Personhood, and Colonialism in the American Tropics*. Minneapolis: University of Minnesota Press, 2013.

Amin, Kadji. *Disturbing Attachments: Genet, Modernism, and Queer Pederasty*. Durham, NC: Duke University Press. 2017.

Amin, Kadji, Amber Jamilla Musser, and Roy Pérez. "Queer Form: Aesthetics, Race, and the Violences of the Social." *ASAP/Journal* 2, no. 2 (2017): 227–39.

Anker, Elizabeth R. *Ugly Freedoms*. Durham, NC: Duke University Press, 2022.

Arimitsu, Michio. "From Voodoo to Butoh: Katherine Dunham, Hijikata Tatsumi, and Trajal Harrell's Transcultural Refashioning of Blackness." *MoMA*, n.d., 1–10. https://assets.moma.org/momaorg/shared/pdfs/docs/calendar/Trajal_Harell_Michio_Arimitsu_.pdf.

Aschenbrenner, Joyce. "Katherine Dunham: Anthropologist, Artist, Humanist." In *African American Pioneers in Anthropology*, edited by Ira E. Harrison and Faye Venetia Harrison, 129–45. Chicago: University of Illinois Press, 1999.

Asia Society. "This ember state." Accessed June 28, 2023. https://asiasociety.org/new-york/events/ember-state-sold-out-3.

Attali, Jacques. *Noise: The Political Economy of Music*. Translated by Brian Massumi. Minneapolis: University of Minnesota Press, 1977.

Bailey, Moya. "The Ethics of Pace." *South Atlantic Quarterly* 120, no. 2 (April 2021): 285–99.

Baldwin, Andrew, and Bruce Erickson. "Introduction: Whiteness, Coloniality, and the Anthropocene." *Society and Space* 38, no. 1 (2020): 3–11.

Bambara, Celia. "Yanvalou's Elliptic Displacements: Staging Spirit Time in the United States." *Journal of Haitian Studies* 15, no. 1/2, Haitian Studies Association 20th Anniversary Issue (Spring/Fall 2009): 290–303.

Barlow, Jos, Filipe França, Toby A. Gardner, Christina C. Hicks, Gareth D. Lennox, Erika Berenguer, Leandro Castello et al. "The Future of Hyperdiverse Tropical Ecosystems." *Nature* 559 (2018): 517–26.

Barounis, Cynthia. *Vulnerable Constitutions: Queerness, Disability, and the Remaking of American Manhood*. Philadelphia: Temple University Press, 2019.

Barzel, Ann, dir. *Shango*. Filmed at the Studebaker Theater, Chicago, 1947. Katherine Dunham Collection. Library of Congress. https://www.loc.gov/item/ihas.200003834/.

Beauvoir, Simone de. *The Second Sex*. Edited and translated by H. M. Parshley. New York: Vintage, 1989.

Belyk, Michel, Joseph F. Johnson, and Sonja Kotz. "Science Explains Why Humans Are Better at Whistling Than Singing." Inverse. June 14, 2018. https://www.inverse.com/article/45162-whistling-better-than-singing-instruments-voice.

Benedicty-Kokken, Alessandra. *Spirit Possession in French, Haitian, and Vodou Thought: An Intellectual History*. Lanham, MD: Lexington, 2015.

Bersani, Leo. "Is the Rectum a Grave?" *October* 43 (Winter 1987): 197–222.

Best, Stephen. *None Like Us: Blackness, Belonging, Aesthetic Life*. Durham, NC: Duke University Press, 2018.

Best, Stephen, and Sharon Marcus. "Surface Reading: An Introduction." *Representations* 108.1 (Fall 2009): 1–21.

Beyoncé. "Formation." Recorded 2015. *Lemonade*, track 12. Parkwood Entertainment and Columbia Records, 2016.

Bhabha, Homi. "Foreword: Framing Fanon." In Frantz Fanon, *Wretched of the Earth*, vii–xli. Translated by Richard Philcox. New York: Grove, 2004.

Bonilla, Yarimar. "The Coloniality of Disaster: Race, Empire, and the Temporal Logics of Emergency in Puerto Rico, USA." *Political Geography* 78 (April 2020). https://doi.org/10.1016/j.polgeo.2020.102181.

Bradley, Laura. "How *Men in Black*, *Get Out*, and Meryl Streep Inspired *Us*'s Climactic Fight." *Vanity Fair*, March 29, 2019. https://www.vanityfair.com/hollywood/2019/03/us-jordan-peele-ending-dance-fight-scene-choreographer-madeline-hollander.

Bradley, Regina. "SANDRA BLAND: #SayHerName Loud or Not at All." *Sounding Out!*, November 16, 2015. https://soundstudiesblog.com/2015/11/16/sandra-bland-sayhername-loud/.

Brenner, Corina. Yin yoga teacher training. October 23–26, 2020. Integral Yoga Center.

Briefel, Aviva. "'We Want to Take Our Time': The Hard Work of Leisure in Jordan Peele's *Us* (2019)." In *Labors of Fear: The Modern Horror Film Goes to Work*, edited by Aviva Briefel and Jason Middleton, 133–51. Austin: University of Texas Press, 2023.

Brinkley, M. Kent. "A Historical Overview of Greenhouses in the Seventeenth and Eighteenth Centuries." In *The Green Spring Plantation Greenhouse/Orangery and the Probable Evolution of the Domestic Area Landscape*, 117–32. Richmond, VA: United States Department of the Interior, 2004.

Brooks, Daphne A. *Liner Notes for the Revolution: The Intellectual Life of Black Feminist Sound*. Cambridge, MA: Harvard University Press, 2021.

Brooks, LeRonn P. "Vision & Justice Online: Ming Smith and the Kamoinge Workshop." *Aperture*, 2016. https://aperture.org/editorial/vision-justice-online-kamoinge-workshop/.

Brown, Jayna. *Black Utopias: Speculative Life and the Music of Other Worlds*. Durham, NC: Duke University Press, 2021.

Brown, Karen McCarthy. *Mama Lola: A Vodou Priestess in Brooklyn*. Berkeley: University of California Press, 2001.

Buckley, Chris, and Adam Wu. "In China, the 'Noisiest Park in the World' Tries to Tone Down Retirees." *New York Times*, July 3, 2016. https://www.nytimes.com/2016/07/04/world/asia/china-chengdu-park-noise.html.

Butler, Judith. "Sex and Gender in Simone de Beauvoir's *Second Sex*." *Yale French Studies*, no. 72 (1986): 35–49. https://doi.org/10.2307/2930225.

Campt, Tina. "Black Visuality and the Practice of Refusal." *Women and Performance*, February 25, 2019. https://www.womenandperformance.org/ampersand/29-1/campt.

Campt, Tina. *Listening to Images*. Durham, NC: Duke University Press, 2017.

Carby, Hazel. *Imperial Intimacies: A Tale of Two Islands*. New York: Verso, 2019.

"Carib Song." *Playbill*. Accessed July 21, 2023. https://playbill.com/production/carib-song-adelphi-theatre-vault-0000003761.

Casid, Jill H. *Scenes of Projection: Recasting the Enlightenment Subject*. Minneapolis: University of Minnesota Press, 2014.

Cervenak, Sarah Jane. *Wandering: Philosophical Performances of Racial and Sexual Freedom*. Durham, NC: Duke University Press, 2014.

Césaire, Aimé. *Discourse on Colonialism*. New York: New York University Press, 2001.

Césaire, Aimé. *Solar Throat Slashed: The Unexpurgated 1948 Edition*. Edited and translated by A. James Arnold and Clayton Eshleman. Middletown, CT: Wesleyan University Press, 2011.

Césaire, Suzanne. "Surrealism and Us: 1943." *Surrealist Women: An International Anthology*. Edited by Penelope Rosemont, 136–37. Austin: University of Texas Press, 1998.

Chambers-Letson, Joshua. *After the Party: A Queer of Color Manifesto*. New York: New York University Press, 2018.

Chambers-Letson, Joshua. *A Race So Different: Performance and Law in Asian America*. New York: New York University Press, 2013.

Chapman, Dasha. "The Diasporic Re-membering Space of Jean Appolon's Afro-Haitian Dance Classes." *Black Scholar* 46, no. 1 (2016): 54–65. https://doi.org/10.1080/00064246.2015.1119622.

Chemaly, Soraya. *Rage Becomes Her: The Power of Women's Anger*. New York: Atria, 2018.

Chen, Mel. *Animacies: Biopolitics, Racial Mattering, and Queer Affect*. Durham, NC: Duke University Press, 2012.

Cheng, Anne Anlin. *Melancholy of Race: Psychoanalysis, Assimilation, and Hidden Grief*. Oxford: Oxford University Press, 2001.

Cheng, William. "Black Noise, White Ears: Resilience, Rap, and the Killing of Jordan Davis." *Current Musicology*, no. 102 (2018): 115–89. https://doi.org/10.7916/cm.v0i102.5367.

Childers, Kristen Stromberg. *Seeking Imperialism's Embrace: National Identity, Decolonization, and Assimilation in the French Caribbean*. New York: Oxford University Press, 2016.

Chion, Michel. *Sound: An Acoustological Treatise*. Translated by James Steintrager. Durham, NC: Duke University Press, 2016.

Chuh, Kandice. *The Difference Aesthetics Makes: On the Humanities "After Man."* Durham, NC: Duke University Press, 2019.

Chuh, Kandice. "It's Not About Anything." *Social Text* 32, no. 4 (2014): 125–34.

Cirino, Erica. "What Is Chimerism?" Healthline. November 29, 2018. https://www.healthline.com/health/chimerism.

Clare, Stephanie D. *Earthly Encounters: Sensation, Feminist Theory, and the Anthropocene*. Albany: SUNY Press, 2019.

Clark, VèVè. "On Stage with the Dunham Company: An Interview with Vanoye Aikens." In *Kaiso! Writings by and about Katherine Dunham*, edited by VèVè A. Clark and Sara E. Johnson, 274–87. Madison: University of Wisconsin Press, 2005.

Clark, VèVè. "Performing the Memory of Difference in Afro-Caribbean Dance: Katherine Dunham's Choreography, 1938–1987." In *Kaiso! Writings by and about Katherine Dunham*, edited by VèVè A. Clark and Sara E. Johnson, 320–40. Madison: University of Wisconsin Press, 2005.

Cohen, Ed. *A Body Worth Defending: Immunity, Biopolitics, and the Apotheosis of the Modern Body*. Durham, NC: Duke University Press, 2009.

Cook's Country. "All About Acid, Cooking's Most Versatile Ingredient." August 1, 2018. https://www.cookscountry.com/articles/1212-all-about-acid-cooking-s-most-versatile-ingredient.

Cooper, Brittney. *Eloquent Rage: A Black Feminist Discovers Her Superpower*. New York: Picador, 2019.

Coulombe, Charles A. *Rum: The Epic Story of the Drink That Conquered the World*. New York: Citadel, 2004.

Cox, Aimee Meredith. *Shapeshifters: Black Girls and the Choreography of Citizenship*. Durham, NC: Duke University Press, 2015.

Crawley, Ashon. *Blackpentecostal Breath: The Aesthetics of Possibility*. New York: Fordham University Press, 2016.

Cutruzzula, Kara. "The Key to Productivity Is Tapping into Your Flow State. Here's How." *Ideas.TED.com*, May 4, 2020. https://ideas.ted.com/the-key-to-productivity-is-tapping-into-your-flow-state-heres-how/.

Daniel, Yvonne. *Dancing Wisdom: Embodied Knowledge in Haitian Vodou, Cuban Yoruba, and Bahian Candomblé*. Chicago: University of Illinois Press, 2005.

Das, Joanna Dee. "Choreographing a New World: Katherine Dunham and the Politics of Dance." PhD diss., Columbia University, 2014.

Das, Joanna Dee. *Katherine Dunham: Dance and the African Diaspora*. Oxford: Oxford University Press, 2017.

Davis, Angela. "Reflections on the Black Woman's Role in the Community of Slaves." *Black Scholar* 3, no. 4 (1971): 2–15.

Deleuze, Gilles. *The Fold: Leibniz and the Baroque*. Translated by Tom Conley. Minneapolis: University of Minnesota Press, 1988.

Demos, T. J. "Blackout: The Necropolitics of Extraction." In *Beyond the World's End: Arts of Living at the Crossing*, 43–67. Durham, NC: Duke University Press, 2020.

Derrida, Jacques. *Of Grammatology*. 1976. Translated by Gayatri Chakravorty Spivak. Baltimore: Johns Hopkins University Press, 1998.

Díaz, Junot. "The Silence: The Legacy of Childhood Trauma." *New Yorker*, April 16, 2018. https://www.newyorker.com/magazine/2018/04/16/the-silence-the-legacy-of-childhood-trauma.

Dunham, Katherine. *Dances of Haiti*. Los Angeles: UCLA Center for Afro-American Studies, 1983.

Dunham, Katherine. *Islands Possessed*. 1969. Chicago: University of Chicago Press, 1994.

Dunham, Katherine. "The Negro Dance." In *Kaiso! Writings by and about Katherine Dunham*, edited by VèVè A. Clark and Sara E. Johnson, 217–26. Madison: University of Wisconsin Press, 2005.

Edwards, Bryan. *The History, Civil and Commercial, of British Colonies in the West Indies*, Vol. II. Dublin: 1793.

Edwards, Erica. *The Other Side of Terror: Black Women and the Culture of US Empire*. New York: New York University Press, 2021.

Ellis, Nadia. *Territories of the Soul: Queered Belonging in the Black Diaspora*. Durham, NC: Duke University Press, 2015.

Eng, David L. *The Feeling of Kinship: Queer Liberalism and the Racialization of Intimacy*. Durham, NC: Duke University Press, 2010.

English, Darby. *To Describe a Life: Notes from the Intersection of Art and Race Terror*. New Haven, CT: Yale University Press, 2019.

Estés, Clarissa Pinkola. *Women Who Run With the Wolves: Myths and Stories of the Wild Woman Archetype*. New York: Ballantine, 1995.

Eyestone, Emily. "Cannibalizing Paradise: Suzanne Césaire's Ecofeminist Critique of Tourist Literature." *Island Studies Journal* 17, no. 2 (2022): 1–22.

Fanon, Frantz. *Black Skin, White Masks*. Translated by Charles Markmann. New York: Grove, 1967.

Fanon, Frantz. *The Wretched of the Earth*. Translated by Richard Philcox. New York: Grove, 2004.

Federici, Silvia. "Wages against Housework." Montpelier, UK: Power of Women Collective and Falling Wall Press, 1975.

Felman, Shoshana. *Jacques Lacan and the Adventure of Insight: Contemporary Culture and Psychoanalysis*. Cambridge, MA: Harvard University Press, 2012.

Ferguson, Roderick. *The Reorder of Things: The University and Its Pedagogies of Minority Difference (Difference Incorporated)*. Minneapolis: University of Minnesota Press, 2012.

Field, Corinne T., Tammy C. Owens, Marcia Chatelain, LaKisha Simmons, Abosede George, and Rhian Keyse. "The History of Black Girlhood: Recent Innovations and Future Directions." *Journal of the History of Childhood and Youth* 9, no. 3 (Fall 2016): 383–401.

Freeman, Elizabeth. *Beside You in Time: Sense Methods and Queer Sensibilities in the American Nineteenth Century*. Durham, NC: Duke University Press, 2019.

Fretwell, Erica. *Sensory Experiments: Psychophysics, Race, and the Aesthetics of Feeling*. Durham, NC: Duke University Press, 2020.

Freud, Sigmund. *The Uncanny*. New York: Penguin, 1919.

Furlonge, Nicole. *Race Sounds: The Art of Listening in African American Literature*. Des Moines: University of Iowa Press, 2018.

Gaines, Malik. *Black Performance on the Outskirts of the Left: A History of the Impossible*. New York: New York University Press, 2017.

Gaines, Mikal. "Racing Work and Working Race in Buppie Horror." In *Labors of Fear: The Modern Horror Film Goes to Work*, edited by Aviva Briefel and Jason Middleton, 151–68. Austin: University of Texas Press, 2023.

Gehred, Kathryn. "Did George Washington's False Teeth Come from His Slaves?" Washington Papers. October 19, 2016. https://washingtonpapers.org/george-washingtons-false-teeth-come-slaves-look-evidence-responses-evidence-limitations-history/.

Gendzier, Irene L. "Frantz Fanon: In Search of Justice." *Middle East Journal* 20, no. 4 (1966): 534–44.

Gill, Lyndon. *Erotic Islands: Art and Activism in the Queer Caribbean*. Durham, NC: Duke University Press, 2018.

Gilles, Jerry M., and Yvrose S. Gilles. *Remembrance: Roots, Rituals, and Reverence in Vodou*. Davie, FL: Bookmanlit, 2009.

Gillespie, Michael Boyce. *Film Blackness: American Cinema and the Idea of Black Film*. Durham, NC: Duke University Press, 2016.

Ginsberg, Elaine K. *Passing and the Fictions of Identity*. Durham, NC: Duke University Press, 1996.

Gladstone Gallery. "Allora & Calzadilla, Cadastre, September 13–November 2, 2019." https://www.gladstonegallery.com/exhibition/5934/cadastre/info.

Glaser, Daniel. "How to Describe What It Feels Like to Be in a Hurricane." *Guardian*, September 17, 2017. https://www.theguardian.com/lifeandstyle/2017/sep/17/how-to-describe-what-it-feels-like-to-be-in-a-hurricane.

Glissant, Édouard. *Poetics of Relation*. Translated by Betsey Wing. Detroit: University of Michigan Press, 1997.

Gluibizzi, Amanda. "On Edge(s)." *Brooklyn Rail*, October 2020. https://brooklynrail.org/2020/10/criticspage/EdgesLimits-EdgesTableau.

Goeman, Mishuana. *Mark My Words: Native Women Mapping Our Nations*. Minneapolis: University of Minnesota Press, 2013.

Gómez-Barris, Macarena. "The Colonial Anthropocene: Damage, Remapping, and Resurgent Resources." *Antipode Online*, March 19, 2019. https://antipodeonline.org/2019/03/19/the-colonial-anthropocene/.

Gopinath, Gayatri. *Unruly Visions: The Aesthetic Practices of Queer Diaspora*. Durham, NC: Duke University Press, 2018.

Gordon, Lewis R. *What Fanon Said: A Philosophical Introduction to His Life and Thought*. New York: Fordham University Press, 2015.

Grande, Sandy. "Care." In *Keywords for Gender and Sexuality Studies*, edited by the Keywords Feminist Editorial Collective, 43–46. New York: New York University Press, 2021.

Greenberger, Alex. "Ming Smith Shook Up Photography in the '70s. Now, She Is Coming into Full View." *ARTnews*, November 16, 2020. https://www.artnews.com/art-news/artists/ming-smith-photography-aperture-kamoinge-workshop-1234576646/.

Griffiths, David. "Queer Theory for Lichens." *UnderCurrents: Journal of Critical Environmental Studies* 19 (2015): 36–45.

Gumbs, Alexis Pauline. "End Capitalism." *Boston Review*, February 16, 2021. https://bostonreview.net/science-nature/alexis-pauline-gumbs-end-capitalism.

Hainge, Greg. *Noise Matters: Toward an Ontology of Noise*. London: Bloomsbury Academic, 2013.

Hantel, Max. "Plasticity and Fungibility: On Sylvia Wynter's Pieza Framework." *Social Text* 38, no. 2 (2020): 97–119.

Haraway, Donna. "Situated Knowledges: The Science Question in Feminism and the Privilege of Partial Perspective." *Feminist Studies* 14, no. 3 (1988): 575–99.

Harper, Phillip Brian. *Abstractionist Aesthetics: Artistic Form and Social Critique in African American Culture*. New York: New York University Press, 2015.

Harris, Dawn P. "Confined Spaces, Constrained Bodies: Land, Labor, and Confinement in Barbados after 1834." In *Punishing the Black Body: Marking Social and Racial Structures in Barbados and Jamaica*, 92–117. Atlanta: University of Georgia Press, 2017.

Harrison, Sheri-Marie. "Us and Them: Between Race and Class, the Tether." *Commune* (Winter 2020): 5. https://communemag.com/us-and-them/.

Hartman, Saidiya V. *Scenes of Subjection: Terror, Slavery, and Self-Making in Nineteenth-Century America*. New York: Oxford University Press, 1997.

Hartman, Saidiya V. "Venus in Two Acts." *Small Axe* 26, no. 2 (June 2008): 1–14.

Hartman, Saidiya V. *Wayward Lives, Beautiful Experiments: Intimate Histories of Social Upheaval*. New York: W. W. Norton, 2019.

Harvey, David. *A Brief History of Neoliberalism*. New York: Oxford University Press, 2005.

Harvey, David. *The New Imperialism*. New York: Oxford University Press, 2003.

Hathaway, Bill. "Sugar Targets Gut Microbe Linked to Lean and Healthy People." *YaleNews*, December 17, 2018. https://news.yale.edu/2018/12/17/sugar-targets-gut-microbe-linked-lean-and-healthy-people.

Hellwig, Rachel. "Sugar Plum Fairy Exposé: Dissolving the Sugar Coating." *Dance Advantage*, December 21, 2015. https://www.danceadvantage.net/sugarplum-fairy-exposed.

"Hematopoiesis." *ScienceDirect: Books and Journals*. Elsevier. https://www.sciencedirect.com/topics/neuroscience/hematopoiesis.

Hillel, Alexander. "Spasmodic Dysfonia." *Hopkins Medicine*. Accessed June 28, 2023. https://www.hopkinsmedicine.org/health/conditions-and-diseases/spasmodic-dysphonia.

Holmes, Jessica A. "Expert Listening Beyond the Limits of Hearing: Music and Deafness." *Journal of the American Musicological Society* 70, no. 1 (2017): 171–220.

Hong, Grace Kyungwon. *Death beyond Disavowal: The Impossible Politics of Difference*. Minneapolis: University of Minnesota Press, 2015.

Hulse, Patricia. "Black History Month in the Adventure Garden." *New York Botanical Garden*, February 13, 2020. https://www.nybg.org/planttalk/black-history-month-in-the-adventure-garden/.

Ibrahim, Azeem. "Modi's Slide Toward Autocracy." *Foreign Policy.com*, July 13, 2020. https://foreignpolicy.com/2020/07/13/modi-india-hindutva-hindu-nationalism-autocracy/.

Ibrahim, Habiba. *Black Age: Oceanic Lifespans and the Time of Black Life*. New York: New York University Press, 2021.

Jackson, Zakiyyah Iman. *Becoming Human: On Blackness and Being*. New York: New York University Press, 2020.

Jafa, Arthur, and Greg Tate. "The sound she saw." In *Ming Smith*, 217–26. New York: Aperture Foundation; Dallas: Documentary Arts, 2020.

James, Joy. "The Womb of Western Theory: Trauma, Time Theft and the Captive Maternal." *Carceral Notebooks*, vol. 12 (2016): 253–96.

James, Robin. *The Sonic Episteme: Acoustic Resonance, Neoliberalism, and Biopolitics*. Durham, NC: Duke University Press, 2020.

Jennings, Eric T. *Escape from Vichy: The Refugee Exodus to the French Caribbean*. Cambridge, MA: Harvard University Press, 2018.

"Jing (Essence) - Vital Substances in TCM." Sacred Lotus Chinese Medicine. Accessed June 28, 2023. https://www.sacredlotus.com/go/foundations-chinese-medicine/get/jing-essence-vital-substance.

Juhan, Deane. *Job's Body: A Handbook for Bodywork, Third Edition*. Barrytown, NY: Stationhill, 2003.

Kapadia, Ronak. *Insurgent Aesthetics: Security and the Queer Life of the Forever War*. Durham, NC: Duke University Press, 2019.

Kaphar, Titus. "A Fight for Remembrance." *Georgia Review* 69, no. 2 (2015): 199–208.

Kaphar, Titus, and Jason Stanley. "Titus Kaphar." *BOMB*, no. 147 (2019): 81–88.

Kaplan, Caren. *Aerial Aftermaths: Wartime from Above*. Durham, NC: Duke University Press, 2018.

Keeling, Kara. *Queer Times, Black Futures*. New York: New York University Press, 2019.

Keeling, Patrick J., and John P. McCutcheon. "Endosymbiosis: The Feeling Is Not Mutual." *Journal of Theoretical Biology* 434 (2017): 75–79.

Kelley, Robin D. G. *Freedom Dreams: The Black Radical Imagination*. Boston: Beacon, 2002.

Kelley, Robin D. G. "Introduction: Invisible Surrealists." In *Black, Brown, and Beige: Surrealist Writings from Africa and the Diaspora*, edited by Robin D. G. Kelley and Franklin Rosement, 1–19. Austin: University of Texas Press, 2009.

Kheshti, Roshanak. *Modernity's Ear: Listening to Race and Gender in World Music*. New York: New York University Press, 2015.

Kheshti, Roshanak. "Toward a Rupture in the Sensus Communis: On Sound Studies and the Politics of Knowledge Production." *Current Musicology* 99/100 (2017). https://doi.org/10.7916/cm.v0i99/100.5341.

Kim, Christine Sun, dir. *[Closer Captions]*. 2020. 7 min., 46 sec. In "Artist Christine Sun Kim Rewrites Closed Captions." YouTube, posted by Pop-Up Magazine, October 13, 2020. https://www.youtube.com/watch?v=tfe479qL8hg.

Kim, Jina B. "Toward a Crip-of-Color Critique: Thinking with Minich's 'Enabling Whom?'" *Lateral* 6, no. 1 (Spring 2017). https://csalateral.org/issue/6-1/forum-alt-humanities-critical-disability-studies-crip-of-color-critique-kim/.

Kim, Jina B., and Sami Schalk. "Reclaiming the Radical Politics of Self-Care: A Crip-of-Color Critique." *South Atlantic Quarterly* 120, no. 2 (April 2021): 325–42.

Kim, Julie. "The Caribs of St. Vincent and Indigenous Resistance during the Age of Revolutions." *Early American Studies* (Winter 2013): 117–32.

Kincaid, Jamaica. *A Small Place*. New York: Farrar, Straus and Giroux, 2000.

King, Tiffany Lethabo. *The Black Shoals: Offshore Formations of Black and Native Studies*. Durham, NC: Duke University Press, 2019.

King, Tiffany Lethabo. "In the Clearing: Black Female Bodies, Space, and Settler Colonial Landscapes." PhD diss., University of Maryland, College Park, 2013.

Kinsley, David. *Hindu Goddesses: Visions of the Divine Feminine in the Hindu Religious Tradition*. Berkeley: University of California Press, 1986

Knight, Lisa. *Contradictory Lives: Baul Women in India and Bangladesh*. Oxford: Oxford University Press, 2011.

Kraut, Anthea. "Between Primitivism and Diaspora: The Dance Performances of Josephine Baker, Zora Neale Hurston, and Katherine Dunham." *Theatre Journal* 55, no. 3 (October 2003): 433–50.

Lacan, Jacques. "The Subversion of the Subject and the Dialectic of Desire." In *Écrits: The First Complete Edition in English*, translated by Bruce Fink, 671–702. New York: W. W. Norton, 2006.

Lazcano, Antonio, and Juli Peretó. "On the Origin of Mitosing Cells: A Historical Appraisal of Lynn Margulis Endosymbiotic Theory." *Journal of Theoretical Biology* 434 (2017): 80–87.

Lee, Rachel. *The Exquisite Corpse of Asian America: Biopolitics, Bioscocialities, and Posthuman Ecologies*. New York: New York University Press, 2014.

Leland, Kurt. "The Rainbow Body: How the Western Chakra System Came to Be." *Quest* 105, no. 2 (Spring 2017): 25–29. https://www.theosophical.org/publications/quest-magazine/4246-the-rainbow-body-how-the-western-chakra-system-came-to-be.

Leroy, Justin. "Black History in Occupied Territory: On the Entanglements of Slavery and Settler Colonialism." *Theory and Event* 19, no. 4 (2016). https://www.proquest.com/docview/1866315134?parentSessionId=DstvcjsEGwYXdS95EcEhfMo2WBCV8FckrMIg4qQTzQs%3D.

Lewis, Robin Coste. *Voyage of the Sable Venus and Other Poems*. New York: Alfred A. Knopf, 2015.

Libson, Laura. "Edges/Limits. Edges/Tableau." *Brooklyn Rail*, October 2020. https://brooklynrail.org/2020/10/criticspage/EdgesLimits-EdgesTableau.

Livingston, Julie. *Debility and the Moral Imagination in Botswana*. Bloomington: Indiana University Press, 2005.

Livingston, Julie. *Self-Devouring Growth: A Planetary Parable As Told from Southern Africa*. Durham, NC: Duke University Press, 2019.

Lorde, Audre. *The Cancer Journals*. San Francisco: Aunt Lute Books, 1980.

Lorde, Audre. "Eye to Eye: Black Women, Hatred, and Anger." In Lorde, *Sister Outsider*, 145–75.

Lorde, Audre. "The Master's Tools Will Never Dismantle the Master's House." In Lorde, *Sister Outsider*, 110–14.

Lorde, Audre. *Sister Outsider: Essays and Speeches by Audre Lorde*. Feminist Series. New York: Crossing Press, 2007.

Lorde, Audre. "Uses of Anger." In Lorde, *Sister Outsider*, 124–33.

Lorde, Audre. "Uses of the Erotic." In Lorde, *Sister Outsider*, 53–59.

Lorde, Audre. *Zami: A New Spelling of My Name*. Freedom, CA: Crossing Press, 1982.

Lowe, Lisa. *The Intimacies of Four Continents*. Durham, NC: Duke University Press, 2015.

MacLeod, Jessie. "Tom." George Washington's Mount Vernon. Accessed June 28, 2023. https://www.mountvernon.org/library/digitalhistory/digital-encyclopedia/article/tom/#1.

Magloire, Marina. "An Ethics of Discomfort: Katherine Dunham's Vodou Belonging." *Small Axe* 23, no. 3 (60) (November 2019): 1–17.

Malatino, Hil. *Trans Care*. Minneapolis: University of Minnesota Press, 2020.

Manning, Susan. "Watching Dunham's Dances, 1937–1945." In *Kaiso! Writings by and about Katherine Dunham*, edited by VèVè A. Clark and Sara E. Johnson, 256–66. Madison: University of Wisconsin Press, 2005.

Manring, Rebecca. "Review of *Contradictory Lives: Baul Women in India and Bangladesh*." *Journal of Hindu Studies* 8, no. 3 (November 2015): 330–32.

Marya, Rupa, and Raj Patel. *Inflamed: Deep Medicine and the Anatomy of Injustice*. New York: Farrar, Straus and Giroux, 2021.

Masé, Guido. *The Wild Medicine Solution: Healing with Aromatic, Bitter, and Tonic Plants*. New York: Healing Arts Press, 2013.

Mathur, Avantika, Suhas Vijayakumar, Bhismadev Chakrabarti, and Nandini Singh. "Emotional Response to Hindustanti *Raga* Music: The Role of Musical Structure." *Frontiers in Psychology* 6 (2015). https://www.ncbi.nlm.nih.gov/pmc/articles/PMC4415143/.

Matthews, Timothy. "Singularity and Collision: Aimé Césaire, Pablo Picasso, *Corps perdu*." *L'Esprit créateur* 55, no. 1 (Spring 2015): 134–51.

Mbembe, Achille. *Critique of Black Reason*. Translated by Laurent Dubois. Durham, NC: Duke University Press, 2017.

Mbembe, Achille. "On the Universal Right to Breathe." *Zürcher Theater Spektakel*. https://www.theaterspektakel.ch/en/article/essay-achille-mbembe.

McDonald, Jim. *Foundational Herbcraft*. Self-published, n.d. Available at https://herbcraft.podia.com/foundational-herbcraft.

McKittrick, Katherine. *Dear Science and Other Stories*. Durham, NC: Duke University Press, 2021.

McKittrick, Katherine. *Demonic Ground: Black Women and Cartographies of Struggle*. Minneapolis: University of Minnesota Press, 2006.

McMaster, James. Review of *Matters of Care: Speculative Ethics in More than Human Worlds*, by María Puig de la Bellacasa. *Women and Performance* 27, no. 3 (2017): 352–58.

McMillan, Uri. *Embodied Avatars: Genealogies of Black Feminist Art and Performance*. New York: New York University Press, 2015.

McMillan, Uri. "Introduction: Surface, Skin, Sensorium." Special issue, "Surface Aesthetics: Race, Performance, Play." *Women and Performance: A Journal of Feminist Theory* 28, no. 1 (2018): 1–15.

McRuer, Robert. *Crip Times: Disability, Globalization, and Resistance*. New York: New York University Press, 2018.

Meaney, Thomas. "History Unclassified: Frantz Fanon and the CIA Man." *American Historical Review* 124, no. 3 (June 2019): 983–95.

Mills, Mara. "Do Signals Have Politics? Inscribing Abilities in Cochlear Implants." In *The Oxford Handbook of Sound Studies*, edited by Trevor Pinch and Karin Bijsterveld, 320–46. New York: Oxford University Press, 2012.

Minet, Carla. "María's Death Toll: On the Crucial Role of Puerto Rico's Investigative Journalists." In *Aftershocks of Disaster: Puerto Rico Before and After the Storm*, edited by Yarimar Bonilla and Marisol Le Bron, 73–79. Chicago: Haymarket, 2019.

Mintz, Sidney. *Sweetness and Power: The Place of Sugar in Modern History*. New York: Penguin, 1987.

Mishan, Ligaya. "How Sourness Has Come to Dominate Our Dining Habits, and Our Discourse." *New York Times Style Magazine*, May 14, 2019. https://www.nytimes.com/2019/05/14/t-magazine/sour-food.html.

Moi, Toril. *What Is a Woman? And Other Essays*. Oxford: Oxford University Press, 2001.

Morell, Virginia. "Like Humans, Flamingos Make Friends for Life." *National Geographic*, April 24, 2020. https://www.nationalgeographic.com/animals/article/flamingos-make-friends-for-life.

Moten, Fred. *Black and Blur*. Durham, NC: Duke University Press, 2017.

Muñoz, José Esteban. "Brown Commons." In *The Sense of Brown*, 1–7. Durham, NC: Duke University Press, 2020.

Muñoz, José Esteban. *Cruising Utopia: The Then and There of Queer Futurity*. New York: New York University Press, 2009.

Musser, Amber Jamilla. "Infinity Folds: Sonic Sculptures and Dancing Shapes." In *collective terrain/s*, edited by Lydia Bell, 18–22. New York: Danspace Projects, 2019.

Musser, Amber Jamilla. "Racialized Femininity and Representation's Ambivalences in Trajal Harrell's *The Return of La Argentina*." Special issue, "Ambivalent Criticisms," edited by Tina Post and Michael Dango. *Post45*, no. 8 (October 2022). https://post45.org/2022/10/racialized-femininity-and-representations-ambivalences/.

Musser, Amber Jamilla. *Sensational Flesh: Race, Power, and Masochism*. New York: New York University Press, 2014.

Musser, Amber Jamilla. *Sensual Excess: Queer Femininity and Brown Jouissance*. New York: New York University Press, 2018.

Musser, Amber Jamilla. "Specimen Days: Diversity, Labor, and the University." *Feminist Formations* 27, no. 3 (Winter 2015): 1–20.

Musser, Amber Jamilla. "Tamarind and the Politics of Rest." Special issue, "Black Ecologies," edited by Imani Jacqueline Brown and Sarrita Hunn. *MARCH* 2 (Fall 2021): 42–52.

Musser, Amber Jamilla. "*Tear* and the Politics of Brown Feeling." *ASAP/J*, September 30, 2021. https://asapjournal.com/tear-and-the-politics-of-brown-feelings-amber-jamilla-musser/.

Musser, Amber Jamilla. "Toward Mythic Feminist Theorizing: Simone Leigh and the Power of the Vessel." *differences* 30, no. 3 (December 2019): 63–91.

Nancy, Jean-Luc. *Listening*. Translated by Charlotte Mandel. New York: Fordham University Press, 2007.

The Nap Ministry. "Resources from 'a Space to Rest' Virtual Experience with Wa Na Wari, Central District Forum Ideas and Langston." August 3, 2020. https://thenapministry.wordpress.com/.

Nash, Jennifer. "Practicing Love: Black Feminism, Love-Politics, and Post-Intersectionality." *Meridians* 19, no. 1 (2020): 439–62.

Neptune, Harvey R. *Caliban and the Yankees: Trinidad and the United States Occupation*. Chapel Hill: University of North Carolina Press, 2007.

Neyria, Ren. "Towards an Un-American Solidarity." *Independent Curators International Research Journal* (October 30, 2017). https://curatorsintl.org/research/towards-an-un-american-solidarity-thinking-with-puerto-rico-after-hurricane.

Nguyen, Mimi Thi. *The Gift of Freedom: War, Debt, and Other Refugee Passages*. Durham, NC: Duke University Press, 2012.

Nichols, Lewis. "'Carib Song' with Katherine Dunham and Avon Long, Makes Its Bow at the Adelphi Theatre." *New York Times*, September 28, 1945, 17.

Nyong'o, Tavia. *Afro-Fabulations: The Queer Drama of Black Life*. New York: New York University Press, 2018.

Osumare, Halifu. "Dancing the Black Atlantic: Katherine Dunham's Research-to-Performance Method." *AmeriQuests* 7, no. 2 (2010). https://ejournals.library.vanderbilt.edu/index.php/ameriquests/article/view/165.

Owens, Emily. "'Yes Means Yes' and the Problem of Consent in the Law." African American Intellectual History Society, October 21, 2014. http://aaihs.org/yes-means-yes-and-the-problem-of-consent-in-the-law/.

Owusu, Nadia. *Aftershocks: A Memoir*. New York: Simon and Schuster, 2021.

Ozkan, Mert. "Thousands of Flamingos Die in Drought in Central Turkey." *Reuters*, July 15, 2021. https://www.reuters.com/business/environment/thousands-flamingos-die-drought-central-turkey-2021-07-15/.

Patterson, Orlando, and David Reich, "Ancient DNA Is Changing How We Think about the Caribbean." *New York Times*, December 23, 2020. https://www.nytimes.com/2020/12/23/opinion/dna-caribbean-genocide.html?action=click&module=Opinion&pgtype=Homepage.

Peele, Jordan, dir. *Get Out*. Universal Pictures Home Entertainment. 104 min. 2017.

Peele, Jordan, dir. *Us*. Universal Pictures Home Entertainment. 116 min. 2019.

Peterson, Marina. *Atmospheric Noise: The Indefinite Urbanism of Los Angeles*. Durham, NC: Duke University Press, 2021.

Peterson, Marina. *Sound, Space, and City: Civic Performance in Downtown Los Angeles*. Philadelphia: University of Pennsylvania Press, 2012.

Petro, Brian. "Classic Cocktails in History: the Whiskey Sour." Alcohol Professor. January 27, 2015. https://www.alcoholprofessor.com/blog-posts/blog/2015/01/27/classic-cocktails-in-history-the-whiskey-sour.

Pinto, Samantha, and Shoniqua Roach. "Black Privacy." *Black Scholar* 51, no. 1 (2021): 1–2.

Posmentier, Sonya. *Cultivation and Catastrophe: The Lyric Ecology of Modern Black Literature*. Baltimore, MD: Johns Hopkins University Press, 2017.

Post, Tina. *Deadpan: The Aesthetics of Black Inexpression*. New York: New York University Press, 2023.

Powell, Elliott H. *Sounds from the Other Side: Afro–South Asian Collaborations in Black Popular Music*. Minneapolis: University of Minnesota Press, 2020.

Priest, Myisha. "Salvation Is the Issue." *Meridians* 8, no. 2 (2008): 116–22.

Puar, Jasbir. *The Right to Maim: Debility, Capacity, Disability*. Durham, NC: Duke University Press, 2017.

Puig de la Bellacasa, María. *Matters of Care: Speculative Ethics in More Than Human Worlds*. Minneapolis: University of Minnesota Press, 2017.

Quashie, Kevin. *Black Aliveness, or A Poetics of Being*. Durham, NC: Duke University Press, 2021.

Rabbitt, Kara. "In Search of the Missing Mother: Suzanne Césaire, *Martiniquaise*." *Research in African Literatures* 44, no. 1 (2013): 36–54.

Raengo, Alessandra. *On the Sleeve of the Visual, Race as Face Value*. Hanover, NH: Dartmouth College Press, 2013.

Ramsey, Kate. *The Spirits and the Law: Vodou and Power in Haiti*. Chicago: University of Chicago Press, 2015.

Rancière, Jacques. *The Ignorant Schoolmaster: Five Lessons in Intellectual Emancipation*. Translated by Kristin Ross. Palo Alto, CA: Stanford University Press, 1991.

Rault, Jasmine. "Window Walls and Other Tricks of Transparency: Digital, Colonial, and Architectural Modernity." *American Quarterly* 72, no. 4 (December 2020): 937–60.

Redmond, Shana. "*Us* Liner Notes." *Us: Original Motion Picture Soundtrack*. Waxworks Records, 2023.

Renda, Mary. *Taking Haiti: Military Occupation and the Culture of U.S. Imperialism, 1915–1940*. Chapel Hill: University of North Carolina Press, 2001.

Rivera-Servera, Ramón H. "José E. Muñoz's Queer Gestures." *QED: A Journal in GLBTQ Worldmaking* 1, no. 3 (Fall 2014): 146–49.

Roberts, Justin. "Working Between the Lines: Labor and Agriculture on Two Barbadian Sugar Plantations, 1796–97." *William and Mary Quarterly* 63, no. 3 (July 2006): 551–86.

Robles, Frances. "Puerto Rico Spent 11 Months Turning the Power Back On. They Finally Got to Her." *New York Times*, August 14, 2018. https://www.nytimes.com/2018/08/14/us/puerto-rico-electricity-power.html.

Rodriguez, Juana María. *Sexual Futures, Queer Gestures, and Other Latina Longings*. New York: New York University Press, 2014.

Roos, Dave. "How Crude Smallpox Inoculations Helped George Washington Win the War." *History Channel*, May 13, 2020. https://www.history.com/news/smallpox-george-washington-revolutionary-war.

Ruiz, Sandra. *Ricanness: Enduring Time in Anticolonial Performance*. New York: New York University Press, 2019.

Ruiz, Sandra, and Hypatia Vourloumis. *Formless Formation: Vignettes for the End of this World*. New York: Minor Compositions, 2021. https://www.minorcompositions.info/wp-content/uploads/2021/05/formlessformation-web.pdf.

Rusert, Britt. *Fugitive Science: Empiricism and Freedom in Early African American Culture*. New York: New York University Press, 2017.

Sagan [Margulis], Lynn. "On the Origin of Mitosing Cells." *Journal of Theoretical Biology* 14 (1967): 225–74.
Sartre, Jean Paul. *Being and Nothingness: An Essay on Phenomenological Ontology.* 1943. Translated by Mary Warnock. New York and London: Routledge, 2003.
Schuller, Kyla. "Biopower Below and Before the Individual." *GLQ* 22, no. 4 (2016): 629–36.
Schuller, Kyla. "Losing Paradise." *Rumpus*, June 2020. https://therumpus.net/2020/06/losing-paradise/?fbclid=IwAR1Tmt3F2EdDXlNkHke8fYJqqij4CtR7q41KUPK-BYkoofHFL5OP5_xzoPk.
Schuller, Kyla. *The Trouble with White Women*. New York: Bold Type, 2021.
Schuller, Kyla, and Jules Gill-Peterson. "Introduction: Race, the State, and the Malleable Body." *Social Text* 38, no. 2 (2020): 1–17.
Scott, Darieck. *Extravagant Abjection: Blackness, Power, and Sexuality in the African American Literary Imagination*. New York: New York University Press, 2010.
Scott, Emmy. "The Native Imagery of Jordan Peele's *Us*, Explained." *Vulture*, March 29, 2019. https://www.vulture.com/2019/03/the-native-imagery-of-jordan-peele-s-us-explained.html.
Sedgwick, Eve Kosofsky. "Art, Writing, Performativity." In conversation with Gavin Butt. In *Frieze Projects and Frieze Talks, 2006–2008*. London: Frieze, 2009.
Sellin, Eric. "Soleil cou coupé." *Romance Notes* 14, no. 1 (Autumn 1972): 13–16.
Serpell, Namwali. "The Shimmering Go-Between." In *Ming Smith*,, 53–59. New York: Aperture Foundation; Dallas: Documentary Arts, 2020.
Shange, Savannah. *Progressive Dystopia: Abolition, Antiblackness, and Schooling in San Francisco*. Durham, NC: Duke University Press, 2019.
Sharpe, Christina. *In the Wake: On Blackness and Being*. Durham, NC: Duke University Press, 2016.
Sheller, Mimi. *Island Futures: Caribbean Survival in the Anthropocene*. Durham, NC: Duke University Press, 2020.
Sheller, Mimi. *Mobility Justice: The Politics of Movement in an Age of Extremes.* New York: Penguin, 2018.
Shimikawa, Karen. *National Abjection: The Asian American Body On Stage*. Durham, NC: Duke University Press, 2002.
Silva, Denise Ferreira da. *Toward a Global Idea of Race*. Minneapolis: University of Minnesota Press, 2007.
Simmons, LaKisha Michelle. *Crescent City Girls: The Lives of Young Black Women in Segregated New Orleans*. Chapel Hill: University of North Carolina Press, 2015.
Simpkins, Kate, Juniper Johnson, and Dannie Brice. "Makandal Exhibit." *Early Caribbean Digital Archive*. Northeastern University, 2019. https://ecda.northeastern.edu/makandal-exhibit-introduction/.
Sinha, Samita. Interview with *Sound American*. Accessed May 5, 2020. http://soundamerican.org/sa_archive/Rubin/samita-sinha.html.
Smith, Valerie. "Reading the Intersection of Race and Gender in Narratives of Passing." *Diacritics* 24, no. 2/3 (1994): 43–57.

Snorton, C. Riley. *Black on Both Sides: A Racial History of Trans Identity*. Minneapolis: University of Minnesota Press, 2017.

Spillers, Hortense J. "Interstices: A Small Drama of Words." In *Pleasure and Danger: Exploring Female Sexuality*, edited by Carol Vance, 73–100. New York: Routledge, 1984.

Spillers, Hortense J. "Mama's Baby, Papa's Maybe: An American Grammar Book." *Diacritics* 17, no. 2 (1987): 65–81.

Spivak, Gayatri Chakravorty. "Can the Subaltern Speak?" In *Marxism in Culture*, edited by C. Nelson and L. Grossberg, 271–313. Basingstoke, UK: Macmillan Education, 1988.

Stephens, Michelle. "Skin, Stain and Lamella: Fanon, Lacan, and Inter-racializing the Gaze." *Psychoanalysis, Culture, and Society* 23, no. 4 (September 2018): 310–29. https://doi.org/10.1057/s41282-018-0104-1.

Sterne, Jonathan. *Diminished Faculties: A Political Phenomenology of Impairment*. Durham, NC: Duke University Press, 2022.

Stoever, Jennifer Lynn. *The Sonic Color Line: Race and the Cultural Politics of Listening*. New York: New York University Press, 2016.

Stoler, Ann Laura. *Race and the Education of Desire: Foucault's History of Sexuality and the Colonial Order of Things*. Durham, NC: Duke University Press, 1995.

Strongman, Roberto. "Transcorporeality in Vodou." *Journal of Haitian Studies* 14, no. 2 (2008): 4–29.

Sullivan, Mecca Jamilah. *Poetics of Difference: Queer Feminist Forms in the African Diaspora*. Chicago: University of Illinois Press, 2021.

Tadimalla, Ravi Teja. "7 Health Benefits of Tamarind + Possible Side Effects." *StyleCraze*, January 27, 2020. https://www.stylecraze.com/articles/amazing-benefits-of-tamarind/.

Tagore, Rabindrath. *The Religion of Man*. 1931. London: Ravenio Books, 2015.

Talbert, Janet Hill, and Ming Smith. "Portrait of the Artist." In *Ming Smith*, 10–20. New York: Aperture Foundation; Dallas: Documentary Arts, 2020.

Tallbear, Kim. "A Sharpening of the Already Present: An Indigenous Materialist Reading of Settler Apocalypse 2020." Talk presented virtually for Speaker Series, Department of Political Science, University of Alberta, October 2020. https://www.youtube.com/watch?v=eO14od9mlTA.

"Tamarindus." Medicine Traditions. June 12, 2021. https://www.medicinetraditions.com/tamarindus-tamarind.html.

Tinsley, Omise'eke Natasha. "Black Atlantic, Queer Atlantic: Queer Imaginings of the Middle Passage." *GLQ* 14, no. 2–3 (2008): 191–215.

Tinsley, Omise'eke Natasha. *Ezili's Mirrors: Imagining Black Queer Genders*. Durham, NC: Duke University Press, 2018.

Tobias, Tobi. "Some Like It Hot." *New York Magazine*, January 4, 1988.

Tompkins, Kyla Wazana. "Crude Matter, Crude Form." *ASAP Journal* 2, no. 2 (May 2017): 264–68.

Tompkins, Kyla Wazana. "Sweetness, Capacity, Energy." *American Quarterly* 71, no. 3 (2019): 849–56.

Tongson, Karen. *Why Karen Carpenter Matters*. Austin: University of Texas Press, 2019.

Twitty, Michael. *Fighting Old Nep: The Foodways of Enslaved Afro-Marylanders, 1634–1864*. Self-published, 2006.

Tyler, Dennis. *Disabilities of the Color Line: Redressing Antiblackness from Slavery to the Present*. New York: New York University Press, 2022.

Van Middeldyk, R. A. *The History of Puerto Rico*. New York: Arno, 1975.

Vassell, Nicola. "On Ming Smith: A Life of Magical Thinking." *Gagosian Quarterly*, Spring 2021. https://gagosian.com/quarterly/2021/03/03/interview-ming-smith-magical-thinking/.

Vazquez, Alexandra. *Listening in Detail: Performances of Cuban Music*. Durham, NC: Duke University Press, 2013.

Vogel, Shane. *Stolen Time: Black Fad Performance and the Calypso Craze*. Chicago: University of Chicago Press, 2018.

Voight, Ginger. "The Difference Between Sour and Bitter." *Sciencing*, April 25, 2017. https://sciencing.com/difference-between-sour-bitter-8551852.html.

Waddington, Peter. "Katherine Dunham Raises Primitive Dance Art to New Heights of Sophistication." In *Kaiso! Writings by and about Katherine Dunham*, edited by VèVè A. Clark and Sara E. Johnson, 302–9. Madison: University of Wisconsin Press, 2005.

Walcott, Rinaldo. *On Property: Policing, Prisons, and the Call for Abolition*. Windsor, ON: Biblioasis, 2021.

Wald, Gayle. *Crossing the Line: Racial Passing in Twentieth-Century U.S. Literature and Culture*. Durham, NC: Duke University Press, 2000.

Walsh, Mary Williams. "Puerto Rico's Governor Warns of Fiscal 'Death Spiral.'" *New York Times*, October 14, 2016. https://www.nytimes.com/2016/10/15/business/dealbook/puerto-rico-financial-oversight-board.html.

Wanzo, Rebecca Ann. "Moten's Magical Meditations: Black Ontology and Genealogies of Hope." *European Journal of American Culture* 39, no. 2 (2020): 226–32.

Warren, Calvin. *Ontological Terror: Blackness, Nihilism, and Emancipation*. Durham, NC: Duke University Press, 2018.

Warren, Jack D., Jr., "Washington's Journey to Barbados." George Washington's Mount Vernon. Accessed June 28, 2028. https://www.mountvernon.org/george-washington/washingtons-youth/journey-to-barbados/.

Weheliye, Alexander Ghedi. *Habeas Viscus: Racializing Assemblages, Biopolitics, and Black Feminist Theories of the Human*. Durham, NC: Duke University Press, 2014.

Weinbaum, Alys. *Wayward Reproductions: Genealogies of Race and Nation in Transatlantic Modern Thought*. Durham, NC: Duke University Press, 2004.

Wiley, Roland John. *Tchaikovsky's Ballets*. Oxford: Oxford University Press, 1985.

Wilson, Elizabeth A. *Gut Feminism*. Durham, NC: Duke University Press, 2015.

Wisely, Rene. "This Gaseous Culprit Could Be Causing Your Stomach Pain and Constipation." Michigan Medicine. January 8, 2018. https://healthblog.uofmhealth.org/digestive-health/gaseous-culprit-could-be-causing-your-stomach-pain-and-constipation.

Wright, Michelle. *The Physics of Blackness: Beyond the Middle Passage Epistemology*. Minneapolis: University of Minnesota Press, 2015.

Wright, Nazera Sadiq. *Black Girlhood in the Nineteenth Century*. Champaign: University of Illinois Press, 2016.

Wu, Cynthia. *Chang and Eng Reconnected: The Original Siamese Twins in American Culture*. Philadelphia: Temple University Press, 2012.

Wyman, Rachel. "Yanvalou." Angeline Gragasin website for *Yanvalou*. https://www.angelinegragasin.com/projects/yanvalou.

Wynter, Sylvia. "Novel and History, Plot and Plantation." *Savacou*, no. 5 (June 1971): 95–102.

Wynter, Sylvia. "Unsettling the Coloniality of Being/Power/Truth/Freedom: Towards the Human, after Man, Its Overrepresentation—An Argument." *CR: New Centennial Review* 3, no. 3 (2003): 257–337.

Zakariya, Nasser. *A Final Story: Science, Myth, and Beginnings*. Chicago: University of Chicago Press, 2017.

Index